HISTORY OF
AMERICAN PRESIDENTIAL ELECTIONS

By Marc Schulman

MultiEducator, Inc.
New Rochelle, NY

MultiEducator, Inc.
New Rochelle, NY
www.multieducator.net

First Edition 2012
ISBN 978-1-885881-19-9

Design Layout & Typesetting by Amy Erani

Printed in the United States of America

ACKNOWLEDGEMENTS

I would like to thank all of the archivists and librarians of

the Library of Congress and the National Archives

who have been so helpful over the years.

~●●●~

For My children

Yael, Tali and Eytan

Table of Contents

CHAPTER
1
Introduction

For more than 200 years, Americans have held presidential elections every four years. There is no other place in the world where a new leader has been elected, or a sitting leader has been given a new mandate to govern, so regularly, for so long. Over the course of US history much has changed in the process of electing a president. Still, much in the way elections take place remains unchanged.

The constitutional framework that governs how presidential elections are conducted; that of Electoral College, (which you can read about in this book) has remained constant since the writing of the US Constitution. At the same time, both the means by which those electors are selected, and the way in which candidates run for office changed a great deal during the early years of the Republic. The first Presidents were chosen by the Electoral College; a body whose electors were selected by the states. Thus, initially Presidential elections had very little in common with today's elections where millions of citizens get out and vote. Rapidly, however, the states began to elect the electors to the Electoral College by popular vote. By 1828 instead of the state legislators selecting the delegates to the Electoral College, electors were selected by popular vote. The popular vote to determine state electors was expanded over the years to include larger and larger proportions of the population. In the early part of the 20th century the popular vote was extended to women and in the 1960's the popular vote finally began to include African Americans, who had often been denied their constitutionally mandated right to vote.

The method of selecting presidential candidates has also changed over time. Initially, presidential candidates were selected by party leaders privately behind the scenes. Those behind the scenes meetings were transformed during the 19th century into public nominating conventions. The delegates to those nominating conventions were themselves selected by party leaders in each state. However, the act of actually nominating the presidential candidates was public–while not totally transparent. Though back room deals were often the norm, the nomination themselves were usually free and fair. Over the course of the 20th century the system by which presidential candidates were chosen was transformed. More and more states instituted election primaries to select delegates to a national convention. The result was two-fold, the extension of the nominating process expanded the American election cycle, which, effectively, begins now after the Congressional elections two years before. From that moment on, prospective candidates form exploratory committees, and begin to raise the money necessary to run in the primary elections. In the past forty years, those primary elections have selected the presidential nominee. As a result, by the time a party holds its convention, the nominee is known. Thus, the party convention has turned into one large political advertisement for the presumptive nominee.

There is one way American elections have not changed much. American Presidential campaigns have always been nasty and negative. In the early years candidates did not personally campaign. Surrogates implemented all campaigns. Those surrogates spared no punches. From the beginning American presidential campaigns were often as nasty as one can imagine. Candidates were attacked both for their policies as well as their morals. The early elections relied on party newspapers to get out the message about and against the candidates. Over the course of the 20th century the United States moved away from party newspapers and developed a more independent press. Thus, while papers endorsed one candidate or another, and despite the fact that newspapers tended to reflect the politics of their owners, the news coverage tended to be less slanted. Candidates were force to rely on paid advertising. That advertising, as well as its cost, exploded, as the main source of news became television. Advertising on television became extremely effective, especially negative advertising.

Two of the most famous presidential television ads are part of this book. The 1964 ad run by President Johnson showed a little girl with flowers, followed by a mushroom cloud. The Johnson ad inferred that if the US were to elect Senator Goldwater nuclear war would follow. In 1988, a Republican Pac ran the Willie Horton ad. This ad inferred that if Governor Dukakis were elected he would release thousands of African American criminals from jail. Most recently, we have seen the devastating effectiveness of the negative campaign ads that Pro-Governor Romney PACs have run against Former House Speaker Gingrich. Now in the 21st century, new mediums have once again changed campaigns. Facebook pages, internet advertisement, and a news cycle that has gone somehow beyond 24 hours has been transforming campaigns in ways that we still do not fully understand.

Despite all these changes, however, once again on the first Tuesday, after the first Monday in November, every four years, the American public votes to select a President. That election will continue to evolve and change, but it will also remain very much the same.

CHAPTER
2
The Electoral Process

OVERVIEW: How Elections Work

Presidential Elections

The President of the United States is elected by the Electoral College, and not directly by the population. Each state is assigned electoral votes based on the number of senators and representatives that state has in Congress. Each state has two Senators. The number of representatives is determined by the states population, but is never less than one. Thus small states with a small population are overly represented in the Electoral College. One candidate wins all of the electoral votes in all states except Maine and Nebraska. Their two electors are chosen by statewide popular vote and a single elector is chosen in each Congressional district.

When does the electoral college meet?

The Electoral College meets on the first Monday after the second Wednesday in December. Their votes are then counted again in the presence of Joint Meeting of Congress sixth day of January to certify the returns. The candidate that wins over 50% of the electoral votes becomes President of the United States.

Who are the members of the Electoral College?

The members of the Electoral College are individual who are active in their party. They are pledged to vote for one or the other candidates. By law they are not required to vote for their pledged candidate, but in fact always do.

What if no one wins the majority of the electoral votes?

The House of Representatives decides the outcome in the case where no candidate receives the majority of electoral votes. The House of Representatives votes individually, state, by, state. Thus, every state in the House of Representative gets one vote.

The Nomination Process

SUMMER SCHEDULE 7/24//1947 Depicts Ohio Senator Robert A. Taft, son of former President William Howard Taft, examining an electoral map of the US planning his "summer schedule" with hopes of becoming the next President. Taft lost the Republican nomination to NY Governor Thomas Dewey.

Candidates wishing to run for the presidency must enter primary elections held by each party in states throughout the United States. The primary season begins in January of the year in which a presidential election is held. Traditionally, the cycle of presidential primaries begin in Iowa. The state caucuses select delegates to the party's national convention. The New Hampshire primary follows the Iowa primary Even though these are small states and have few votes; the momentum gained or lost by a victory or defeat in these early states is critical in obtaining money for the rest of the campaign.

Following the Iowa and New Hampshire primaries there are often blocks of primaries held on certain dates, such as "Super Tuesday," when many states hold their nominations. Candidates may choose not to participate in all the primaries, but they must constantly accumulate delegates for the convention and raise funds to keep their campaigns going.

There are two basic types of primaries: open and closed. In open primaries, all registered voters may vote to nominate a candidate. Most primaries, however, are closed primaries, in which only registered members of the party can vote to nominate the party's candidates. The two major parties, Democratic and Republican, nominate their presidential candidates at a national nominating convention. Until recently, local party officials had appointed the majority of the delegates to the national convention. Today, the overwhelming majority is elected through the primary system. This makes the system more democratic, while at the same time eliminating most of the drama and purpose of the convention. Since today's primaries determine the makeup of the convention floor, the nominations of the presidential candidates are a foregone conclusion. Conventions have turned into "made-for-TV" specials to advertise the parties' presidential choices. Nominees for vice president are also officially selected at conventions. However, the presidential candidate is the person who actually chooses his or her running mate.

SECTION 3
Political Party Conventions

The 1876 Democratic National Convention in Missouri.

A key part of the American political process has included party conventions held every four years to determine the major parties Presidential candidates. The first party to introduce nominating conventions was the Anti-Masons. Delegates from 13 states met in Baltimore Maryland on September 26, 1831 were they selected Attorney General William Wirt of Maryland to be their candidate. The Democrats followed in 1832 and renominated President Jackson. Since that time, many of the conventions have been places of great drama, where it has taken multiple votes to elect a party's Presidential candidate.

In recent years, with the current primary system, in which most of the convention votes are decided, the drama of the conventions has been lost, as the outcomes have been predetermined. Instead, the parties used the conventions as a tool to market their candidates and unveil their party platform. In recent years, the only true disagreements at the conventions have been negotiations over party platform.

Election Campaigns

US presidential election badges

While presidential campaigns traditionally begin after Labor Day, they actual kick off at the nominating conventions held over the summer. Once the conventions have ended, the candidates launch campaigns; some begin even before the conventions. Presidential campaigns are simultaneously national in scope, and local in focus. Candidates run separate campaigns in different states. A candidate must win 281 electoral votes in order to be elected President. When candidates win the majority of electoral votes in a given state, they gain all the electoral votes of that state. Thus, states with many electoral votes; such as California, Texas and New York are the sites of aggressive campaigning. Some states are considered likely victories for one party candidate or another, while other states are "up for grabs." These "swing states", (states that could "swing" and vote for any candidate), usually receive the greatest amount attention from campaigning candidates. These considerations greatly influence presidential candidates, as they decide where to invest their efforts and where to allocate their spending. Presidential campaigns often seem like chess games, with the players making strategic decisions to try to maximize their chances of winning the required number of votes.

SECTION 5
Campaign Financing

The cost of financing campaigns has steadily risen over the last few decades. In 1975-76, $100 million dollars was spent on congressional election campaigns. By 1995-96, that number had grown to $766.4 million. In the same period, direct spending in presidential campaigns has risen from a little over $100 million to $400 million, and this does not even include the amount spent by independent groups, or state and national campaigns. In 2008 it is estimated that $5.5 billion was spent on both Congressional and Presidential elections combined.

Under terms of the Federal Election Campaign Act of 1971, individuals are limited to making contributions of $1,000 per candidate per election, $5,000 a year to a political action committee (PAC) and $20,000 a year to a political party. In total, an individual cannot donate more than $25,000 to an election campaign.

In addition, the act provides for public funding of the presidential campaigns of the major parties. In 2008, both candidates refused to accept public funding. Thus, the candidates were not limited to the limits on spending that public financing requires.

The effectiveness of the Campaign Act has been greatly reduced by three subsequent Supreme Court decisions. In the first decision, "Buckley v. Valeo" (1976), the Court held that individuals could not be made to accept campaign donation limits. According to the Supreme Court, Spending money on a campaign was equivalent to free speech. Candidates can only have their spending limited, if they enter into agreements to limit spending by taking federal campaign funds.

In 1996, in the case of "Colorado Republican Federal Campaigning Committee v. Federal Election Commission", the Supreme Court held that state and local parties cannot be limited in the amount of money spent on behalf of candidate, as long as that spending is not coordinated with the candidate. This ruling extends to PACs and other equivalent groups.

Finally, in 2010 the Supreme Court ruled in the case of "Citizen United vs. Federal Election Committee" that a law limiting corporate spending on political advocacy violated the First Amendment Right of Free Speech of corporations. Thus, corporations are now free to spend unlimited sums on political advocacy. Though they are still limited in their direct contribution to candidates and PACs.

The need for so much money in political campaigns has resulted in an unseemly pursuit of funding. A candidate for the House of Representatives needs to raise nearly $2,000 every day. A Senator requires more than three times that amount. As a result, Congressmen feel they must offer access to their offices in return for donations. The practice was taken to its logical extreme in the 1996 presidential campaign, during which donors to the Democratic Committee were promised tea with the Clintons or, in some cases, an opportunity to sleep in the Lincoln bedroom in the White House.

To most observers of the system, the need for significant campaign reform is clear. Unfortunately, it has been difficult to bring about significant reform, because of the position of the Supreme **Court, which has equated spending money with free speech, and the opposition of people who benefit from the current system.**

The 2012 Presidential election promises to be the most expensive in history.

Electoral College

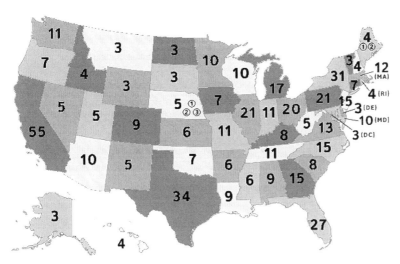

*US Map of electoral votes by state,
after redistricting from the 2000 census.*

The Electoral College was created for two reasons. The first purpose was to create a buffer between population and the selection of a President. The second purpose was, to establish part of the structure of the government that gave extra power to the smaller states. The first reason that the founders created the Electoral College is hard to understand today. The founding fathers were afraid of holding purely direct election to the Presidency. They feared a tyrant could manipulate public opinion and come to power. Hamilton wrote in the Federalist Papers:

"It was equally desirable, that the immediate election should be made by men most capable of analyzing the qualities adapted to the station, and acting under circumstances favorable to deliberation, and to a judicious combination of all the reasons and inducements which were proper to govern their choice. A small number of persons, selected by their fellow-citizens from the general mass, will be most likely to possess the information and discernment requisite to such complicated investigations. It was also peculiarly desirable to afford as little opportunity as possible to tumult and disorder. This evil was not least to be dreaded in the election of a magistrate, who was to have so important an agency in the administration of the government as the President of the United States. But the precautions which have been so happily concerted in the system under consideration, promise an effectual security against this mischief."

Hamilton and the other founders believed the electors would be able to insure that only a qualified person would become President. The founders believed that with the Electoral College no one would be able to manipulate the citizenry. It would act as a check on an electorate that might be duped. Hamilton and the other founders did not trust the population to make the right choice. The founders also believed the Electoral College had the advantage of being a group that met only once, and thus could not be manipulated over time by foreign governments or other entities.

The formation of the Electoral College was also part of the compromises made to satisfy the small states. Under the system of the Electoral College, each state had the same number of electoral votes as they had representative in Congress. Thus no state could have less than three representatives. As a result of this system, in the 2000 election the state of Wyoming cast about 210,000 votes. Each elector represented 70,000 votes. While voters in California cast approximately 9,700,000 votes for 54 electors. Thus, each elector for California represented

179,000 votes. Obviously, this creates an unfair advantage to voters in the small states, whose votes actually count more than those Americans living in medium and large states.

One aspect of the electoral system, that is not mandated in the Constitution, is the fact that winners take all of the votes in the state. Therefore, it makes no difference if you win a state by 50.1%, or by 80%, of the popular vote you receive the same number of electoral votes. This can be a recipe for one individual to win some states by large pluralities, and lose others by small number of votes. This is an easy scenario for one candidate to win the popular vote; while another wins the electoral vote. This "winner take all" methods used in picking electors has been decided by the states themselves. This trend took place over the course of the 19th century.

While there are clear problems with the Electoral College, though there are also some advantages. Changing the Electoral College system is very unlikely. It would take a constitutional amendment ratified by 3/4 of states to change the system. It is hard to imagine the smaller states agreeing to any change. One way of modifying the system is to eliminate the "winner take all" part of it. The method that the states vote for the Electoral College is not mandated by the constitution, but decided by the states. There are two states that do not use the "winner take all" system; Maine and Nebraska. It would be difficult, but not impossible, to get other states to change their systems. Unfortunately, the party that has the advantage in the state is unlikely to agree to a unilateral change.

Disputed Elections

The 2000 presidential election was not the first disputed election in American history.

1800

The first election which ended in a dispute was the election of the 1800; America's fourth presidential election. In that election the Federalists nominated John Adams to be President, and Charles Pinckney to be Vice President. The Democratic-Republicans nominated Jefferson as President, and Aaron Burr as Vice President. The Democratic-Republicans made the mistake of assigning the same number of electoral votes to both Jefferson as Burr. Thus, no one had the majority of votes, and the election was turned over to the House of Representatives. The House deliberated from February 11th to February 17th. They voted 36 times. The Federalists had decided to support Burr, whom many felt was a lesser evil than the "dangerous" Jefferson. The Federalists would have won, since they were the majority of the outgoing House. However, the constitution called for the election of President by the House to be on a state-by-state basis, and the Federalists could not carry enough states.

On the 36th ballot Jefferson was selected. However, the country had come very close to having Aaron Burr as President. In the immediate aftermath of this election, there was a call to amend the constitutional provision requiring double balloting for President and Vice President. This ruling was eliminated by the passage of the 12th amendment. Congress approved the 12th amendment in December 1803. This amendment was ratified in time for the presidential election of 1804.

1824

The election of 1824 was the second and last election decided by the House of Representatives. The four major candidates were John Quincy Adams, Henry Clay, William H Crawford, and Andrew Jackson. When the electors were counted Jackson had 99, Adams 84, Crawford 41 and Clay 37. The election was thrown to the House of Representatives, with the three leading candidates competing. All of the candidates hoped for support from Clay and his supporters. A scandal erupted, before the House met, when a Philadelphia newspaper published an anonymous letter claiming that Clay would support Adams, in return

The 1876 election was hotly contested, as can be seen by this poster published the following year.

A truce - not a compromise, but a chance for high-toned gentlemen to retire gracefully from their very civil declarations of war

for an appointment as Secretary of State. Clay vigorously denied this allegation. Adams won the nomination on the first ballot of the House of Representatives. Later, Adams appointed Clay as his Secretary of State.

1876

The Democratic party nominated Samuel Tilden and the Republican party nominated Rutherford Hayes in 1876. When the election results were tallied, it was confirmed that Samuel Tilden had won the popular vote by 250,000 votes; out of a total of 8.5 million votes cast. The electoral vote, however, was tight. In three southern states the results were hotly contested: South Carolina, Florida, and Louisiana. All three of these states were strongly divided between Whites and newly enfranchised Blacks; between supporters of Reconstruction, and those who wished to bring the wave of Reconstruction to an end. All three of these divided southern states ended up empowering two separate slates of electors.

The Congress passed a special law to decide on these disputed votes. That law created a 15-member commission made up of five senators, five member of the House, and five Supreme Court Justices. Initially, the swing, or fifteenth member of the commission was an independent. However, when he was appointed to the Senate, he resigned, and a Republican replaced him. The commission then met. In each of the three cases of disputed slates, the commission accepted the Republican slate. In accordance with the law, under which the commission had been set up, decisions of the commission could be overturned by a vote of both houses of Congress. The House rejected the commission's findings, while the Senate accepted it. The House Democrats threatened a filibuster to block the resumption of the count of the electoral votes. The Democrats did not go through with their threat. Hayes agreed to withdraw federal troops from the south, and end reconstruction, when he became President. As a result of his promise Hayes was selected.

1888

In the election of 1888 Grover Cleveland, the incumbent Democratic President, faced Republican challenger Benjamin Harrison. Grover Cleveland won the popular vote, but lost the electoral vote. This came about because Cleveland overwhelmingly won states with smaller numbers of electoral votes, while losing certain larger key states, by only a few votes. Benjamin Harrison became President. However, he lost to Cleveland in a rematch four years later.

1960

In this century there have been two very close elections. In 1960, a little over 100,000 votes ended up separating Vice President Richard Nixon and Senator John Kennedy. When it became apparent that Kennedy had won Illinois, Nixon conceded. There have been some references made to the similarities between the 2000 presidential election and Nixon's concession. The similarities are limited. Kennedy held a lead in the popular vote throughout. In the most contested state, Illinois, Kennedy won by 8,000 votes. Even if Nixon had carried Illinois, he still would have lost the election.

1976

The 1976 between President Ford and Governor Carter election was close in the Electoral College. However, Carter won by a commanding 2,000,000 votes in the popular votes.

2000

The closest election in US history began with a night of errors on the part of the major TV networks. The first error occurred when they prematurely declared Al Gore had won the state of Florida. That victory seemed to make an electoral victory by George W. Bush unlikely. As the night went on, the networks retracted their call and placed Florida in the undecided camp. Later in the night it became clear that the Florida decision would determine the elections. A little after 2 AM Eastern Standard Time the networks made their next mistake, declaring the state of Florida had gone to George Bush. That declaration set in motion a concession phone call by Gore to Bush. As Gore was about to make his concession speech, word reached him that the State of Florida was indeed too close to call. Gore called Bush back and recanted his concession. Then the recount of the Florida votes began. Most Americans went to sleep believing Bush had won. They woke up to learn the election had not been decided. As it turned out, the election would not be decided for another month. Then, in one of the most controversial decisions of all times, the Supreme Court decided the election in favor of George W. Bush.

CHAPTER
3
VOTING

SECTION 1
Voter Turnout

One of the subjects studied recently has been the reason the "voter turnout" (the percent of people participating in elections) has been lower in United States, as compared to turnout for elections in other democracies. The chart below demonstrates how election participation differs from country to country. The participatory rate of voters in the United States is substantially lower today than it was in the 19th century. Over the course of the 19th century, over 80% of eligible voters participated in each US election. Of course, in the 19th century, the number of eligible US voters was much lower, since woman and other minorities were effectively unable to vote.

What explains both the overall drop in voter participation, and America's lower voter participation rate, relative other democratic nations? A number of theories have been put forth to explain America's lower turnout. Some of these explanations are plausible, and others are less so.

One of the most popular theories seeking to explain sluggish US voter turnout posits that Americans have a more negative view of their government today compared to citizens of other nations. As a result, Americans, allegedly, do not participate in elections. I completely disagree with this theory. This theory may explain American voting patterns over the course of the last few years. However, I also do not really believe this to be the case. In fact, the truth is quite the opposite. All of the evidence gathered over the course of the last 50 years shows that Americans have a more positive view of their government than that of the citizens of many of the nations that have a larger voter turnout.

A second theory on rates of voter participation posits that Americans feel their vote simply will not count. According to this view, voting is not worth the bother. There is probably some truth to this explanation. However, with the exception of the 2000 election, which was decided by a mere 320 votes, most American elections are decided by large margins. Moreover, the American Electoral College system, where each state, (with two exceptions) gives all of its electoral votes to one candidate, further distances a voter from the election results. In fact, there are so many states that are not considered competitive; as there is a foregone conclusion that one candidate or another will win. In these cases, voting can seem almost like an irrational waste of time.
In many foreign countries votes are cast for a party that will then be part of a coalition government. In those cases, even small changes in the votes received by one party or another can affect the outcome of the government. The coalition system works to empower voters.

A third argument attempting to explain changes in US voter turnout claims the fact that in the United States Election Day is a working day like any other day is a deterrent to potential voters. In other countries Election

Day is a holiday. It is a fact these other countries have greater voter turnout.

The final explanation given to try to explain lower turnout rates in the United States is the requirement for voters to pre-register in order to vote. Americans are required to re-register to vote any time they move residences. Statistics show that Americans move more often than citizens of most other countries. In addition, the US voting process is a two-step process. Registration, which has to take place at least 30 days before an election in most states, has to occur before most people have begun to concentrate on the elections. It is interesting to note that the requirement for voter pre-registration was only mandated in the 20th century. The introduction of required voter pre-registration corresponds with the decrease in voter participation in US elections.

Another fact supporting the view that pre-registration hinders US voter turnout is that the few states that allow same-day voter registration have a higher than average turnout: From Minnesota with 77.7% to a low rate of 63.7 for Idaho in the 2008 elections. These rates must be compared to the overall US voter turnout average of 61.6%.

I do not think there is any one theory that fully explains the patterns of lack luster American voter turnout. In my opinion, a combination of the last three theories: a feeling that your vote will not matter; a busy schedule on election day; and finally the requirement to pre-register combine to keep US voter turnout continually low.

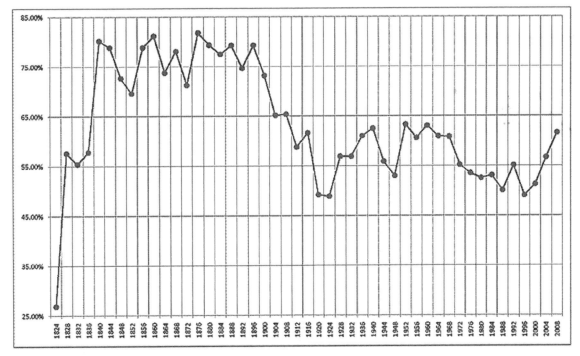

Graph of Voter turnout in the United States presidential elections from 1824 to 2008.

Why People Vote

Political scientists often question why America's voter turnout is lower in presidential elections than voting rates in other countries. Psychologists and some economists prefer to question what factors convince people vote at all. In my opinion, laboring to answer this question seems like an illogical waste of time. After all, rarely, if ever, does any vote determine an election. So why do people actually vote? There is no clear answer to this question. Though a number of good theories have been put forth. One theory holds that people vote to feel better about themselves. Some feel by voting they fulfill their "social responsibility" and that makes them feel better about themselves. Others think voting is a social norm.

In other words, when people belong to a community and everyone in their community votes, they feel they must vote as well. Sometimes that community may be their political party or their church or any other group to which they belong. It is clear that the decision to vote is not chosen rationally, through doing a cost–benefit analysis. If this was the case, one would expect to see the more educated population voting in lower numbers. However, the facts are just the opposite. The higher the level of a potential voter's education, the greater the chance they will in fact vote. Thus, it is clearly not a rational decision that brings people vote. Yet, vote they do.

Ethnic Voting

OVERVIEW

When examining presidential elections, or election results in general, for that matter, clear voting patterns emerge. Traditionally, certain ethnic and religious groups have higher rates of support for either Republican or Democratic candidates and/or their parties as a whole. Sometimes, the reason for this support is predictable. For example, since the 1960's the Democratic Party has been the leading supporter of Civil Rights legislation. As a result, African Americans have responded to that support for Civil Rights with their overwhelming support for the Democratic Party. Other times the reasons are less obvious. Jewish Americans have long been stalwart supporters of the Democratic Party. Jews vote overwhelmingly Democratic. However, based on their income and education levels, one would think Jews would primarily support the Republican Party. That being said, in almost every case there are historic, or cultural, or religious reasons for individual groups' support of one party or another.

THE "AFRICAN AMERICAN VOTE"

In the last US Presidential election 95% of African Americans voted for Barack Obama. That is no surprise, of course, since Obama is the first African American President. However, African American support for President Obama was only slightly higher than the 88% of African Americans who supported Presidential candidate John Kerry (Democrat) over President George W. Bush (Republican) in 2004. Yet, until the Roosevelt Presidency, those African Americans who could vote, voted for the Republicans. After all, the Republicans were the party of Lincoln, and it was Lincoln who freed the slaves. Thus, African Americans remained loyal to the Republicans until the time of Franklin D. Roosevelt.

However, before that time, a large percentage of African Americans were barred from voting by all sorts of poll taxes, literacy tests and the like. Franklin Delano Roosevelt was the first President to take any actions, however small, to improve the plight of African Americans. African Americans responded by increased support for the Democratic Party. African American support for the Democratic Party increased further when President Truman took the significant action to integrate the Armed Forces. President Eisenhower received credit for ordering Federal troops to Little Rock, Arkansas on orders to carry out a Supreme Court mandate. However, it was the words of President Kennedy, followed by the Civil Rights Legislation passed by President Johnson that solidified African American support for the Democratic Party. African American support for the Democratic Party was only strengthened when Richard Nixon developed what became known as the "Southern Strategy" for the Republican Party. The "Southern Strategy" was designed to capitalize on the resentment Southern Whites had toward the support the Democratic Party exhibited for the Civil Rights Legislation. This policy successfully established Republican dominance in the South for at least a generation. However, it also solidified African American support for the Democratic Party.

THE "HISPANIC-AMERICAN VOTE"

Hispanic Americans are not monolithic in their socio-economic standing or history. As a result, Hispanic Americans, have not traditionally identified with any one party. In the past, the Republican Party could count on support from Cuban Americans, because of the traditional Republican strong anti-Castro policy. Other Hispanic groups do not share the same concerns about the Cuban policy. There has always been an expectation that Republicans might gain support from Hispanics due to some of their shared conservative social values.

In the 2004 Presidential election President Bush received 40% of the Hispanic vote. The Hispanic vote represented 19% of the overall vote in that election. President Obama managed to win 57% of the Hispanic vote, even in Florida (a state whose Hispanic population has historically given its vote to Republicans.) The reason for the rapid decline in support for the Republican Party amongst Hispanic voters in the past five years has been the increasingly more stringent anti-immigrant policies endorsed by the party.

(IMPORTANT TO NOTE: The Hispanic vote in the U.S. has grown (from 8% of voters in 2004 to 9% in 2009).

THE "CATHOLIC-AMERICAN VOTE"

Catholics have traditionally been supporters of the Democratic Party. That support goes all the way back to the 1840's. Early Catholic immigrants became Democratic supporters when the "Know Nothing" and "Whig" parties took strongly anti-immigrant stances. Strong Catholic support for the Democratic parties strengthened further when the Democratic Party nominated Al Smith, the first Catholic Presidential candidate. Franklin Delano Roosevelt received overwhelming Catholic support. The election of President Kennedy, the first Catholic President, seemed to solidify Catholic support for the Democratic Party.

President Reagan went after "Blue-Collar" Democrats. Reagan managed to draw a large number of Catholic votes. In subsequent years, abortions became a large wedge issue. The strong Republican "Pro-Life", anti-abortion stance, matches that of the official position of Catholic Church. As a result, additional White Catholics have begun to vote for the Republican Party.

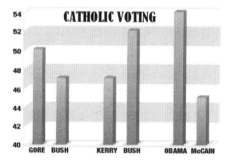

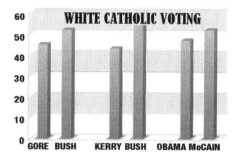

The "EVANGELICAL 'Born Again' CHRISTIAN VOTE"

The votes of Evangelical, sometimes known as "Born Again", Christians have been tallied separately only in the last two Presidential races. This new tally is an important development, as the Evangelical Christian electorate has been growing rapidly. In the two elections that have tallied Evangelical Christians have given their support overwhelmingly to the Republican Presidential candidate. That fact should not come as a surprise. Most Evangelical Christians view abortion as a key issue and the Republicans have been strong opponents of women's "Choice". Support among self-identifying Evangelicals is stronger for the Republican Party than support for Republicans among Catholics who share the same views on abortion. By definition, the religious beliefs Evangelicals maintain are a very important factor in their identity. While many Catholics are simply born Catholic. As a result, their faith is not all that important to them.

THE "JEWISH-AMERICAN VOTE"

Jews have primarily voted for Democratic candidates since the election of Woodrow Wilson in 1914. The continued Jewish support for Democrats over the last thirty years has been perplexing. During this time, Jews have become one of the wealthiest segments of the American population. While their increased fortune should have resulted in their greater support for the Republican Party, it did not.

Jews voted overwhelmingly for Franklin D. Roosevelt starting from his first Presidential election. Jewish support for Roosevelt can be understood in terms of Jewish self-interest. Roosevelt's liberal economic programs reflected the needs and interests of the largely immigrant Jewish community. His strong internationalist position and his inimical position to the rise of Hitler in Europe found overwhelming support in the Jewish community, concerned with the plight of the relatives they left behind in Europe. By the 1950's Roosevelt was long gone. However, Jews were rapidly advancing to middle class and often beyond. Yet, the Jewish vote remained overwhelmingly Democratic. In a year when a very popular Republican, Dwight Eisenhower, won the presidential election by a landslide, Jews retained their steadfast loyalty to the Democratic Party. This Jewish vote was perceived by some to be against their own self-interest. According to scholars, here began the "paradox of the Jewish vote". Scholars asked: Why do Jews continue to vote for Democratic candidates, while others with similar backgrounds and economic standing repeatedly vote for the Republican Party?

There has been no clear answer to this question. In some regards, the situation is particularly confusing, taking into account the fact that for the last 20 years (or more), Republican candidates (with the exception of the first President Bush) have all been perceived as more supportive of Israel than many of their Democratic counterparts. There have been a number of explanations posited over the years attempting to explain Jewish voting patterns. The first explanation cites the importance of social welfare in Jewish tradition. According to this theory, values of social welfare are so entrenched in the Jewish psyche, that Jews, whatever their economic standing, identify more closely with the social welfare positions of the Democratic Party. A second theory suggests that Jews, as opposed to other groups, more stringently maintain their family traditions. In this case, the tradition is voting for Democratic candidates.

In recent years, an argument can be made that the social conservative positions of most Republican candidates have been just too conservative for most Jews. This premise also explains the increased support religious Jews (who are more culturally conservative and often have greater connection to Israel) have given to the Republican Party. However, I believe another factor is at work determining Jewish voting in America. There is a sense among American Jews that the Republican Party is the party of exclusion. While Republican candidates are not anti-Semitic, the Republican Party has the veneer of being a party of anti-Semites. Furthermore, Jews consider the strict separation of State and religion sacrosanct. Separation of Church and State is a founding value that has made America different from any other country. It is separation of Church and State that has limited anti-Semitism to the fringes. The Republican position over the past two decades has been to decry that separation. In some cases Republican candidates have claimed the very idea of that separation is a misinterpretation of the Constitution. To Jews, separation of Church and State has been the major barrier against anti-Semitism in America. Therefore, the Republican party's more recent assault on that separation, combined with the earlier perception of Republicans as being "exclusionary, country club members", has made it difficult for Jews to support the Republican Party.

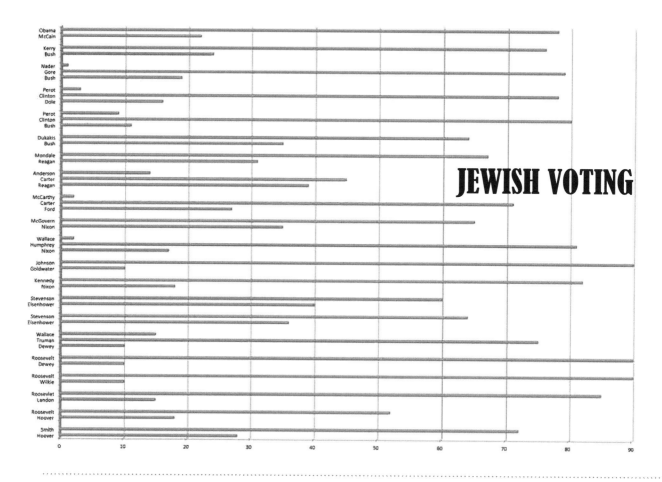

CHAPTER
4
FIFTY-SIX and COUNTING...

Flag of the President of the United States of America

America has gone to vote for a President 56 times between 1789 and 2008. In the first few elections, only the few and the privileged voted. By the 1832, nearly all white males could, and usually did, vote. The vote was slowly extended to African Americans and women. Over the years, as you will see as you read about individual elections, the issues change with the times. The promotional material has changed as well. However, the message has remained largely uniform: attack the opponent, and promote your candidate's good points.

The mediums have also changed over the years, as technology has evolved. In the early elections, local newspapers and flyers were the key. As the telegraph united the country political campaign messages soon became more national in nature. In the 20th century, radio and then TV became the dominant medium. In this book you will see many of the TV ads that used to promote recent candidates. In the past few elections, especially the Presidential election of 2008, the Internet, and specifically "social media", (such as Facebook and Twitter) became influential in presidential campaigns.

Now, Turn the virtual page and enter into the history of each and every US presidential election. Learn who won and why. Check out how many states each candidate carried and how many votes they received. In many of the elections there are photo galleries, where you can examine campaign photos, memorabilia and ads. Explore. Get a feel for each election, and of course, when you get to the later part of the 20th century, make sure you view the campaign videos.

History of U.S. Presidential Elections

UNITED STATES
PRESIDENTIAL ELECTION OF 1789

The Presidential Election of 1789 was an uncontested election. General George Washington was the only candidate for President. There was no question in anyone's mind that General Washington should be the first President. The only one who questioned that idea, was General Washington himself. General Washington was enjoying his retirement in Mt. Vernon. However, ultimately, there was no denying the need of the country. As Alexander Hamilton wrote to General Washington: "every public and personal consideration will demand from you an acquiescence in what will certainly be the unanimous wish of your country." In the end, Washington agreed. George Washington was elected the first President of the United States by a vote of acclamation.

George Washington
ELECTED

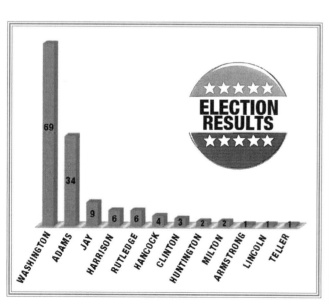

THE ISSUES

THE PRESIDENCY

Would George Washington agree to run for a second term?

President Washington hoped to retire after his first term as President. Washington believed his health was failing. He did not believe he was physically fit for the job of President. Washington also believed that it was important to show that American leaders, in contrast to European leaders, would seek to peacefully turn over power. Unfortunately for President Washington the one thing all of his lieutenants agreed on was the need for him to continue as President for a second term. Washington acquiesced and agreed to run for a second term. Once again, the electors unanimously selected Washington. John Adams won again, for the position of Vice President. However, Adams only received 77 votes, compared to 50 votes received by Governor George Clinton.

US MAP OF STATES CARRIED

◆WASHINGTON (FEDERALIST)

ELECTION RESULTS

George Wasshington
ELECTED

ELECTORAL VOTE

- WASHINGTON 132
- ADAMS 77
- CLINTON 50
- JEFFERSON 4
- BURR 1

UNITED STATES
PRESIDENTIAL ELECTION OF 1796

THE ISSUES

FRANCE OR ENGLAND

Should the United States support the French Revolution, or try to be closer to Great Britain?

The presidential election of 1796 was the first disputed election. With Washington retiring, the two loosely organized parties; the Federalists and the Republicans, were ready to face off. The Federalist's natural candidate was Vice President John Adams. The Republican Vice Presidential candidate was Secretary of State, Thomas Jefferson. Neither of the two candidates took direct part in the election. The two men remained on good terms throughout the presidential race. Their surrogates, however, became involved in a very nasty fight. Jefferson was attacked for not being religious and for his closeness to the French Revolution. Adams was attacked for being fond of the monarchy and for being too aloof. Adams won the election, receiving 71 votes to Jefferson's 68 votes. An oddities of this election came to light when the Electoral College met in February 1797. Two of the electors who were pledged to the Federalists voted for Jefferson. As was the case before the ratification of the 12th amendment in 1804, the runner up in electoral votes became the Vice President. Thus, Jefferson became the Vice President of his Presidential rival.

PRESIDENTIAL CANDIDATES

Thomas Jefferson (Democrat/Republican)

John Adams (Federalist)

US MAP OF STATES CARRIED

ELECTION RESULTS

◆JEFFERSON (DEMOCRATIC-REPUBLICAN)
◆ADAMS (FEDERALIST)

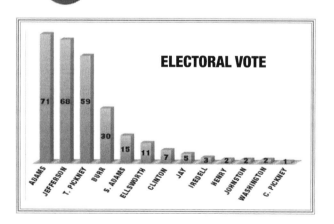

ELECTORAL VOTE

71 68 59 30 15 11 7 5 3 2 2 2 1

ADAMS JEFFERSON T. PCKNEY BURR S. ADAMS ELLSWORTH CLINTON JAY IREDELL HENRY JOHNSTON WASHINGTON C. PCKNEY

John Adams
ELECTED

UNITED STATES
PRESIDENTIAL ELECTION OF 1800

THE ISSUES   **ALIEN AND SEDITION ACT**

Was the Alien and Sedition Act legal?

The election campaign of 1800 was a partial replay of the campaign of 1796, with the Jeffersonians opposing Federalist policies. The attacks of the Jeffersonians were somewhat muted by the Alien and Sedition Act. However, the attacks of the Federalists on the Jeffersonians were not similarly muted. Federalist newspapers went as far as to claim that the election of Jefferson would cause the "teaching of murder robbery, rape, adultery and incest".

Foreign issues were not as important in this campaign. As, the rise of Napoleon dampened Jefferson's support for the French. Issues of domestic power and state rights took the spotlight in the campaign instead. Jefferson had been one of the authors of the controversial Virginia and Kentucky Resolutions, which declared the Alien and Sedition Act unconstitutional. Although the issue of state nullification of Federal laws would ultimately be settled in favor of the national government, it was a popular issue for discussion.

Adams faced substantial opposition within his own party. Hamilton opposed Adams' reelection. Hamilton schemed to have Pinckney, Adams' Vice Presidential candidate, receive more electoral votes, and thus become President. The election was settled when the New York legislature became dominated by supporters of Jefferson. The New York electors provided Jefferson with 12 key electoral votes. The defeat to the Federalists, however, did not end with the Election of 1800.

The Democratic-Republicans made the mistake of assigning the same number of electoral votes to both Jefferson, as to Burr. Thus, no one had the majority of votes. The election was turned over to the House of Representatives for a final decision. The House deliberated from February 11th to February 17th. They voted 36 times. The Federalists decided to support Burr, whom many felt was a "lesser evil" than the "dangerous" Jefferson. The Federalists should have won, since they were the majority of the outgoing House. However, the Constitution called for the election of the President by the House to be on a state by state basis, and the Federalists could not carry enough states. On the 36th ballot Jefferson was selected, but the country had come very close to having Aaron Burr as President.

Thomas Jefferson
ELECTED

UNITED STATES PRESIDENTIAL Election of 1800

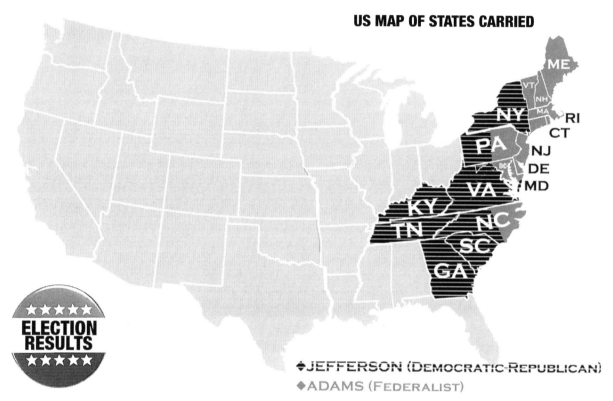

US MAP OF STATES CARRIED

◆JEFFERSON (Democratic-Republican)
◆ADAMS (Federalist)

ELECTION RESULTS

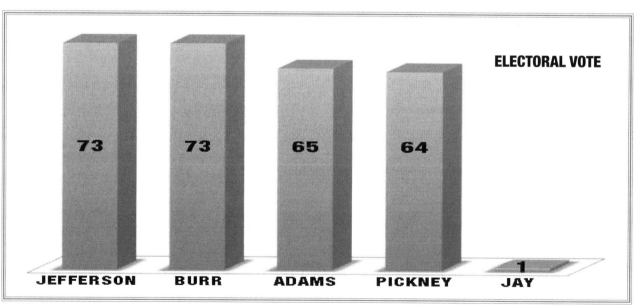

ELECTORAL VOTE

JEFFERSON	BURR	ADAMS	PICKNEY	JAY
73	73	65	64	1

THE ISSUES

JEFFERSON AND PICKNEY

Was Vice President Thomas Jefferson a radical?

PRESIDENTIAL CANDIDATES

Thomas Jefferson (Democrat/Republican)

Charles Pickney (Federalist)

1804 marked the first time there was a nominating caucus for President. One hundred Republican Congressmen met and nominated Jefferson, by vote of acclamation. The Federalist Party nominated Charles Pickney for President and Rufus King to be Vice President. The Federalists attacked President Jefferson on a number of points; claiming the Louisiana Purchase as unconstitutional. The Federalists also attacked Jefferson's defense policies. They further claimed Jefferson had children with Sally Heming, a slave of his at Monticello. These attacks were not effective. Jefferson was immensely popular. His first term had been peaceful, and the Louisiana Purchase was very popular. In addition, the Federalists were discredited by radical elements in their party. The final results of the election even surprised Jefferson supporters. Jefferson won an overwhelming victory winning, gaining 162 electoral votes compared to Pinckney's 14 electoral votes.

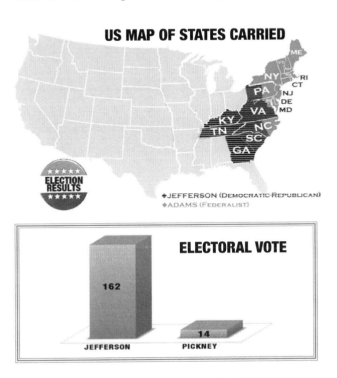

US MAP OF STATES CARRIED

ELECTION RESULTS

◆JEFFERSON (DEMOCRATIC-REPUBLICAN)
◆ADAMS (FEDERALIST)

ELECTORAL VOTE

162 JEFFERSON

14 PICKNEY

Thomas Jefferson
ELECTED

THE ISSUES   **LOUISIANA PURCHASE**

Was the Louisiana Purchase constitutional?

PRESIDENTIAL CANDIDATES

James Madison (Democrat/Republican)
Charles Pickney (Populist)
George Clinton (Democrat/Republican)

Thomas Jefferson followed the precedent Washington set. Jefferson felt that two terms in office was enough for any President to serve. Jefferson's second term had not been successful as his first. The war between England and France, and the failure of both countries to observe American neutrality resulted in the passage of the Embargo Act. The Embargo Act was very unpopular among the shippers of New England, as well as farmers who exported their crops. It also failed to have any effect of England or France. The Federalist hoped to exploit that unhappiness to unseat the Republicans.

Jefferson's hand-picked successor was his long-term friend, and Secretary of State, James Madison. Madison was the unanimous selection of the Republican party. The Federalists ran Charles Pinckney as their candidate once again. The campaign was very spirited, with the Federalists bitterly attacking Madison for the Embargo Act. However, when the electors were selected, it was clear that the opposition to the Embargo Act was not as widespread as the Federalists had hoped. James Madison easily defeated Charles Pinckney. Madison garnered almost three times as many electoral votes as Pinckney had received.

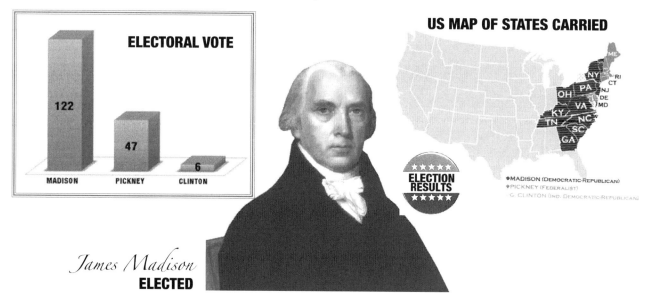

ELECTORAL VOTE

MADISON	PICKNEY	CLINTON
122	47	6

US MAP OF STATES CARRIED

ELECTION RESULTS

◆MADISON (DEMOCRATIC-REPUBLICAN)
◆PICKNEY (FEDERALIST)
G. CLINTON (IND. DEMOCRATIC-REPUBLICAN)

James Madison
ELECTED

THE ISSUES

US INTERESTS ON THE HIGH SEAS

As Secretary of State, did James Madison do enough to protect American interests on the seas?

PRESIDENTIAL CANDIDATES

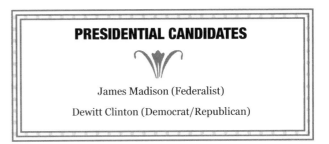

James Madison (Federalist)

Dewitt Clinton (Democrat/Republican)

The election of 1812 was the first war time election of a President. It began a tradition that continued in the re-election of war time Presidents. The war, had begun a month after Madison was renominated. While the war was largely popular, there were many who either opposed the war or, opposed how it was being prosecuted.

The Republicans selected Dewitt Clinton of New York to run against Madison by the Federalist. Clinton hoped to defeat Madison by both getting the United States into war, while at the same time, not fighting the war vigorously enough. Clinton also hoped to win support of those wishing for someone other than a Virginian to serve as President. Former President Adams was so disgusted by what he thought was a two-faced campaign by the Federalists that he established a committee in his home town of Quincy. The committee was called "Federalists for Madison". The results of the election showed that whatever qualms Americans might have had about the implementation of the war, they were not willing to change leaders in the middle of the war. Madison was re-elected by a comfortable majority.

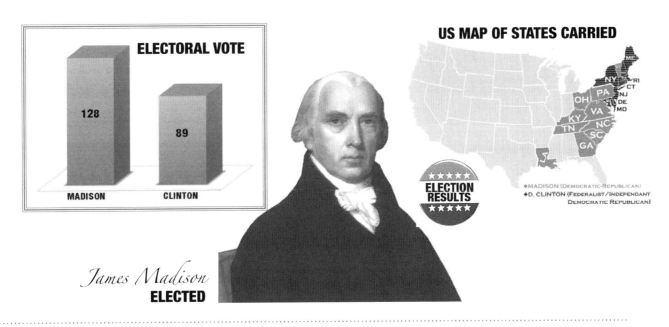

ELECTORAL VOTE

128 MADISON

89 CLINTON

US MAP OF STATES CARRIED

ELECTION RESULTS

◆MADISON (DEMOCRATIC-REPUBLICAN)
◆D. CLINTON (FEDERALIST/INDEPENDANT DEMOCRATIC REPUBLICAN)

James Madison
ELECTED

THE ISSUES

THE PRESIDENTIAL ELECTION OF 1816 WAS UNCONTESTED

PRESIDENTIAL CANDIDATES

James Monroe (Democrat/Republican)

Rufus King (Federalist)

ON THIS ... ELECTION

James Monroe was the favorite candidate of both former Presidents, Thomas Jefferson and James Madison to become the next President of the United States. Secretary of War, William Crawford, opposed Monroe, but Monroe received the Republican nomination without difficulty.

Monroe's opponent in the general election was Rufus King. King was a Federalist Senator from New York. King was an early opponent of slavery. The election campaign of 1816 itself was highly one-sided. The early opposition of the Federalists to the War of 1812 had, for all practical purposes, destroyed the party. The war ended with the American victory at the Battle of New Orleans. As a result, those who opposed the war were discredited. Monroe went on to win an overwhelming victory.

US MAP OF STATES CARRIED

ELECTION RESULTS

◆MONROE (DEMOCRATIC-REPUBLICAN)
◆KING (FEDERALIST)

James Monroe
ELECTED

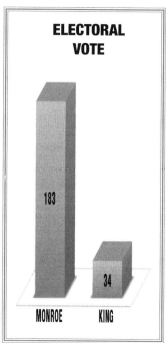

ELECTORAL VOTE

183

34

MONROE   KING

THE ISSUES

THE PRESIDENTIAL ELECTION OF 1820 WAS UNCONTESTED

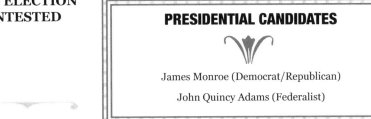

PRESIDENTIAL CANDIDATES

James Monroe (Democrat/Republican)

John Quincy Adams (Federalist)

President James Monroe was re-elected without opposition in 1820. Even former President John Adams came out of retirement to cast an electoral vote for Monroe. Monroe won all but one electoral vote. The lone dissenter was former Senator William Plumer, who voted for John Quincy Adams. Plumer reasoned that he did not want Monroe to be elected unanimously, leaving that honor to President Washington alone.

US MAP OF STATES CARRIED

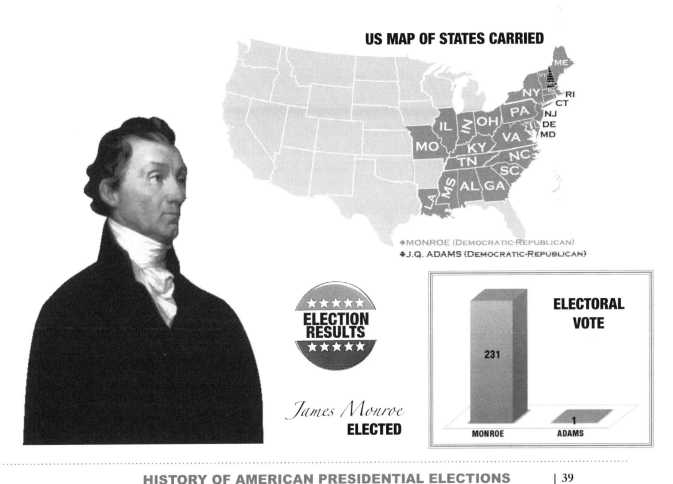

◆ MONROE (DEMOCRATIC-REPUBLICAN)
◆ J.Q. ADAMS (DEMOCRATIC-REPUBLICAN)

★★★★★
ELECTION RESULTS
★★★★★

James Monroe
ELECTED

ELECTORAL VOTE

MONROE	ADAMS
231	1

THE ISSUES

NEW BLOOD

Should an outsider (General Jackson), considered to be represent "the common man", be elected President?

The campaign to succeed Monroe as President began early, with many different candidates being suggested. It soon came down to four viable candidates. William Crawford, Secretary of Treasury, John Q. Adams, Henry Clay and General Andrew Jackson. Crawford was the first to be an official candidate, being selected by caucus of Republican Congressmen. Being selected by a caucus actually hurt Crawford's chances, when he became identified with a system of selection that was out of favor.

Each of those nominated represented a different geographic part of the country. As had become common in Presidential campaigns, the newspapers of the time wrote very favorable items about those they supported. Conversely, newspapers attacked those they opposed with venom. They made fun of how poorly Adams dressed and his "English" wife. They called Clay "a drunkard and gambler". They charged that Crawford had done unlawful acts while in office, and accused Andrew Jackson of murder.

It became clear that no candidate received the majority of either the popular vote or the electoral vote. Though Andrew Jackson was in the clear lead, with 99 electoral votes and 152,901 popular votes. Adams had 84 electoral votes and 11,023 popular votes. Crawford was a poor third, and Clay brought up the rear.

PRESIDENTIAL CANDIDATES

Andrew Jackson (Democratic Republican)

John Quincy Adams (Democratic Republican)

Henry Clay (Democratic Republican)

William Crawford (Democratic Republican)

As no candidate received 50% of the electoral votes, under the provisions of twelfth amendment to the constitution, the House voted for the President. Each state had one vote and only the top three vote recipients participated. Clay who came in fourth could not compete. Clay believed that Adams was the best qualified to be President. He did not believe that Jackson's success as a general meant he was ready for the Presidency and thus supported Adams. Adams laters selected Clay to be his Secretary of State thus opening the way for charges that it was a "corrupt bargain."

John Quincy Adams
ELECTED

STATES	JOHN QUINCY ADAMS		ANDREW JACKSON		HENRY CLAY		WILLIAM CRAWFORD		TOTAL VOTES
	VOTES	PERCENT	VOTES	PERCENT	VOTES	PERCENT	VOTES	PERCENT	
Alabama	2,422	17.8	9,429	69.3	96	0.07	1,656	12.2	13,600
Connecticut	7,494	70.4	0	0	0	0	1,965	18.5	9,459
Illinois	1,516	32.5	1,272	27.2	1,036	22.2	847	18.1	4,671
Indiana	3,071	19.4	7,444	47	5,316	33.6	0	0	15,831
Kentucky	0	0	6,356	27.2	16,982	72.8	0	0	23,338
Maine	10,289	81.5	0	0	0	0	2,336	18.5	12,625
Maryland	14,631	44.1	14,522	43.7	695	2.1	3,364	10.1	33,212
Massachusetts	30,687	73	0	0	0	0	11,369	0	42,056
Mississippi	1,654	33.8	3,121	63.8	0	0	119	2.4	4,894
Missouri	159	4.6	1,166	34	2,042	59.5	32	0.9	3,399
New Hampshire	9,389	93.6	0	0	0	0	643	6.4	10,032
New Jersey	8,309	41.9	10,333	52.1	0	0	1,196	6	19,838
North Carolina	0	0	20,231	56	0	0	15,622	43.3	35,853
Ohio	12,280	24.5	18,489	37	19,255	38.5	0	0	50,024
Pennsylvania	5,441	11.6	35,736	75.9	1,690	3.6	4,206	8.9	47,073
Rhode Island	2,144	91.5	0	0	0	0	2,344	8.5	4,488
Tennessee	216	1	20,197	97.5	0	0	312	1.5	20,725
Virginia	3,419	22.2	2,975	19.4	419	2.7	8,558	55.7	15,371
TOTALS	113,122	30.9	151,271	41.3	47,531	13.0	40,856	11.2	365,833

1824 ELECTION: STATE-BY-STATE RESULTS (JQ ADAMS vs. JACKSON vs. CLAY vs. CRAWFORD)

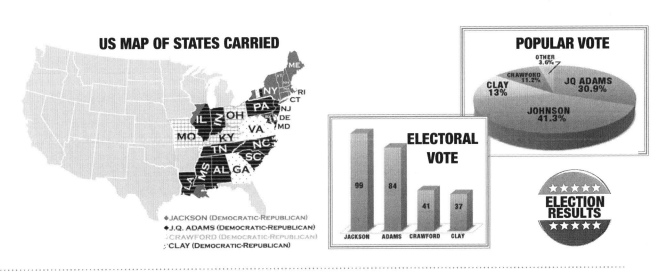

US MAP OF STATES CARRIED

◆ JACKSON (DEMOCRATIC-REPUBLICAN)
◆ J.Q. ADAMS (DEMOCRATIC-REPUBLICAN)
CRAWFORD (DEMOCRATIC-REPUBLICAN)
CLAY (DEMOCRATIC-REPUBLICAN)

ELECTORAL VOTE

JACKSON 99 ADAMS 84 CRAWFORD 41 CLAY 37

POPULAR VOTE

OTHER 3.6%
CRAWFORD 11.2%
CLAY 13%
JQ ADAMS 30.9%
JOHNSON 41.3%

ELECTION RESULTS

THE ISSUES

A QUESTION OF CHARACTER

Was Andrew Jackson fit to be President of the United States?

PRESIDENTIAL CANDIDATES

Andrew Jackson (Democratic)

John Quincy Adams (National Republican)

The election of 1828 was a seminal election in American history. It was the first election which was to be decided by popular vote. It was an election which pitted Andrew Jackson, who projected an image of a populist, against President Adams, who was a member of "the ruling class".

Once again the election campaign included numerous personal attacks on each of the candidates. Adams was attacked for living in "kingly pomp and splendor". Adam was also attacked for traveling on Sunday and having premarital relations with his wife. Jackson was attacked as being uneducated and reckless. They also attacked Jackson, branding him a murderer, for his executions of deserters. Jackson's marriage to his wife also came under attack, based on a technicality. Jackson's wife was an adulterer when she initially began her relationship with him.

Beyond personality traits, there were actual policy differences between the two candidates. Adams supported the National Bank. He wanted high tariffs and supported federal funds for internal improvements. Jackson opposed the bank. He wanted lower tariffs and was in favor of only limited federal support for internal improvements.

Adams continued the tradition of presidential candidates not personally campaigning at all.

Jackson, on the other hand, was intimately involved in organizing his campaign. Jackson won the southern and western states, which were enough to insure his victory. Adams maintained his support in New England.

Andrew Jackson
ELECTED

STATES	ANDREW JACKSON		JOHN QUINCY ADAMS		TOTAL VOTES
	VOTES	PERCENT	VOTES	PERCENT	
Alabama	16,736	89.9	1,878	10.1	18,618
Connecticut	4,448	23.0	1,829	71.4	19,378
Georgia	19,362	96.8	642	3.2	20,004
Illinois	9,560	67.2	4,662	32.8	14,222
Indiana	22,201	56.6	17,009	43.4	39,210
Kentucky	39,308	55.5	31,468	44.5	70,776
Louisiana	4,605	53.0	4,082	47.0	8,687
Maine	13,927	40.0	20,773	59.7	34,789
Maryland	22,782	49.7	23,014	50.3	45,796
Massachusetts	6,012	15.4	29,836	76.4	39,074
Mississippi	6,763	81.1	1,581	18.9	8,344
Missouri	8,232	70.6	3,422	29.4	11,654
New Hampshire	20,212	45.9	23,823	54.1	44,035
New Jersey	21,809	47.9	23,753	52.1	45,570
New York	139,412	51.4	131,563	48.6	270,975
North Carolina	37,814	73.1	13,918	26.9	51,747
Ohio	67,596	51.6	63,453	48.4	131,049
Pennsylvania	101,457	66.7	50,763	33.3	152,220
Rhode Island	820	22.9	2,755	77.0	3,580
Tennessee	44,293	95.2	2,240	4.8	46,533
Vermont	8,350	25.4	24,363	74.2	32,833
Virginia	26,854	69.0	12,070	31.0	38,924
TOTALS	642,553	56.0	500,897	43.6	1,148,018

1828 ELECTION: STATE-BY-STATE RESULTS (JACKSON vs. JQ ADAMS)

US MAP OF STATES CARRIED

◆ JACKSON (DEMOCRATIC)
◆ J.Q. ADAMS (NATIONAL REPUBLICAN)

ELECTION RESULTS

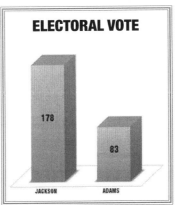

ELECTORAL VOTE

178

83

JACKSON   ADAMS

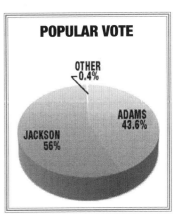

POPULAR VOTE

OTHER 0.4%

ADAMS 43.6%

JACKSON 56%

UNITED STATES
PRESIDENTIAL ELECTION OF 1832

THE ISSUES

SECOND BANK OF THE U.S.

Should President Jackson have vetoed the charter of the Second Bank?

1832 was the first election in which the candidates in were nominated by national nominating conventions. The Democrats met in Baltimore, and overwhelmingly nominated Andrew Jackson. Henry Clay was nominated by the National Republicans at their convention in Baltimore, Maryland.

The major issue in the campaign was Jackson's determination to eliminate the Bank of the United States. Jackson had vetoed the bill reauthorizing the bank shortly before being renominated. Henry Clay decided to make that veto the major issue in the campaign. Clay's campaign headquarters were in Pennsylvania, where the bank was head-quartered. Thus, Clay was very popular at home. However, Clay's strategy backfired. The bank was widely considered a tool of the rich. As a result, the bank was extremely unpopular. Jackson won by an overwhelming margin.

The DEMOCRATIC CONVENTION

PLACE: Baltimore, Maryland

DATE: May 21 to 23, 1832

NOMINATED: Andrew Jackson, of Tennessee, for President

NOMINATED: Martin Van Buren, of New York, for Vice President

334 Democrats came together to renominate President Andrew Jackson. The convention also replaced Vice President Clay with Martin Van Buren.

PRESIDENTIAL CANDIDATES

Andrew Jackson (Democratic)

Henry Clay (National Republican)

John Floyd (Independent Democrat)

William Wirt (Anti-Mason)

Andrew Jackson
ELECTED

STATES	ANDREW JACKSON		HENRY CLAY		WILLIAM WIRT		JOHN FLOYD		TOTAL VOTES
	VOTES	PERCENT	VOTES	PERCENT	VOTES	PERCENT	VOTES	PERCENT	
Alabama	14,286	100.0	5	0	0	0.0	0	0.0	14,291
Connecticut	11,269	34.3	18,155	55.3	3,409	10.4	0	0.0	32,833
Delaware	4,110	49.0	4,276	51.0	0	0.0	0	0.0	8,386
Georgia	20,750	100.0	0	0	0	0.0	0	0.0	20,750
Illinois	14,609	68.0	6,745	31.4	97	0.5	30	0.1	21,481
Indiana	31,652	55.4	25,473	44.6	27	0.0	0	0.0	57,152
Kentucky	36,292	45.5	43,449	54.5	0	0.0	0	0.0	79,741
Louisiana	3,908	61.7	2,429	38.3	0	0.0	0	0.0	6,337
Maine	33,978	54.7	27,331	44.0	844	1.4	0	0.0	62,153
Maryland	19,156	50.0	19,160	50.0	0	0.0	0	0.0	38,316
Massachusetts	13,933	20.6	31,963	47.3	14,692	21.7	7,031	10.4	67,619
Mississippi	5,750	100.0	0	0	0	0.0	0	0.0	5,750
Missouri	5,192	100.0	0	0	0	0.0	0	0.0	5,192
New Hampshire	24,855	56.8	18,938	43.2	0	0.0	0	0.0	43,793
New Jersey	23,826	49.9	23,466	49.1	468	1.0	0	0.0	47,760
New York	168,497	52.1	154,896	47.9	0	0.0	0	0.0	323,393
North Carolina	25,261	84.8	4,538	15.2	0	0.0	0	0.0	29,799
Ohio	81,246	51.3	76,566	48.4	538	0.3	0	0.0	158,350
Pennsylvania	90,973	57.7	0	0	66,706	42.3	0	0.0	157,679
Rhode Island	2,051	35.7	2,871	50.0	819	14.3	6	0.1	5,747
Tennessee	28,078	95.4	1,347	4.6	0	0.0	0	0.0	29,425
Vermont	7,865	24.3	11,161	34.5	13,112	40.5	206	0.6	32,344
Virginia	34,243	75.0	11,436	25.0	3	0.0	0	0.0	45,682
TOTALS	701,780	54.2	484,205	37.4	100,715	7.8	7,273	.0.6	1,293,973

1832 ELECTION: STATE-BY-STATE RESULTS (JACKSON vs. CLAY vs. WIRT vs. FLOYD)

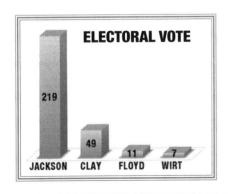

ELECTORAL VOTE

219 — JACKSON
49 — CLAY
11 — FLOYD
7 — WIRT

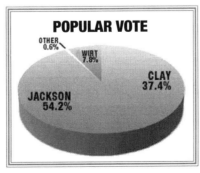

POPULAR VOTE

OTHER 0.6%
WIRT 7.8%
CLAY 37.4%
JACKSON 54.2%

US MAP OF STATES CARRIED

◆JACKSON (DEMOCRATIC)
◆CLAY (NATIONAL REPUBLICAN)
FLOYD (INDEPENDANT DEMOCRAT)
WIRT (ANTI-MASON)

ELECTION RESULTS

THE ISSUES — POWER OF THE PRESIDENCY

Had the institution of the Presidency become too strong under the stewardship of Andrew Jackson?

The DEMOCRATIC CONVENTION

PLACE: Baltimore, Maryland

DATE: May 20 to 22, 1836

NOMINATED: Martin Van Buren, of New York, for President

NOMINATED: Richard M. Johnson, of Kentucky, for Vice President

The party convention was held a year earlier to insure that the party would support President Jackson's candidate, Vice President Van Buren. The convention duly and unanimously, but reluctantly, approved the selection. Richard M. Johnson, best known for having shot Tecumseh in the War of 1812, was nominated to be Vice President.

President Jackson decided not to run for re-election. He called on the Democrats to hold a convention of the people. The convention unanimously selected Martin Van Buren to be the Democratic Presidential nominee, since Van Buren was the hand picked successor chosen by President Jackson. The Whig party was not strong enough to hold a national convention. As a result, they were not able to nominate one national candidate. Instead, the Whigs nominated several regional candidates. With multiple candidates, the Whig party hoped to deny Van Buren a majority, and throw the election to House of Representatives.

In the 1836 campaign the issue of slavery became important for the first time. Van Buren attempted to keep both the South and North happy. He claimed Congress had the right to outlaw slavery in the District of Columbia. Though, he personally opposed such a move. Van Buren's major opponent was William Henry Harrison. Harrison was a strong supporter of federal money for internal improvements. This gave Harrison strong support in the West. In addition, Harrison promised he would be willing to reopen the Bank of the United States— if economic conditions warranted it. Van Buren maintained Jackson's staunch opposition to the Bank. In the end, the superior organization of the Democrats determined the election in favor of Van Buren. With Democratic support, Van Buren was able to gain more than 50% of the vote.

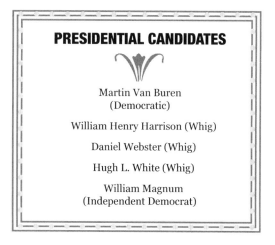

PRESIDENTIAL CANDIDATES

Martin Van Buren
(Democratic)

William Henry Harrison (Whig)

Daniel Webster (Whig)

Hugh L. White (Whig)

William Magnum
(Independent Democrat)

Martin Van Buren
ELECTED

STATE	MARTIN VAN BUREN		W.H. HARRISON		HUGH L. WHITE		DANIEL WEBSTER		WILLIE MANGUM		TOTAL
	VOTE	PERCENTAGE	VOTE	PERCENTAGE	VOTE	PERCENTAGE	VOTE	PERCENTAGE	VOTE	PERCENTAGE	VOTES
Alabama	20,638	55.3	0	0.0	16,658	44.7	0	0.0	0	0.0	37,296
Arkansas	2,380	64.1	0	0.0	1,334	35.9	0	0.0	0	0.0	3,714
Connecticut	19,294	50.6	18,799	49.4	0	0.0	0	0.0	0	0.0	38,093
Delaware	4,154	46.7	4,736	53.2	0	0.0	0	0.0	5	0.1	8,895
Georgia	22,778	48.2	0	0.0	24,481	51.8	0	0.0	0	0.0	47,259
Illinois	18,369	54.7	15,220	45.3	0	0.0	0	0.0	0	0.0	33,589
Indiana	33,084	44.5	41,339	55.5	0	0.0	0	0.0	0	0.0	74,423
Kentucky	33,229	47.4	36,861	52.6	0	0.0	0	0.0	0	0.0	70,090
Louisiana	3,842	51.7	0	0.0	3,583	48.3	0	0.0	0	0.0	7,425
Maine	22,825	58.9	14,803	32.8	0	0.0	0	0.0	1,112	2.9	38,740
Maryland	22,267	46.3	25,852	53.7	0	0.0	0	0.0	0	0.0	48,119
Massachusetts	33,486	44.8	0	0.0	0	0.0	41,201	55.1	45	0.1	74,732
Michigan	6,507	54.0	5,545	46.0	0	0.0	0	0.0	0	0.0	12,052
Mississippi	10,297	51.3	0	0.0	9,782	48.7	0	0.0	0	0.0	20,079
Missouri	10,995	60.0	0	0.0	7,337	40.0	0	0.0	0	0.0	18,332
New Hampshire	18,697	75.0	6,228	25.0	0	0.0	0	0.0	0	0.0	24,925
New Jersey	25,592	49.5	26,137	50.5	0	0.0	0	0.0	0	0.0	51,729
New York	166,795	54.6	135,548	45.4	0	0.0	0	0.0	0	0.0	305,343
North Carolina	26,631	53.1	0	0.0	23,521	46.9	0	0.0	1	0.0	50,153
Ohio	97,122	47.9	105,809	52.1	0	0.0	0	0.0	0	0.0	202,931
Pennsylvania	91,466	51.2	87,235	48.8	0	0.0	0	0.0	0	0.0	178,701
Rhode Island	2,962	52.2	2,710	47.8	0	0.0	0	0.0	1	0.0	5,673
Tennessee	26,170	42.1	0	0.0	36,027	57.9	0	0.0	0	0.0	62,197
Vermont	14,040	40.0	20,994	59.8	0	0.0	0	0.0	65	0.2	35,099
Virginia	30,556	56.6	0	0.0	23,384	43.3	0	0.0	5	0.0	53,945
TOTALS	764,176	50.8	550,816	36.6	146,107	9.7	41,201	2.7	1,234	0.1	1,503,534

1836 ELECTION: STATE-BY-STATE RESULTS (VAN BUREN vs. WH HARRISON vs. WHITE vs. WEBSTER vs. MANGUM)

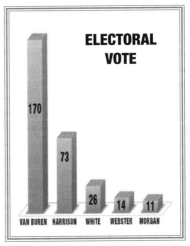

ELECTORAL VOTE

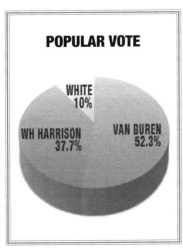

POPULAR VOTE

US MAP OF STATES CARRIED

THE ISSUES ECONOMIC WOES

Should President Van Buren have done more to fight the economic depression?

The DEMOCRATIC CONVENTION

PLACE: Baltimore, Maryland

DATE: May 5 to 6, 1840

NOMINATED: Martin Van Buren, of New York, for President

NOMINATED: Richard M. Johnson, of Kentucky, for Vice President

The 1840 Democratic nominating convention renominated Martin Van Buren for President. The convention body also changed the name of the party from the "Democratic-Republicans" to the "Democratic Party".

... ON THIS ELECTION

President Van Buren was very unpopular by the time the election of 1840 neared. Van Buren was blamed for the depression that followed the Panic of 1837. President Van Buren was reviled for not doing anything to improve the economy. As a result, the Whig Party felt they had a good chance to capture the White House.

Henry Clay, of Kentucky, was the early favorite at the Whig convention in Harrisburg, PA, in December 1839. Clay, however, was a Mason. The anti-mason feeling was strong enough to block his nomination. In the final ballot Harrison was nominated, with 148 votes to Clay's 90, and Scott's 16. John Tyler was nominated as the Vice Presidential candidate. Meanwhile, President Van Buren was unanimously renominated by the Democrats.

The election of 1840 was the first campaign with slogans, songs, and modern campaign paraphernalia. The campaign slogan that became best known was: "Tippecanoe and Tyler too". Tippecanoe was the battle Harrison won against the Indians in 1811. Harrison was portrayed as a man of the people.

Though Harrison's views on most major issues were unknown. The cconomy was the major issue of the campaign. Van Buren shouldered the blame for the poor state of the economy. Harrison promised to get the economy moving again. By this time, Van Buren was so wildly unpopular that he even lost the vote of his own home state.

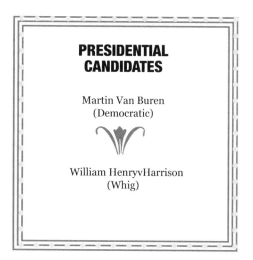

PRESIDENTIAL CANDIDATES

Martin Van Buren
(Democratic)

William HenryvHarrison
(Whig)

William Henry Harrison
ELECTED

STATES	W.H. HARRISON		MARTIN VAN BUREN		JAMES BIRNEY		TOTAL VOTES
	VOTES	PERCENTAGE	VOTES	PERCENTAGE	VOTES	PERCENTAGE	
Alabama	28,515	45.6	33,996	54.4	0	0.0	62,511
Arkansas	5,160	43.6	6,679	56.4	0	0.0	11,839
Connecticut	31,598	55.6	25,281	44.4	0	0.0	56,879
Delaware	5,967	55.0	4,872	44.9	0	0.0	10,852
Georgia	40,339	55.8	31,983	44.2	0	0.0	72,322
Illinois	45,574	48.9	47,441	50.9	160	0.2	93,175
Indiana	65,280	55.5	51,696	44.0	30	0.0	117,605
Kentucky	58,488	64.2	32,616	35.8	0	0.0	91,104
Louisiana	11,296	59.7	7,616	40.3	0	0.0	18,912
Maine	46,612	50.2	46,190	49.8	0	0.0	92,802
Maryland	33,528	53.8	28,752	46.2	0	0.0	62,280
Massachusetts	72,852	57.4	52,355	41.3	1,618	1.3	126,825
Michigan	22,933	52.1	21,096	47.9	0	0.0	44,029
Mississippi	19,515	53.4	17,010	46.6	0	0.0	36,525
Missouri	22,954	43.4	29,969	56.6	0	0.0	52,923
New Hampshire	26,310	43.9	32,774	54.7	872	1.5	59,956
New Jersey	33,351	51.7	31,034	48.1	69	0.1	64,454
New York	226,001	51.2	212,733	48.2	2,809	0.6	441,543
North Carolina	46,567	57.7	34,168	42.3	0	0.0	80,735
Ohio	148,043	54.3	123,944	45.4	903	0.3	272,890
Pennsylvania	144,023	50.1	143,672	49.9	0	0.0	287,695
Rhode Island	5,213	60.4	3,263	37.8	19	0.2	8,631
Tennessee	60,194	55.7	47,951	44.3	0	0.0	108,145
Vermont	32,440	63.9	18,006	35.5	317	0.6	50,782
Virginia	42,637	49.4	43,757	50.6	0	0.0	86,394
TOTALS	1,275,390	52.9	1,128,854	46.8	6,797	0.3	2,411,808

1840 ELECTION: STATE-BY-STATE RESULTS (WH HARRISON vs. VAN BUREN vs. BIRNEY)

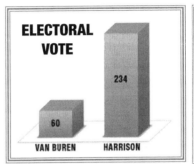

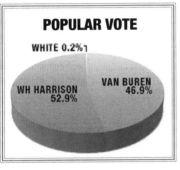

US MAP OF STATES CARRIED

UNITED STATES
PRESIDENTIAL ELECTION OF 1844

THE ISSUES AMERICAN EXPANSIONISM

Should the United States decide to annex Texas?

The DEMOCRATIC CONVENTION

PLACE: Baltimore, Maryland

DATE: May 27 to 29, 1844

NOMINATED: James Polk, of Tennessee, for President

NOMINATED: George Dallas, of Pennsylvania, for Vice President

The 1844 Democratic convention was the first truly divided convention. The Democratic party was split over whether to annex Texas as part of the United States. This was the beginning of the split that would ultimately divide the party over the issue of slavery. Texas would be a slave state, and many opposed adding another slave state. Those in the south, however, were enthusiastic in their support for the annexation. Former President Van Buren was the official leader of the party. He had the majority of convention votes pledged to him. Van Buren opposed annexation, and had never been popular within the party. Thus, there was a determined effort to stop his nomination. Robert Walker of Mississippi led the opposition. Walker passed a resolution requiring a 2/3 vote to nominate a President. On the first vote Van Buren received 146 of the 266 votes cast; a

majority, but not enough to be selected. Van Buren's support quickly diminished on subsequent votes. Lewis Cass seemed likely to receive the nomination, but the convention adjourned for the night. The Van Buren forces decided to support James Polk who endorsed the annexation of Texas. Polk received 44 votes on the eighth ballot. On the next vote, Van Buren threw his support to Polk and he was soon nominated unanimously.

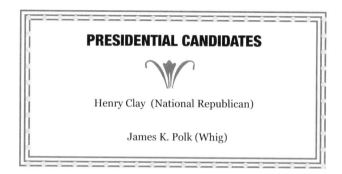

PRESIDENTIAL CANDIDATES

Henry Clay (National Republican)

James K. Polk (Whig)

James K. Polk
ELECTED

Pre he election of 1840 had been fought over the economy. The election of 1844 was fought over American expansion. The question of the annexation of Texas had become a political issue. However, both the expected Democratic nominee, former President Van Buren, and the expected Whig nominee Clay, agreed not to make Texas an issue in the campaign.

At the Democratic convention, in Baltimore, in May 1844, many Democrats opposed President Van Buren's position on Texas. Van Buren did not receive the required 2/3 vote. As a result the convention seemed near a deadlock. Finally, on the ninth ballot the convention swung behind James Polk. This was the first time that a dark horse, (an unknown), received the Democratic nomination.

The Democratic party endorsed a platform that called for the annexation of Texas and the reoccupation of Oregon. It also stood against federal improvement and the resurrection of the Bank of the United States. The Whigs nominated Henry Clay, unanimously.

In April of 1844, President Tyler dropped his "Texas bombshell", as it had become known, when he submitted a treaty for the annexation of Texas. This framed the election campaign. Questions of Manifest Destiny and Slavery dominated the campaign.

Clay was the early front runner, and expected to have an easy victory. His opposition to the annexation of Texas lost him support in the South. The fact he was a slave owner lost him support in the North. A third party, abolitionist candidate named James Birney siphoned off enough support in the North to deny Clay a win in New York, which would have guaranteed his election victory. This election was very personal, with newspaper attacks calling Polk "a coward" and Clay a "drunkard". James Polk won this election.

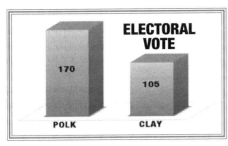

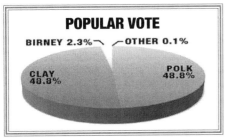

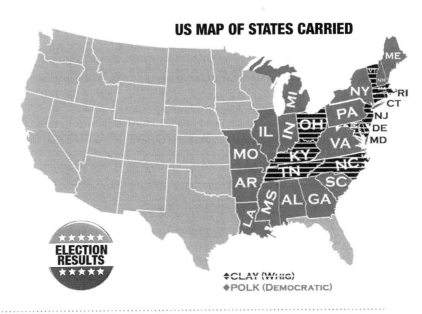

US MAP OF STATES CARRIED

◇CLAY (WHIG)
◆POLK (DEMOCRATIC)

STATES	JAMES POLK		HENRY CLAY		JAMES BIRNEY		TOTAL
	VOTES	PERCENTAGE	VOTES	PERCENTAGE	VOTES	PERCENTAGE	VOTES
Alabama	37,401	59.0	26,002	41.0	0	0.0	63,403
Arkansas	9,546	63.0	5,604	37.0	0	0.0	15,150
Connecticut	29,841	46.2	32,832	50.8	1,943	3.0	64,616
Delaware	5,970	48.7	6,271	51.2	0	0.0	12,247
Georgia	44,147	51.2	42,100	48.8	0	0.0	86,247
Illinois	58,795	53.9	45,854	42.0	3,469	3.2	109,057
Indiana	70,183	50.1	67,866	48.4	2,108	1.5	140,157
Kentucky	51,988	45.9	61,249	54.1	0	0.0	113,237
Louisiana	13,782	51.3	13,083	48.7	0	0.0	26,865
Maine	45,719	53.8	34,378	40.5	4,836	5.7	84,933
Maryland	32,706	47.6	35,984	52.4	0	0.0	68,690
Massachusetts	53,039	40.2	67,062	50.8	10,830	8.2	132,037
Michigan	27,737	49.9	24,185	43.5	3,638	6.5	55,560
Mississippi	25,846	57.4	19,158	42.6	0	0.0	45,004
Missouri	41,322	57.0	31,200	43.0	0	0.0	72,522
New Hampshire	27,160	55.2	17,866	36.3	4,161	8.5	49,187
New Jersey	37,495	49.4	38,318	50.5	131	0.2	75,944
New York	237,588	48.9	232,482	47.8	15,812	3.3	485,882
North Carolina	39,287	47.6	43,232	52.4	0	0.0	82,521
Ohio	149,127	47.8	155,091	49.7	8,082	2.6	312,300
Pennsylvania	167,311	50.4	161,195	48.6	3,139	0.9	331,645
Rhode Island	4,867	39.9	7,322	60.0	0	0.0	12,194
Tennessee	59,917	49.9	60,040	50.1	0	0.0	119,957
Vermont	18,041	37.0	26,770	54.9	3,954	8.1	48,765
Virginia	50,679	53.0	44,860	47.0	0	0.0	95,539
TOTALS	1,339,494	49.5	1,300,004	48.1	62,103	2.3	2,703,659

1844 ELECTION: STATE-BY-STATE RESULTS (WH HARRISON vs. VAN BUREN vs. BIRNEY)

THE ISSUES

EXPANSION OF SLAVERY

Should the new states in the Union be able to decide independently if they are to be "Free" or "Slave" states?

The DEMOCRATIC CONVENTION

PLACE: Baltimore, Maryland

DATE: May 22 to 25, 1848

NOMINATED: Lewis Cass, of Michigan, for President

NOMINATED: William O. Butler, of Kentucky, for Vice President

When Democrats gathered in Baltimore they were divided into three distinct groups. One group, led by former President Van Buren, totally opposed slavery. The second group, led by Senator Calhoun, opposed anything that would diminish slavery in the United States. The third group, led by Lewis Cass, championed the idea of popular sovereignty; the notion that new territories should be free to determine whether they were to be free or slave states. Lewis Cass, being the compromise candidate between two extremes, won the nomination on the fourth ballot. He won the votes of 179 out of the 254 able to vote. Van Buren and his supporters were not willing to accept the outcome of the convention. They left the Democratic party to found a new party, called "the Free Soil Party".

PRESIDENTIAL CANDIDATES
Zachary Taylor (Whig)
Lewis Cass (Democratic)

In the aftermath of the the Mexican-American War it was questioned whether or not to extend slavery to the territory gained in the war. This issue framed the election of 1848. As a war hero, Zachary Taylor was a clear favorite at the Whig convention in June 1848. He received the needed two-thirds of the votes on the fourth ballot. The Democrats nominated Lewis Cass as their presidential candidate.

Taylor said very little on the question of whether slavery should be extended or not. Taylor did, however, own 200 slaves. His views were inferred from his actions. Cass, on the other hand, supported the view that each territory should decide for itself whether to allow slavery. Van Buren ran as a third party candidate on the Free Soil ticket, in total opposition to the expansion of slavery.

This presidential campaign was characteristic of the campaigns of the times, with each side slinging mud at the other. Taylor was attacked as a military autocrat, Democrats went on to call Taylor "semi-literate". The Whigs responded by calling Cass a "vagabond of evil".

The election was decided by Van Buren. Though the ex-President did not win any states, the 10% of the vote he did receive was enough to ensure Taylor's victory.

Zachary Taylor

ELECTED

STATES	ZACHARY TAYLOR		LEWIS CASS		MARTIN VAN BUREN		TOTAL VOTES
	VOTES	PERCENTAGE	VOTES	PERCENTAGE	VOTES	PERCENTAGE	
Alabama	30.482	49.4	31,173	50.6	0	0.0	61,659
Arkansas	7,587	44.9	9,301	55.1	0	0.0	16,888
Connecticut	30,318	48.6	27,051	43.4	5,005	8.0	62,398
Delaware	6,440	51.8	5,910	47.5	82	0.7	12,432
Florida	4,120	57.2	3,083	42.8	0	0.0	7,203
Georgia	47,532	51.3	44,785	48.5	0	0.0	92,317
Illinois	52,853	42.4	55,952	44.9	15,702	12.6	124,596
Indiana	69,668	45.7	74,695	49.0	8,031	5.3	152,394
Iowa	9,930	44.6	11,238	50.5	1,103	5.0	22,271
Kentucky	67,145	57.5	49,720	42.5	0	0.0	116,865
Louisiana	18,487	54.6	15,379	45.4	0	0.0	33,866
Maine	35,273	40.3	40,195	45.9	12,157	13.9	87,625
Maryland	37,702	52.1	34,528	47.7	129	0.2	72,359
Massachusetts	61,072	45.3	35,281	26.2	38,333	28.4	134,748
Michigan	23,947	36.8	30,742	47.2	10,393	16.0	65,082
Mississippi	25,911	49.4	26,545	50.6	0	0.0	52,456
Missouri	32,671	44.9	40,077	55.1	0	0.0	72,748
New Hampshire	14,781	29.5	27,763	55.4	7,560	15.1	50,104
New Jersey	40,015	51.5	36,901	47.5	829	1.1	77,745
New York	218,583	47.9	114,319	25.1	120,497	26.4	455,944
North Carolina	44,054	55.2	35,772	44.8	0	0.0	79,826
Ohio	138,656	42.1	154,782	47.0	35,523	10.8	328,987
Pennsylvania	285,730	50.3	172,186	46.7	11,176	3.0	369,092
Rhode Island	6,705	60.7	3,613	32.7	726	6.6	11,049
Tennessee	64,321	52.5	58,142	47.5	0	0.0	122,463
Texas	5,281	31.1	11,644	68.5	0	0.0	17,000
Vermont	23,117	48.3	10,943	22.8	13,837	28.9	47,897
Virginia	45,265	49.2	46,739	50.8	0	0.0	92,004
Wisconsin	13,747	35.1	15,001	38.3	10,418	26.6	39,166
TOTAL	1,361,393	47.3	1,223,460	42.5	291,501	10.1	2,879,184

1848 ELECTION: STATE-BY-STATE RESULTS (TAYLOR vs. CASS vs. VAN BUREN)

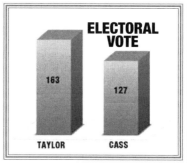

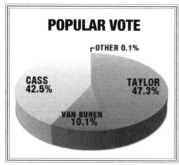

THE ISSUES

CAREER ARMY MAN vs. CITIZEN SOLDIERS

Should Americans elect a career army officer or a citizen soldier to serve as the next President of the United States?

The DEMOCRATIC CONVENTION

PLACE: Baltimore, Maryland

DATE: June 1 to 5, 1852

NOMINATED: Franklin R. Pierce, of New Hampshire, for President

NOMINATED: William O. Butler, of Kentucky, for Vice President

The Democratic party opened its 1852 convention in Baltimore, in June, with four competing candidates for the Presidency. By this time, most of those who had left the party with Van Buren to form the "Free Soilers" had returned. Before deciding on a Presidential candidate, the convention adopted a platform designed to unite the factions fighting over slavery. The platform opposed any further "agitation" over the issue of slavery. When it came to the vote to select a candidate for President, there were four contenders: Stephen Douglas, William Marcy, James Buchanan and Lewis Cass. The convention was hopelessly deadlocked. On the 49th ballot, the convention turned to a "dark horse", Franklin Pierce of New Hampshire. Pierce's views on slavery had not yet been clearly articulated, and thus, had not offended anyone. Franklin Pierce's service as a General in the Mexican American War allowed the party to play the military hero card.

The Whigs nominated Winfield Scott, a military hero from the Mexican American War. The Whigs were hopelessly divided in the campaign. While the Southern Whigs enthusiastically supported their candidate, the Northern Whigs were reluctant supporters. The Democrats, in contrast, were united; with many of those who had deserted the party in 1848 having returned. The returnees included former President Van Buren, who supported Pierce.

This campaign was very personal, with both candidates accusing the other of being a drunk. Scott was accused of being pompous and too in love with his rank. Pierce was accused of collapsing and being a coward during the Mexican American War, where he served as a General; a citizen soldier. Pierce who had been both a Congressman and Senator from New Hampshire, was also a recovering alcoholic.

In the end, the voters chose the "dark horse", Pierce, over the well known general, whom they did not seem to like. This effectively brought an end to the Whig party. Pierce, who was 48 years old at the time, became the youngest man to be elected President of the United States.

PRESIDENTIAL CANDIDATES

Zachary Taylor (Whig)

Lewis Cass (Democratic)

Franklin Pierce
ELECTED

UNITED STATES PRESIDENTIAL **Election of 1852**

STATES	FRANKLIN PIERCE		WINFIELD SCOTT		JOHN HALE		TOTAL VOTES
	VOTES	PERCENTAGE	VOTES	PERCENTAGE	VOTES	PERCENTAGE	
Alabama	26,881	60.9	15,061	34.1	0	0.0	44,147
Arkansas	12,173	62.2	7,404	37.8	0	0.0	19,577
California	40,721	53.0	35,972	46.8	61	0.1	76,810
Connecticut	33,249	49.8	30,359	45.5	3,161	4.7	66,781
Delaware	6,318	49.9	6,293	49.7	62	0.5	12,673
Florida	4,318	60.0	2,875	40.0	0	0.0	7,193
Georgia	40,516	64.7	16,660	26.6	0	0.0	62,626
Illinois	80,378	51.9	64,733	41.8	9,863	6.4	154,974
Indiana	95,340	52.0	80,907	44.2	6,929	3.8	183,176
Iowa	17,763	50.2	15,856	44.8	1,606	4.5	35,364
Kentucky	53,949	48.3	57,428	51.4	266	0.2	111,643
Louisiana	18,647	51.9	17,255	48.1	0	0.0	35,902
Maine	41,609	50.6	32,543	39.6	8,030	9.8	82,182
Maryland	40,022	53.3	35,077	46.7	21	0.0	75,120
Massachusetts	44,569	35.1	52,683	41.4	28,023	22.0	127,103
Michigan	41,842	50.4	33,860	40.8	7,237	8.7	82,939
Mississippi	26,896	60.5	17,558	39.5	0	0.0	44,454
Missouri	38,817	56.4	29,984	43.6	0	0.0	68,801
New Hampshire	28,503	56.4	15,486	30.6	6,546	13.0	50,535
New Jersey	44,301	52.8	38,551	45.9	336	0.4	83,926
New York	262,083	50.2	234,882	45.0	25,329	4.8	522,294
North Carolina	39,788	50.4	39,043	49.5	0	0.0	78,891
Ohio	169,193	47.9	152,577	43.2	31,133	8.8	352,903
Pennsylvania	198,568	51.2	179,182	46.2	8,500	2.2	387,920
Rhode Island	8,735	51.4	7,626	44.8	644	3.8	17,005
Tennessee	56,900	49.3	58,586	50.7	0	0.0	115,486
Texas	14,857	73.5	5,356	26.5	0	0.0	20,223
Vermont	13,044	29.8	22,173	50.6	8,621	19.7	43,838
Virginia	73,872	55.7	58,732	44.3	0	0.0	132,604
Wisconsin	33,658	52.0	22,240	34.4	8,842	13.7	64,740
TOTAL	1,607,510	50.8	1,386,942	43.9	155,210	4.9	3,161,830

1852 ELECTION: STATE-BY-STATE RESULTS (PIERCE vs. SCOTT vs. HALE)

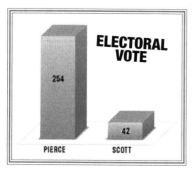

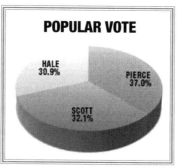

THE ISSUES

EXPANSION OF SLAVERY

Should slavery be allowed to expand to new additional states?

NATIONAL IMPROVEMENTS

Should slavery be allowed to expand to new additional states?

The REPUBLICAN CONVENTION

PLACE: Musical Fund Hall Philadelphia, PA

DATE: June 17 to 19, 1856

NOMINATED: John C. Freemont, of California, for President

NOMINATED: William Dayton, of New Jersey, for VP

The Republicans selected John Charles Freemont in their first national convention. They hoped his celebrity status, as a famous explorer, would help elect him. The Republicans adopted a platform stating that Congress should not allow either slavery nor bigamy in the new territories.

James Buchanan

ELECTED

The DEMOCRATIC CONVENTION

PLACE: Cincinnati, Ohio

DATE: June 2 to 6, 1856

NOMINATED: James Buchanan, of Pennsylvania, for President

NOMINATED: John Breckinridge, of Kentucky, for Vice President

In early June of 1856, when the Democratic party met in Cincinnati, the party was torn by the issues of slavery and states rights. The convention, once again, passed a platform that called for non-interference by Congress in the issue of slavery. Both President Pierce and Stephen Douglas sought their party's nominations. However, both had been severely tarnished by events in "Bloody Kansas"; as had Lewis Cass. The only candidate not tarred by recent event was James Buchanan; who had been US Ambassador to England at the time. On the first ballot Buchanan led with 135 1/2 votes; to 122 1/2 votes for Pierce; 33 for Douglas and 5 for Cass. Support for Pierce faded rapidly, while support for Douglas grew. Buchanan seemed unable to reach the two thirds required to win. On the sixteenth ballot Douglas instructed that his name be removed, thus allowing Buchanan to receive the nomination.

PRESIDENTIAL CANDIDATES

John Freemont (Republican)

James Buchanan (Democratic)

Millard Fillmore (Know Nothing)

The passing of the Kanas Nebraska Act in 1854 brought an end to the Whig party. It also forged the creation of new parties. The act was highly divisive. It gave Kansas and Nebraska the right to decide whether or not to allow slavery in their borders. The result was a mini "civil war" fought in Kansas, between opponents and supporters of slavery. The Whig party had always been divided between Northern opponents of slavery and Southern slavery supporters. The Whig party fell apart, as the central divide in the United States became slavery. This led to the founding of two new parties: the Republican party and the American Party. The Republican party was founded in 1854. The main goal of the Republican party was to stop the expansion of slavery. The American party, otherwise known as the "Know Nothing" Party, was founded in 1855. The main goal of the American party was to stop immigration.

The Democrats met in Cincinnati, in June 1856. President Pierce hoped to be nominated for a second term. That was not going to happen. Instead, the Democrats settled on James Buchanan. His major appeal was the fact he had been abroad during the previous few years. However, Buchanan had not been involved in any of the controversy surrounding the Kanas Nebraska Act. Buchanan was nominated unanimously on the 17th ballot. The Democratic platform, supported the compromise of 1850, opposed federal interference in slavery, and supported the building of the transcontinental railroad.

Buchanan had two opponents in the election; John Fremont of the newly organized Republican party, and former President Millard Fillmore of the Know-Nothing party.

The Republicans opposed the extension of slavery. They held Pierce responsible for the violence in Kansas at the time. The Know-Nothing Party consisted of those opposed to immigration and to Catholic influence. Pierce had a lock on the South, so the fight was over the Northern vote.

The slogan of the Republican party in the candidate was "Free Speech, Free Press, Free Soil, Free Men, Fremont and Victory!" The Democrats claimed the South would not stand for a Fremont victory and would secede. In addition, they claimed that Fremont was a Catholic (which he was not, although he was married in a church). That rumor caused Fremont the loss of substantial support. Pierce narrowly won the election. Fillmore came in third. He won 21.6 percent, the highest percentage vote received by a third party in the 19th century.

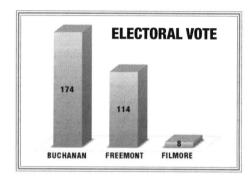

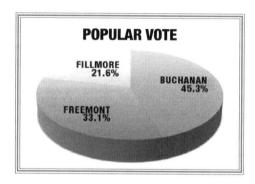

STATES	JAMES BUCHANAN		JOHN FREMONT		MILLARD FILLMORE		TOTAL VOTES
	VOTES	PERCENTAGE	VOTES	PERCENTAGE	VOTES	PERCENTAGE	
Alabama	46,739	62.1	0	0.0	28,552	37.9	75,291
Arkansas	21,910	67.1	0	0.0	10,732	32.9	32,642
California	53,342	48.4	20,704	18.8	36,195	32.8	110,255
Connecticut	35,028	43.6	42,717	53.2	2,615	3.3	80,360
Delaware	8,004	54.8	310	2.1	6,275	43.0	14,598
Florida	6,358	56.8	0	0.0	4,833	43.2	11,191
Georgia	56,581	57.1	0	0.0	42,439	42.9	99,020
Illinois	105,528	44.1	96,275	40.2	37,531	15.7	239,334
Indiana	118,670	50.4	94,375	40.1	22,356	9.5	235,401
Iowa	37,568	40.7	45,073	48.8	9,669	10.5	92,310
Kentucky	74,642	52.5	0	0.0	67,416	47.5	142,058
Louisiana	22,164	51.7	0	0.0	20,709	48.3	42,873
Maine	39,140	35.7	67,279	61.3	3,270	3.0	109,689
Maryland	39,123	45.0	285	0.3	47,452	54.6	86,860
Massachusetts	39,244	23.1	108,172	63.6	19,626	11.5	170,048
Michigan	52,136	41.5	71,762	57.2	1,660	1.3	125,558
Mississippi	35,456	59.4	0	0.0	24,191	40.6	59,647
Missouri	57,964	54.4	0	0.0	48,522	45.6	106,486
New Hampshire	31,891	45.7	37,473	53.7	410	0.6	69,774
New Jersey	46,943	47.2	28,338	28.5	24,115	24.3	99,396
New York	195,878	32.8	276,004	46.3	124,604	20.9	596,486
North Carolina	48,243	56.8	0	0.0	36,720	43.2	84,963
Ohio	170,874	44.2	187,497	48.5	28,121	7.3	386,640
Pennsylvania	230,772	50.1	147,963	32.1	82,202	17.8	460,937
Rhode Island	6,680	33.7	11,467	57.8	1,675	8.5	19,822
Tennessee	69,704	52.2	0	0.0	63,878	47.8	133,582
Texas	31,995	66.6	0	0.0	16,010	33.4	48,005
Vermont	10,569	20.9	39,561	78.1	545	1.1	50,675
Virginia	90,083	60.0	0	0.0	60,150	40.0	150,233
Wisconsin	52,843	43.8	67,090	55.7	580	0.5	120,513
TOTAL	1,836,072	45.3	1,342,345	33.1	873,053	21.5	4,054,647

1856 ELECTION: STATE-BY-STATE RESULTS (TAYLOR vs. CASS vs. VAN BUREN)

US MAP OF STATES CARRIED

♦FREEMONT (REPUBLICAN)
♦BUCHANAN (DEMOCRATIC)
--FILLMORE (KNOW NOTHING)

THE ISSUES EXPANSION OF SLAVERY

EXPANSION OF SLAVERY Would the South decide to secede from the Union?

The REPUBLICAN CONVENTION

PLACE: Chicago, IL

DATE: May 16 to 18, 1860

NOMINATED: Abraham Lincoln, of Illinois, for President

NOMINATED: Hannibal Hamlin, of New Jersey, for VP

Abraham Lincoln was nominated on the third ballot. He defeated Senator Seward of New York. Seward was considered by many to be too radical. The Republicans issued a platform that criticized slavery, while making it clear they would not interfere with slavery in the South. The Republicans also promised to support the building of a transcontinental railroad.

The DEMOCRATIC CONVENTION

DATE/PLACE: Charleston, SC
April 23 to May 3, 1860

DATE/PLACE: Baltimore MD
June 18 to 23, 1860

NOMINATED: Stephen Douglas, of Illinois, for President

NOMINATED: Benjamin Fitzpatrick, of Alabama,, for Vice President

The Democratic party that met in Charleston, in 1860, was deeply divided. Stephen Douglas was the clear favorite of Northern Democrats. Southern Democrats. However, he demanded that the party come out with a platform in clear defense of slavery. Douglas and his supporters could not agree. As a result, many Southern delegates walked out. The convention then went through 54 ballots. Yet Douglas still failed to achieve the needed 2/3 of the votes needed to receive the nomination. The convention adjourned. They planned to reconvene in June, in Baltimore. When the party reconvened, the fight continued. This time, the disagreement was over recognition of the delegations. Some of the delegations walked out, once again. Douglas was still unable to achieve the required 2/3 of the votes needed. Finally, the convention voted to state that since Douglas received 2/3 of the votes present at the convention, he would receive the nomination.

PRESIDENTIAL CANDIDATES

Abraham Lincoln
(Republican)

Stephan Douglas
(Democrat)

John Breckinridge
(Southern Democrat)

John Bell
(Constitutional Union)

Abraham Lincoln
ELECTED

ON THIS ... ELECTION

The Democratic party met in April 1860, in Charleston, South Carolina. The convention body was split between Northerners, who supported popular sovereignty (the ability of a state to decide itself whether to allow slavery or not,) and Southerners, who wanted the Democratic party to defend the right to hold slaves. The convention refused the Southern demand and the Southern delegates walked out. The Northern members then tried to nominate Stephen Douglas as their nominee. However, with the Southern delegate no longer present they did not have the 2/3 votes needed to select a party nominee. The Democrats met again in Baltimore. Once again the convention deadlocked, and the Southern delegates walked out. The Northerners went ahead and nominated Douglas. The Southerners returned to Charleston and nominated Vice President John Breckinridge to represent the party they now called the "National Democrats".

When the Republicans met in Chicago in May of 1860, William Seward was their front runner to receive their presidential nomination. Seward was the most respected Republican in the country. Delegates, however, were afraid that Sewards' outspoken views against slavery, as well as his attacks against the "Know Nothing Party" could limit the support the party would gain in the election. So the party turned to Abraham Lincoln of Illinois. Lincoln won the nomination on the third ballot. The Republican platform opposed slavery in the territories, but upheld the right of slavery in the South. It also opposed the Dred-Scott decision. Furthermore, in order to gain support from the former Whigs the Republicans came out in favor of Federal support for national improvements. This included support for the building of the Trans Continental Railroad.

A fourth political party was established by those who wanted to preserve slavery, but, at the same time, preserve the Union. They were called the "Constitutional Union party". They selected John Bell to be their presidential nominee. The Republicans were all united behind Lincoln, while the other parties were divided by regions. Most of the 1860 presidential campaign was implemented by the party organizations. At this time, presidential candidates took a very small part in active campaigning. Stephen Douglas became the first presidential candidate in history to undertake a nationwide speaking tour. Douglas traveled to the South. Though, he did not expect to win many electoral votes in that region. Douglas spoke to Southerners about the importance of maintaining the Union.

In the 1860 campaign, the presidential contest was in effect two contests. One contest was between Douglas and Lincoln in the North and West. The other contest was between Breckinridge and Bell in the South. The Republicans ran a very vigorous campaign. Their better organization won the day. Lincoln won a clear majority of the electoral vote. He gained 180 electoral votes, versus just 123 for all his opponents combined. His opponents, however, in aggregate (all together) won a greater percentage of the overall vote, and Lincoln would govern after winning considerably less than half (just 39.9%) of the popular vote.

UNITED STATES PRESIDENTIAL Election of 1860

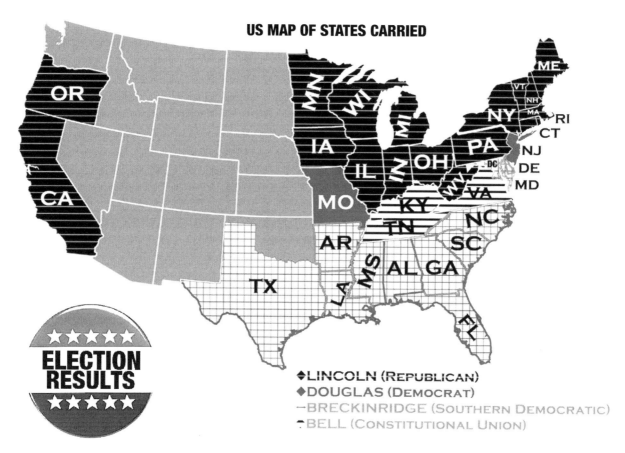

US MAP OF STATES CARRIED

ME
OR
VT
NH
MA
NY
RI
CT
IA
NJ
IL
OH
DC
DE
CA
MD
VA
MO
KY
NC
TN
SC
AR
AL GA
TX
LA MS
FL

★ LINCOLN (REPUBLICAN)
♦ DOUGLAS (DEMOCRAT)
— BRECKINRIDGE (SOUTHERN DEMOCRATIC)
⌐ BELL (CONSTITUTIONAL UNION)

ELECTION RESULTS

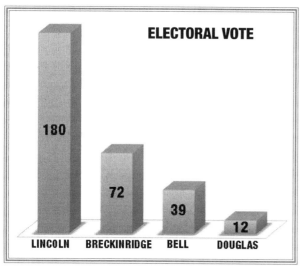

ELECTORAL VOTE

LINCOLN	180
BRECKINRIDGE	72
BELL	39
DOUGLAS	12

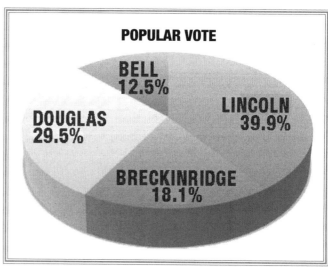

POPULAR VOTE

BELL 12.5%
LINCOLN 39.9%
DOUGLAS 29.5%
BRECKINRIDGE 18.1%

STATE	ABRAHAM LINCOLN		STEPHAN DOUGLAS		JOHN BRECKINRIDGE		JOHN BELL		TOTAL VOTE
	VOTES	PERCENTAGE	VOTES	PERCENTAGE	VOTES	PERCENTAGE	VOTES	PERCENTAGE	
Alabama	0	0.0	13,618	15.1	48,669	54	27,835	30.9	90,122
Arkansas	0	0.0	5,357	9.9	28,732	53.1	20,063	37	54,152
California	38,733	32.3	37,999	31.7	33,969	28.3	9,111	7.6	119,827
Connecticut	43,488	58.1	15,431	20.6	14,372	19.2	1,528	2	74,819
Delaware	3,822	23.7	1,066	6.6	7,339	45.5	3,888	24.1	16,115
Florida	0	0.0	223	1.7	8,277	62.2	4,801	36.1	13,301
Georgia	0	0.0	11,581	10.9	52,176	48.9	42,960	40.3	106,717
Illinois	172,171	50.7	160,215	47.2	2,331	0.7	4,914	1.4	339,666
Indiana	139,033	51.1	115,509	42.4	12,295	4.5	5,306	1.9	272,143
Iowa	70,302	54.6	55,639	43.2	1,035	0.8	1,763	1.4	128,739
Kentucky	1,364	0.9	25,651	17.5	53,143	36.3	66,058	45.2	146,216
Louisiana	0	0.0	7,625	15.1	22,681	44.9	20,204	40	50,510
Maine	62,811	62.2	29,693	29.4	6,368	6.3	2,046	2	100,918
Maryland	2,294	2.5	5,966	6.4	42,482	45.9	41,760	45.1	92,502
Massachusetts	106,684	62.8	34,370	20.2	6,163	3.6	22,331	13.1	169,876
Michigan	88,481	57.2	65,057	42	805	0.5	415	0.3	154,758
Minnesota	22,069	63.4	11,920	34.2	748	2.1	50	0.1	34,804
Mississippi	0	0.0	3,282	4.7	40,768	59	25,045	36.2	69,095
Missouri	17,028	10.3	58,801	35.5	31,362	18.9	58,372	35.3	165,563
New Hampshire	37,519	56.9	25,887	39.3	2,125	3.2	412	0.6	65,943
New Jersey	58,346	48.1	62,869	51.9	0	.			121,215
New York	362,646	53.7	312,510	46.3	0	.			675,156
North Carolina	0	0.0	2,737	2.8	48,846	50.5	45,129	46.7	96,712
Ohio	231,709	52.3	187,421	42.3	11,406	2.6	12,194	2.8	442,866
Oregon	5,329	36.1	4,136	28	5,075	34.4	218	1.5	14,758
Pennsylvania	268,030	56.3	16,765	3.5	178,871	37.5	12,776	2.7	476,442
Rhode Island	12,244	61.4	7,707	38.6	0	.			19,951
Tennessee	0	0.0	11,281	7.7	65,097	44.6	69,728	47.7	146,106
Texas	0	0.0	18	0	47,454	75.5	15,383	24.5	62,855
Vermont	33,808	75.7	8,649	19.4	218	0.5	1,969	4.4	44,644
Virginia	1,887	1.1	16,198	9.7	74,325	44.5	74,481	44.6	166,891
Wisconsin	86,110	56.6	65,021	42.7	887	0.6	161	0.1	152,179
TOTALS	1,865,908	39.9	1,380,202	29.5	848,019	18.1	590,901	12.6	4,685,561

1860 ELECTION: STATE-BY-STATE RESULTS (LINCOLN vs. DOUGLAS vs. BRECKINRIDGE vs. BELL)

UNITED STATES
PRESIDENTIAL ELECTION OF 1864

THE ISSUES

LINCOLN AS COMMANDER AND CHIEF

Could Abraham Lincoln prove to be a competent Commander and Chief?

The DEMOCRATIC CONVENTION

PLACE: Chicago, IL

DATE: August 29 to 31, 1864

NOMINATED: George B. McClellan, of New Jersey, for President

NOMINATED: George H. Pendelton, of Ohio, for Vice President

The REPUBLICAN CONVENTION

PLACE: Baltimore, MD

DATE: June 7 to 8, 1864

NOMINATED: Abraham Lincoln, of Illinois, for President

NOMINATED: Andrew Johnson, of Tennessee, for VP

At their convention Republicans nominated Abraham Lincoln for a second term in office. They also changed the name of their party to the "National Union Party", with the hope of expanding its base. The most fateful decision taken at the convention was the decision to replace Vice President Hannibal Hamlin, of Maine, who was from a state the Republicans were sure to carry, with candidate Andrew Johnson, the pro-Union governor of Tennessee.

The 1864 Democratic convention took place as the tide of the civil war was finally turning in favor of the North. The Democrats passed a platform which was highly critical of President Lincoln. It accused Lincoln of violating civil rights. They also attacked President Lincoln for issuing the Emancipation Proclamation. The Democrats endorsed the idea of a negotiated peace with the South. The plan to work toward a negotiated agreement with the South passed and became part of the Democratic platform. Then the convention body moved to nominate the failed, but still popular, General George B. McClellan as their Presidential candidate.

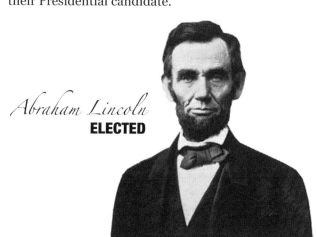

Abraham Lincoln
ELECTED

PRESIDENTIAL CANDIDATES

Abraham Lincoln (Republican)

George B. McClellan (Democratic)

UNITED STATES PRESIDENTIAL Election of 1864

As the election of 1864 neared, the re-election of President Lincoln was very much in doubt. It had been a long a terrible war, that had not started well for the Union. To further call into question Lincoln's re-election prospects, no President had been elected for a second term in the United States, since Andrew Jackson. Despite these challenges, the Republicans chose to renominate Lincoln. When Lincoln was informed he stated: "I do not allow myself to suppose that either the convention, or league have concluded that I am either the greatest or best man in America, but rather they have concluded it is not best to swap horses while crossing the river, and have further concluded that I am not so poor a horse that they might not make a botch of it in trying to swap".

The Democrats nominated General McClellan. The platform of the Democratic party called for a cease-fire. McClellan repudiated the Democratic platform saying the only basis for ceasefire was the restoration of the Union. McClellan strongly criticized Lincoln for the Emancipation of the slaves.

The Democrats attacked Lincoln for being a liar, despot, braggart and much more. The Democrats were accused of treason, and McClellan's war record was ridiculed.

Between the Democratic convention and the election, there were spectacular Union victories. Union victories included Sherman's capture of Atlanta, which radically increased support for Lincoln. In addition, Lincoln received an estimated 80% of votes of Union soldiers. This sealed his overwhelming victory.

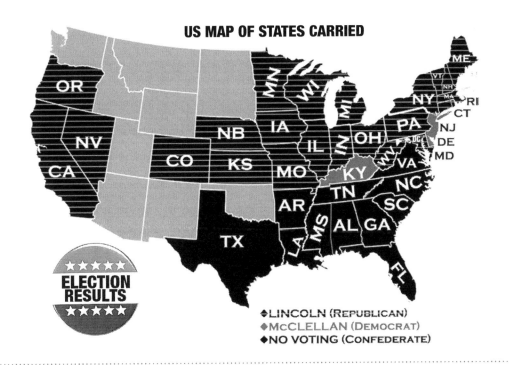

US MAP OF STATES CARRIED

ELECTION RESULTS

◆LINCOLN (Republican)
◆McCLELLAN (Democrat)
◆NO VOTING (Confederate)

STATES	ABRAHAM LINCOLN		GEORGE McCLELLAN		TOTAL VOTES
	VOTES	PERCENTAGE	VOTES	PERCENTAGE	
California	62,053	58.6	43,837	41.4	105,890
Connecticut	44,673	51.4	42,285	48.6	86,958
Delaware	8,155	48.2	8,767	51.8	16,922
Illinois	189,512	54.4	158,724	45.6	348,236
Indiana	149,887	53.5	130,230	46.5	280,117
Iowa	83,858	63.1	49,089	36.9	138,025
Kansas	17,089	79.2	3,836	17.8	21,580
Kentucky	27,787	30.2	64,301	69.8	92,088
Maine	67,805	59.1	46,992	40.9	115,099
Maryland	40,153	55.1	32,739	44.9	72,892
Massachusetts	126,742	72.2	48,745	27.8	175,493
Michigan	91,133	55.1	74,146	44.9	160,023
Minnesota	25,031	59	17,376	40.9	42,433
Missouri	72,750	69.7	31,596	30.3	104,346
Nevada	9,826	59.8	6,594	40.2	16,420
New Hampshire	36,596	52.6	33,034	47.4	69,630
New Jersey	60,724	47.2	68,020	52.8	128,744
New York	368,735	50.5	361,986	49.5	730,721
Ohio	265,674	56.4	205,609	43.6	471,283
Oregon	9,888	53.9	8,457	46.1	18,350
Pennsylvania	296,292	51.6	277,443	48.4	572,707
Rhode Island	14,349	62.2	8,718	37.8	23,067
Vermont	42,419	76.1	13,321	23.9	55,740
West Virginia	23,799	68.2	11,078	31.8	34,877
Wisconsin	83,458	55.9	65,884	44.1	149,342
TOTAL	2,220,846	55.1	1,809,445	44.9	4,030,291

1864 ELECTION: STATE-BY-STATE RESULTS (LINCOLN vs. McCLELLAN)

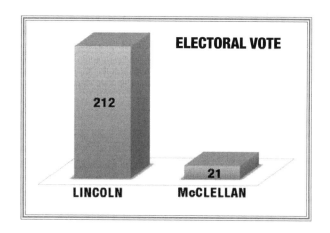

ELECTORAL VOTE

212 LINCOLN

21 McCLELLAN

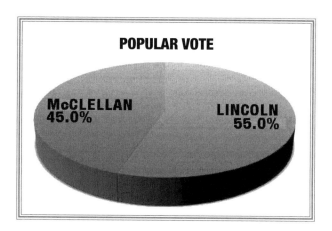

POPULAR VOTE

McCLELLAN 45.0%

LINCOLN 55.0%

THE ISSUES

RECONSTRUCTION

How should Reconstruction be handled? Had Democrats been loyal to the Union?

The REPUBLICAN CONVENTION

PLACE: Chicago, IL

DATE: May 20-21, 1868

NOMINATED: Ulysses S. Grant, of Illinois, for President, for President

NOMINATED: Schuyler Colfax, of Indiana, for VP

The 1868 Republican convention unanimously chose General Grant as their nominee. There were no other nominees. Schuyler Colfax, who was the speaker of the House was selected to be Grant's vice presidential candidate.

PRESIDENTIAL CANDIDATES

Ulysses S. Grant
(Republican)

Horatio Seymour
(Democratic)

The DEMOCRATIC CONVENTION

PLACE: New York, NY

DATE: July 4-9, 1868

NOMINATED: Horatio Seymour, of New York, for President

NOMINATED: Francis P. Blair, of Missouri, for Vice President

The Democratic convention of 1868 opened on the 4th of July in New York City. Before the convention opened it was hoped that Supreme Court Chief Justice Samuel Chase would be the Democratic candidate. However, in keeping with his position, Chase did not mount a campaign for the job. When the convention opened George Pendelton, (the 1864 Democratic candidate for Vice President) was in the lead.

Andrew Johnson was not renominated by the Republicans, (on whose ticket he ran and served as Vice President in 1864). Prior to the Civil War Johnson had always been a Democrat. As a result, Johnson sought re-election in 1868 as a Democrat.

After twenty-two ballots, in which no one achieved the required votes to win, a draft movement quickly developed to nominate the convention chairman, Horatio Seymour. He was a supporter of Chase. However, the momentum was too great. Seymour was unanimously nominated to be the next Democratic candidate for President.

Ulysses S. Grant
ELECTED

General Ulysses Grant received a unanimous vote on the first ballot at the Republican convention. Grant had emerged from the Civil War as the most popular hero.

Grant's Democratic opponent was Horatio Seymour of New York. Seymour was an extremely reluctant nominee, saying he would not be the candidate. In the end, the Democrats forced Seymour to run. Seymour gained the nickname "the Great Decliner".

Grant did not campaign and made no promises. Seymour broke with tradition and campaigned actively in the North. The Republicans promised continued radical reconstruction in the South. Democrats, on the other hand, promised more swift reintegration of the South. The Democrats attacked the Republicans for their promises of reconstruction. Republicans claimed the Democrats were going to give up all that was accomplished in the Civil War. They also attacked Grant for being a drunkard.

Ultimately, it was Grant's personal popularity that determined the outcome of the election.

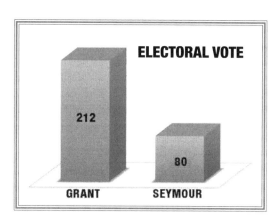

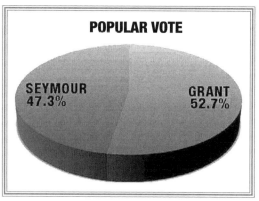

US MAP OF STATES CARRIED

ELECTION RESULTS

◆ GRANT (REPUBLICAN)
◆ SEYMOUR (DEMOCRAT)
◆ NO VOTING (RECONSTRUCTION)

STATES	ULYSSES GRANT		HORATIO SEYMOUR		TOTAL VOTES
	VOTES	PERCENTAGE	VOTES	PERCENTAGE	
Alabama	76,667	51.3	72,921	48.7	149,594
Arkansas	22,112	53.7	19,078	46.3	41,190
California	54,588	50.2	54,068	49.8	108,656
Connecticut	50,789	51.5	47,781	48.5	98,570
Delaware	7,614	41	10,957	59	18,571
Georgia	57,109	35.7	102,707	64.3	159,816
Illinois	250,304	55.7	199,116	44.3	449,420
Indiana	176,548	51.4	166,980	48.6	343,528
Iowa	120,399	61.9	74,040	38.1	194,439
Kansas	30,027	68.8	13,600	31.2	43,630
Kentucky	39,566	25.5	115,889	74.5	155,455
Louisiana	33,263	29.3	80,225	70.7	113,488
Maine	70,502	62.4	42,460	37.6	112,962
Maryland	30,438	32.8	62,357	67.2	92,795
Massachusetts	136,379	69.8	59,103	30.2	195,508
Michigan	128,563	57	97,069	43	225,632
Minnesota	43,545	60.8	28,075	39.2	71,620
Missouri	86,860	57	65,628	43	152,488
Nebraska	9,772	63.9	5,519	36.1	15,291
Nevada	6,474	55.4	5,215	44.6	11,689
New Hampshire	37,718	55.2	30,575	44.8	68,304
New Jersey	80,132	49.1	83,001	50.9	163,133
New York	419,888	49.4	429,883	50.6	849,771
North Carolina	96,939	53.4	84,559	46.6	181,498
Ohio	280,159	54	238,506	46	518,665
Oregon	10,961	49.6	11,125	50.4	22,086
Pennsylvania	342,280	52.2	313,382	47.8	655,662
Rhode Island	13,017	66.7	6,494	33.3	19,511
South Carolina	62,301	57.9	45,237	42.1	107,538
Tennessee	56,628	68.4	26,129	31.6	82,757
Vermont	44,173	78.6	12,051	21.4	56,224
West Virginia	29,015	58.8	20,306	41.2	49,321
Wisconsin	108,920	56.3	84,708	43.7	193,628
TOTAL	3,013,650	52.7	2,708,744	47.3	5,722,440

1868 ELECTION: STATE-BY-STATE RESULTS (GRANT vs. SEYMOUR)

PRESIDENTIAL ELECTION OF 1872

THE ISSUES

POLITICAL AND CIVIL RIGHTS

How much effort should be invested in securing political and civil rights for all Americans?

The DEMOCRATIC CONVENTION

PLACE: Baltimore, MD

DATE: July 9-10, 1872

NOMINATED: Horace Greeley, of New York, for President

NOMINATED: Benjamin Brown, of Massachusetts, for Vice President

The REPUBLICAN CONVENTION

PLACE: Academy of Music, Philadelphia, PA

DATE: June 5-6, 1872

NOMINATED: Ulysses S. Grant, of Illinois, for President, for President

NOMINATED: Henry Wilson, of Massachusetts, for VP

When the Democrats met in 1872, they knew that if they were going to defeat Grant, they had to change their platform, and reject the anti-Reconstruction platform of 1868. They also knew they had to accept Horace Greeley, who was the choice of the Liberal Republican party.

When the Republican party met in Philadelphia on June 5th, there was only one presidential candidate. That one candidate was Ulysses Grant. Grant's critics in the party had already split from the Republicans and created the Liberal Republican Party.

ELECTED

PRESIDENTIAL CANDIDATES

Ulysses S. Grant
(Republican)

Horace Greeley (Democratic)

President Grant was nominated to run for a second term at the Republican Convention in Philadelphia, in June 1872. Grant was renominated without opposition. The Republican platform condemned racial and religious discrimination. It also called for granting women greater rights. President Grant's opponent was Horace Greeley of New York. Greeley was first nominated by the "Liberal Republicans", who wished to protest the corruption of the Grant administration. The Democrats were in such disarray that they were unable to select a presidential candidate. Therefore, they endorsed Greeley.

Horace Greeley had been the editor of the New York Tribune. Greeley was known to be an eccentric figure. At various times, Greeley had been a supporter of spiritualism, prohibition, vegetarianism, and socialism. This made Greeley an easy target of Republican attacks. Greeley's campaign focused primarily on the theme of "more honest government". He also campaigned for an end to radical reconstruction. Greeley received support from most of the South. Grant received support from most Northerners and from most business interests. Most Americans still found Grant popular. Most Americans were also convinced that Grant was not responsible for the corruption in his administration. Thus, Grant was re-elected, receiving an overwhelming majority of the votes. Grant's victory was one of the largest in American electoral history.

Horace Greeley died on November 29th, 1872, before the electoral college could vote. As a result, his vote was split four ways.

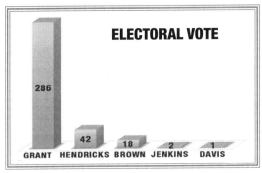

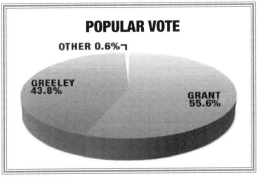

UNITED STATES PRESIDENTIAL Election of 1872

STATES	ULYSSES GRANT		HORACE GREELEY		CHARLES O'CONOR		TOTAL VOTES
	VOTES	PERCENTAGE	VOTES	PERCENTAGE	VOTES	PERCENTAGE	
Alabama	90,272	53.2	79,444	46.8	0	0.0	169,716
Arkansas	41,373	52.2	37,927	47.8	0	0.0	79,300
California	54,007	56.4	40,717	42.5	1,061	1.1	95,785
Connecticut	50,307	52.4	45,685	47.6	0	0.0	95,992
Delaware	11,129	51	10,205	46.8	488	2.2	21,822
Florida	17,763	53.5	15,427	46.5	0	0.0	33,190
Georgia	62,550	45	76,356	55	0	0.0	138,906
Illinois	241,936	56.3	184,884	43	3,151	0.7	429,971
Indiana	186,147	53.2	163,632	46.8	0	0.0	349,779
Iowa	131,566	60.8	71,189	32.9	2,221	1	216,365
Kansas	66,805	66.5	32,970	32.8	156	0.2	100,512
Kentucky	88,766	46.4	99,995	52.3	2,374	1.2	191,552
Louisiana	71,663	55.7	57,029	44.3	0	0.0	128,692
Maine	61,426	67.9	29,097	32.1	0	0.0	90,523
Maryland	66,760	49.7	67,687	50.3	0	0.0	134,447
Massachusetts	133,455	69.3	59,195	30.7	0	0.0	192,650
Michigan	138,768	62.6	78,651	35.5	2,879	1.3	221,569
Minnesota	56,040	61.4	35,131	38.5	0	0.0	91,339
Mississippi	82,175	63.5	47,282	36.5	0	0.0	129,457
Missouri	119,196	43.7	151,434	55.5	2,429	0.9	273,059
Nebraska	18,329	70.7	7,603	29.3	0	0.0	25,932
Nevada	8,413	57.4	6,236	42.6	0	0.0	14,649
New Hampshire	37,168	53.9	31,425	45.6	0	0.0	68,906
New Jersey	91,656	54.5	76,456	45.5	0	0.0	168,467
New York	440,738	53.2	387,282	46.8	0	0.0	829,692
North Carolina	94,772	57.4	70,130	42.5	261	0.2	165,163
Ohio	281,852	53.2	244,320	46.1	1,163	0.2	529,435
Oregon	11,818	58.8	7,742	38.5	547	2.7	20,107
Pennsylvania	349,589	62.2	212,040	37.8	0	0.0	561,629
Rhode Island	13,665	71.9	5,329	28.1	0	0.0	18,994
South Carolina	72,290	75.7	22,699	23.8	204	0.2	95,452
Tennessee	85,655	47.8	93,391	52.2	0	0.0	179.046
Texas	47,910	41.4	67,675	58.5	115	0.1	115,700
Vermont	41,481	79.2	10,927	20.8	0	0.0	52,961
Virginia	93,463	50.5	91,647	49.5	85	0.0	185,195
West Virginia	32,320	51.7	29,532	47.3	615	1	62,467
Wisconsin	105,012	54.6	86,390	44.9	853	0.4	192,255
TOTAL	3,598,468	55.6	2,835,315	43.8	20,609	0.3	6,470,674

1872 ELECTION: STATE-BY-STATE RESULTS (GRANT vs. GREELEY vs. O'CONOR)

THE ISSUES

CIVIL SERVICE

Does the United States require civil service reform? Who bears responsibility for the existence of the country's economic depression?

The REPUBLICAN CONVENTION

PLACE: Exposition Hall
Cincinnati, OH

DATE: June 14 to 16, 1876

NOMINATED: Rutherford B. Hayes, of Ohio, for President

NOMINATED: William A. Wheeler, of New York, for VP

In the period immediately prior to the Republican Convention, the leading Republican candidate was James G. Blaine, the former Speaker of the House. Days before the election Blaine was accused of being tied to the financial scandals that plagued members of the Grant administration. This accusation, combined with questions of Blaine's health, (after he collapsed), established significant opposition to his candidacy. Blaine's opponents blocked his nomination on the first ballot. By the sixth ballot, the convention had nominated Rutherford Hayes.

PRESIDENTIAL CANDIDATES

Rutherford B. Hayes (Republican)

Samuel J. Tilden (Democratic)

The DEMOCRATIC CONVENTION

PLACE: Merchants Exchange, St. Louis, MO

DATE: June 27 to 29, 1876

NOMINATED: Samuel Tilden, of New York, for President

NOMINATED: Thomas Hendricks, of Missouri, for Vice President

The 1876 Democratic Convention opened with three contenders: Samuel J. Tilden of New York, Thomas Hendricks of Indiana, and Union General Winfield Scott Hancock of Pennsylvania. Tilden led on the first vote. However, he was strongly opposed by John Kelley, the leader of Tammany Hall in New York. In the end, Kelley's opposition was not enough to stop the nomination. Tilden won the Democratic nomination on the second ballot.

Rutherford B. Hayes
ELECTED

Rutherford B. Hayes was nominated on the seventh ballot, at the hotly contested Republican convention in 1876. The Republican platform called for the continued control of the South, civil service reform, and investigation of the effects of Oriental immigrations. The Democrats called for the end of reconstruction in the South, restriction of Oriental immigration, and an end to land grants for railroads.

The two presidential candidates were both experienced, albeit, rather dull. Hayes had been a General during the Civil War. He held a law degree from the Harvard Law School and was Governor of Ohio. The Democratic candidate, Samuel Tilden, had been a district attorney fighting corruption in New York, where he became governor.

This campaign revolved around the issue of corruption. The Democrats accused Hayes of being party to the crimes of the Grant administration. At the same time, the Republicans continued to call the Democrats the party of treason. In the final days of the campaign, Tilden was regarded as the favorite presidential candidate. Hayes even believed that he had surely lost the election.

In the end, Tilden won more votes than Hayes had won. However, the election returns in three states: South Carolina, Florida and Louisiana were disputed. As a result, Tilden was one state short of victory. Congress appointed a committee to investigate. The Congressional Committee decided to award all of the disputed votes to Rutherford Hayes. In return, Hayes promised to end reconstruction. Rutherford Hayes became the next President of the United States.

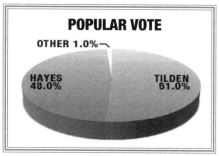

UNITED STATES PRESIDENTIAL Election of 1876

STATES	RUTHERFORD HAYES		SAMUEL TILDEN		PETER COOPER		TOTAL VOTES
	VOTES	PERCENTAGE	VOTES	PERCENTAGE	VOTES	PERCENTAGE	
Alabama	68,708	40	102,989	60	0	0.0	171,699
Arkansas	38,649	39.9	58,086	59.9	211	0.2	96,946
California	79,258	50.9	76,460	49.1	47		155,784
Connecticut	59,033	48.3	61,927	50.7	774	0.6	122,134
Delaware	10,752	44.6	13,381	55.4	0	0.0	24,133
Florida	23,849	51	22,927	49	0	0.0	46,776
Georgia	50,533	28	130,157	72	0	0.0	180,690
Illinois	278,232	50.2	258,611	46.6	17,207	3.1	554,368
Indiana	208,011	48.3	213,529	49.5	9,533	2.2	430,020
Iowa	171,326	58.4	112,121	38.2	9,431	3.2	293,398
Kansas	78,324	63.1	37,902	30.5	7,770	6.3	124,134
Kentucky	97,568	37.4	160,060	61.4	0	0.0	259,614
Louisiana	75,315	51.6	70,508	48.4	0	0.0	145,823
Maine	66,300	56.6	49,917	42.6	0	0.0	117,045
Maryland	71,980	44	91,779	56	0	0.0	163,759
Massachusetts	150,063	57.8	108,777	41.9	0	0.0	259,619
Michigan	166,901	52.4	141,665	44.5	9,023	2.8	318,426
Minnesota	72,962	58.8	48,799	39.3	2,399	1.9	124,119
Mississippi	52,603	31.9	112,173	68.1	0	0.0	164,776
Missouri	145,027	41.4	202,086	57.6	3,497	1	350,610
Nebraska	31,915	64.8	17,343	35.2	0	0.0	49,258
Nevada	10,383	52.7	9,308	47.3	0	0.0	19,691
New Hampshire	41,540	51.8	38,510	48.1	0	0.0	80,143
New Jersey	103,517	47	115,962	52.7	714	0.3	220,193
New York	489,207	48.2	521,949	51.4	1,978	0.2	1,015,503
North Carolina	108,484	46.4	125,427	53.6	0	0.0	233,911
Ohio	330,698	50.2	323,182	49.1	3,058	0.5	658,650
Oregon	15,207	50.9	14,157	47.4	509	1.7	29,873
Pennsylvania	384,157	50.6	366,204	48.2	7,209	0.9	758,973
Rhode Island	15,787	59.6	10,712	40.4	0	0.0	26,499
South Carolina	91,786	50.2	90,097	49.8	0	0.0	182,683
Tennessee	89,566	40.2	133,077	59.8	0	0.0	222,743
Texas	45,013	29.7	106,372	70.2	0	0.0	151,431
Vermont	44,092	68.4	20,254	31.4	0	0.0	64,460
Virginia	95,518	40.4	140,770	59.6	0	0.0	236,288
West Virginia	41,997	42.1	56,546	56.7	1,104	1.1	99,647
Wisconsin	130,050	50.6	-123,922	48.2	1,509	0.6	257,799
TOTAL	4,033,497	48.0	4,288,191	51.0	78,501	0.9	8,411,618

1876 ELECTION: STATE-BY-STATE RESULTS (HAYES vs. TILDEN vs. COOPER)

THE ISSUES

DISENFRANCHISEMENT OF SOUTHERN BLACKS

Did the end of reconstruction, (orchestrated by the Democratic party), act to disenfranchise former slaves in the South? Who was best capable to effectively fight government corruption?

The REPUBLICAN CONVENTION

PLACE: Exposition Hall
Chicago, IL

DATE: June 2 to 8, 1880

NOMINATED: James Garfield, of Ohio, for President

NOMINATED: Chester Arthur, of New York, for VP

The Republican Convention opened with three candidates. However, there was a draft movement to nominate Grant for the third term, after a four year absence. Many opposed the breaking of the two term tradition established by Washington. They supported either Blaine, or Secretary of the Treasury, John Sherman. The convention deadlocked for thirty five ballots. Grant remained 66 votes short to receive the nomination. On the 36th ballot, the anti-Grant vote switched to James Garfield. James Garfield received the Republican nomination.

PRESIDENTIAL CANDIDATES

James A. Garfield (Republican)

Winfield Scott Hancock (Democratic)

The DEMOCRATIC CONVENTION

PLACE: Merchants' Exchange St. Louis, MO

DATE: June 22 to 24, 1880

NOMINATED: Winfield S. Hancock, of New York, for President

NOMINATED: Winfield S. Hancock, of New York, for Vice President

Despite Tilden's near victory in the disputed election of 1876, he was forced to stand down as the leader of the party, due to the many allegations of manipulation of votes during that election. This convention opened with a large field of candidates. However, by the second ballot, the convention voted to nominate General Winfield Hancock.

James A. Garfield
ELECTED

Rutherford Hayes had promised not to run for re-election. Hayes kept his promise. In Chicago, at the 1880 Republican convention, the leading contender for the presidential nomination was former President Grant. Grant wished to run for an unprecedented third term. Anti-Grant forces supported James Blaine of Maine, and John Sherman of Ohio. James Garfield gave a major speech in favor of Sherman. Much of the convention body was impressed by Garfield's speech. The convention remained deadlocked through 34 ballots. Suddenly, Wisconsin voted its 16 votes for James Garfield. Garfield, once again, declared his support for Sherman. Garfield's efforts did not stop the convention for voting for him. On the 36th ballot Garfield was nominated.

Overall, the 1880 election campaign was rather uninspiring. Very few issues divided the candidates. The only issue of substance was the issue of tariffs. The Democratic candidate, Winfield Hancock, supported one for the purposes of revenue only. Led by Garfield, Republicans supported high tariffs. Hancock was a former military officer, who had almost no other experience. This became very evident during the campaign.

The popular election was close. However, the electoral votes were overwhelmingly in favor of Garfield. James Garfield became the next President.

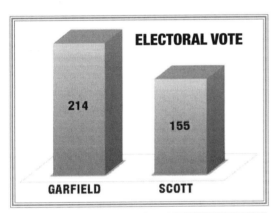

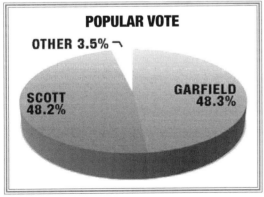

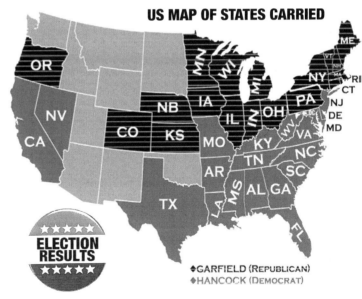

STATES	JAMES GARFIELD		WINFIELD HANCOCK		JAMES WEAVER		TOTAL VOTES
	VOTES	PERCENTAGE	VOTES	PERCENTAGE	VOTES	PERCENTAGE	
Alabama	56,350	37.1	91,130	60	4,422	2.9	151,902
Arkansas	42,436	39	60,775	55.9	4,116	3.8	10,870
California	80,282	48.9	80,426	49	3,381	2.1	164,218
Colorado	27,450	51.3	24,647	46	1,435	2.7	53,546
Connecticut	67,071	50.5	64,411	48.5	868	0.7	132,798
Delaware	14,148	48	15,181	51.5	129	0.4	29,458
Florida	23,654	45.8	27,964	54.2		0	51,618
Georgia	54,470	34.6	102,981	65.4		0	157,451
Illinois	318,036	51.1	277,321	44.6	26,358	4.2	622,305
Indiana	232,169	49.3	225,523	47.9	13,066	2.8	470,758
Iowa	183,904	56.9	105,845	32.8	32,327	10	323,140
Kansas	121,520	60.4	59,789	29.7	19,710	9.8	201,054
Kentucky	106,059	39.7	149,068	55.9	11,499	4.3	266,884
Louisiana	38,978	37.3	65,047	62.3	437	0.4	104,462
Maine	74,052	51.5	65,211	45.3	4,409	3.1	143,903
Maryland	78,515	45.4	93,706	54.1	828	0.5	173,049
Massachusetts	165,198	58.5	111,960	39.6	4,548	1.6	282,505
Michigan	185,335	52.5	131,596	37.3	38,895	9.9	353,076
Minnesota	93,939	62.3	53,314	35.4	3,267	2.2	150,806
Mississippi	34,844	29.8	75,750	64.7	5,797	5	117,068
Missouri	154,647	38.7	208,600	52.5	35,042	8.8	397,289
Nebraska	54,979	62.9	28,523	32.7	3,853	4.4	87,355
Nevada	8,732	47.6	9,611	52.4		0	18,343
New Hampshire	44,856	51.9	40,797	47.2	528	0.6	86,361
New Jersey	120,555	49	122,565	49.8	2,617	1.1	245,928
New York	555,544	50.3	534,511	48.4	12,373	1.1	1,103,945
North Carolina	115,616	48	124,204	51.5	1,126	0.5	240,946
Ohio	375,048	51.7	340,867	47	6,456	0.9	724,984
Oregon	20,619	50.5	19,955	48.9	267	0.7	40,841
Pennsylvania	444,704	50.8	407,428	46.6	20,667	2.4	874,783
Rhode Island	18,195	62.2	10,779	36.9	236	0.8	29,235
South Carolina	57,954	34.1	111,236	65.5	567	0.3	169,793
Tennessee	107,677	44.3	129,569	53.3	6,017	2.5	243,263
Texas	57,225	23.8	155,963	64.8	27,471	11.4	240,659
Vermont	45,567	70	18,316	28.1	1,215	1.9	65,098
Virginia	83,634	39.3	128,647	60.5		0	212,660
West Virginia	46,243	41.1	57,390	50.9	9,008	8	112,641
Wisconsin	144,406	54	114,650	42.9	7,986	3	267,202
TOTAL	4,453,611	48.3	4,445,256	48.2	306,921	3.3	9,220,197

1880 ELECTION: STATE-BY-STATE RESULTS (GARFIELD vs. HANCOCK vs. WEAVER)

UNITED STATES
PRESIDENTIAL ELECTION OF 1884

THE ISSUES

TARIFFS

Should tariffs be decreased?

The DEMOCRATIC CONVENTION

PLACE: Chicago, IL

DATE: July 8 to 11, 1884

NOMINATED: Grover Cleveland, of New Hampshire, for President

NOMINATED: Thomas A. Hendricks, of Indiana, for Vice President

The Democratic Convention opened with four contenders for the presidential nomination. The contenders were: Allen G. Thurman of Ohio, Thomas A Hendricks of Indiana, Thomas Bayard of Delaware, and Grover Cleveland of New York. Cleveland was the governor of New York and the convention favorite. Cleveland's reputation as a reformer made him an enemy of Tammany Hall. They opposed his nomination and tried to engineer the selection of Thomas Hendricks. Cleveland took an early lead on the ballots. On the fourth ballot, delegates switched their support and put Cleveland over the top.

The REPUBLICAN CONVENTION

PLACE: Exposition Hall Chicago, IL

DATE: June 3 to 6, 1884

NOMINATED: James G. Blaine, of Maine, for President

NOMINATED: John A. Logan, of Illinois, for VP

At the opening of the Republican Convention in Chicago, substantial opposition existed to the nomination of Chester Arthur, the incumbent, accidental president. The prevailing view was that it was the time of James G. Blaine to become the Republican nominee. Blaine led on the first ballot. He received the nomination on the fourth ballot.

Grover Cleveland
ELECTED

PRESIDENTIAL CANDIDATES

Grover Cleveland (Democrat)

James Blaine (Republican)

The 1884 Democratic Convention was held in Chicago, in July. Grover Cleveland was the front-runner from the opening of the convention. The only major opposition to Cleveland was from the New York Tammany organization. Cleveland received the nomination on the second ballot, receiving 683 votes. Cleveland's opponent in the election was James Blaine of Maine. President Arthur attempted to receive the Republican nomination, but had little support. Arthur lost support from some of the Republican party by signing the Pendelton Act to reform Civil Service after the assassination of President Garfield. While never having being a member of the reform wing of the party, Arthur signed the reform, without their support. The only individual at the convention who had a chance to receive nomination, other than James Blaine, was General Sherman. The General ended speculation that he would run by making what has become known as 'a Sherman statement': "If nominated, I will not accept, and if elected I will not serve." Blaine won the Republican nomination on the fourth ballot.

There were no major substantive issues that separated the 1884 presidential candidates. As a result, the election turned on the candidates themselves. Blaine was attacked for his close relations with the railroad interests. It was claimed Blaine received financial benefit from the railroads. Blaine's opponents published what were called the "Mulligan Letters", which purported to show Blaine received bribes. Cleveland, on the other hand, was attacked for being "immoral". There were claims Cleveland maintained an affair before his marriage with Maria Halpin. This relationship produced a son. The Republicans would chant "Ma Ma Where's my Papa". Cleveland was able to defuse the story by telling the truth. Cleveland received the support of many reformers including several leading Republicans. Cleveland won the election in a close vote.

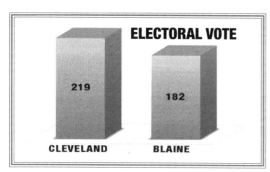

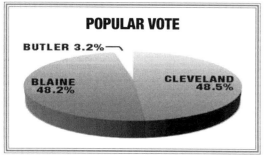

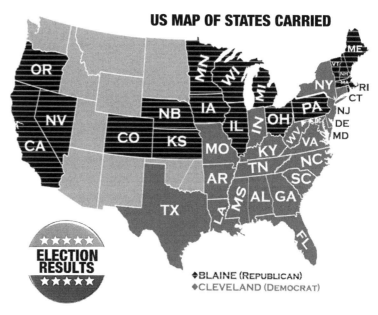

STATES	GROVER CLEVELAND		JAMES BLAINE		BENJAMIN BUTLER		JOHN ST. JOHN		TOTAL VOTES
	VOTES	PERCENTAGE	VOTES	PERCENTAGE	VOTES	PERCENTAGE	VOTES	PERCENTAGE	
Alabama	92,736	60.4	59,444	38.7	762	0.5	610	0.4	153,624
Arkansas	72,734	57.8	51,198	40.7	1,847	1.5	0	0.0	125,779
California	89,288	45.3	102,369	52	2,037	1	2,965	1.5	196.988
Colorado	27,723	41.7	36,084	54.2	1,956	2.9	756	1.1	66,519
Connecticut	67,167	48.9	65,879	48	1,682	1.2	2,493	1.8	137,221
Delaware	16,957	56.6	12,953	43.2	10		64	0.2	29,984
Florida	31,769	53	28,031	46.7	0	0.0	72	0.1	59,990
Georgia	94,667	65.9	48,603	33.8	145	0.1	195	0.1	143,610
Illinois	312,351	46.4	337,469	50.2	10,776	1.6	12,074	1.8	672,670
Indiana	244,989	49.8	238,466	48.5	8,194	1.7	0	0.0	495,423
Iowa	177,316	45.1	197,089	50.1	16,341	4.2	1,499	0.4	393,542
Kansas	90,111	35.9	154,410	61.5	1,691	0.7	4,311	1.7	250,991
Kentucky	152,961	55.6	118,690	43.2	120		3,139	1.1	276,503
Louisiana	62,594	55.3	46,347	40.9	3,955	3.5	338	0.3	109,399
Maine	52,153	41	72,217	56.8	578	0.5	2,160	1.7	130,489
Maryland	96,866	46.2	85,748	40.9	24,382	11.6	2,827	1.3	185,838
Massachusetts	122,352	38.1	146,724	45.7	42,252	13.2	9,923	3.1	303,383
Michigan	149,835	41.1	192,669	52.9	3,583	1	18,403	5	401,186
Minnesota	70,065	37.6	111,685	59.9	0	0.0	4,684	2.5	190,236
Mississippi	77,653	64.3	43,035	35.7	0	0.0	0	0.0	120,688
Missouri	236,023	53.5	203,081	46	0	0.0	2,164	0.5	441,268
Nebraska	54,391	40.5	76,912	57.3	0	0.0	2,899	2.2	134,202
Nevada	5,577	43.6	7,176	56.2	26	0.2	0	0.0	12,779
New Hampshire	39,198	46.3	43,254	51.1	554	0.7	1,580	1.9	84,586
New Jersey	127,747	49	123,436	47.3	3,486	1.3	6,156	2.4	260,853
New York	563,048	48.2	562,001	48.2	16,955	1.5	24,999	2.1	1,167,003
North Carolina	142,905	53.3	125,021	46.6	0	0.0	430	0.2	268,356
Ohio	368,280	46.9	400,092	51	5,179	0.7	11,069	1.4	784,620
Oregon	24,598	46.7	26,845	51	726	1.4	479	0.9	52,683
Pennsylvania	394,772	43.9	472,792	52.5	16,992	1.9	15,154	1.7	899,563
Rhode Island	12,391	37.8	19,030	58.1	422	1.3	928	2.8	32,771
South Carolina	69,845	75.3	21,730	23.4	0	0.0	0	0.0	92,812
Tennessee	133,770	51.5	124,101	47.7	957	0.4	1,150	0.4	259,978
Texas	223,209	69.5	91,234	28.4	3,310	1	3,489	1.1	326,458
Vermont	17,331	29.2	39,514	66.5	785	1.3	1,752	2.9	59,409
Virginia	145,491	51.1	139,356	48.9	0	0.0	130	0.0	284,977
West Virginia	67,311	50.9	63,096	47.7	799	0.6	939	0.7	132,145
Wisconsin	146,447	45.8	161,155	50.4	4,594	1.4	7,651	2.4	319,847
TOTALS	4,915,586	48.6	4,852,916	48.2	135,594	1.3	150,658	1.5	10,058,373

1884 ELECTION: STATE-BY-STATE RESULTS (CLEVELAND vs. BLAINE vs. BUTLER vs. ST. JOHN)

UNITED STATES
PRESIDENTIAL ELECTION OF 1888

THE ISSUES

MORE ON TARIFFS

Should tariffs be increased, or should they be decreased?

The REPUBLICAN CONVENTION

PLACE: Exposition Hall
Chicago, IL

DATE: June 19 to 25, 1888

NOMINATED: Benjamin Harrison,
of Indiana, for President

NOMINATED: Levi P. Morton,
of New York, for VP

When the 1888 Republican Convention opened there were twelve potential presidential nominees. Many Republicans supported Blaine, who came close to defeating Cleveland in 1884. However, after eight ballots, the convention nominated Benjamin Harrison. In their platform, Republicans strongly opposed any change in the tariff system. Democrats proposed and were in favor of a change in the tariff.

The DEMOCRATIC CONVENTION

PLACE: Exposition Building
St. Louis, MO

DATE: June 5 to 7, 1888

NOMINATED: Grover Cleveland,
of New Hampshire, for President

NOMINATED: Thomas A. Hendricks,
of Indiana, for Vice President

The Democratic Convention opened with four contenders for the presidential nomination. The contenders were: Allen G. Thurman of Ohio, Thomas A Hendricks of Indiana, Thomas Bayard of Delaware, and Grover Cleveland of New York. Cleveland was the governor of New York and the convention favorite. Cleveland's reputation as a reformer made him an enemy of Tammany Hall. They opposed his nomination and tried to engineer the selection of Thomas Hendricks. Cleveland took an early lead on the ballots. On the fourth ballot, delegates switched their support and put Cleveland over the top.

Benjamin Harrison
ELECTED

PRESIDENTIAL CANDIDATES

Grover Cleveland (Democrat)

Benjamin Harrison (Republican)

UNITED STATES PRESIDENTIAL **Election of 1888**

President Cleveland was unanimously renominated for a second term by the delegates of the 1888 Democratic convention. The 1888 Republican Convention nominated Benjamin Harrison, on the eighth ballot. The 1888 election campaign was highly restrained. Neither side actively campaigned. The major focus of the campaign was the issue of tariffs. Benjamin Harrison supported a strong tariff policy. Harrison strongly opposed Cleveland's policy of reducing tariffs. Cleveland fervently favored tariff reduction, having said to his advisors: "What is the point of being elected, or being re-elected, unless you stand for something."

As the sitting President, Grover Cleveland did not campaign at all. Benjamin Harrison, on the other hand, carried on an effective front porch campaign. Harrison gave over 80 campaign speeches from the front porch of his home. The election results were exceptionally close. Cleveland won the popular vote, but lost the electoral vote to Harrison. Cleveland lost New York's crucial 34 votes, as a result of efforts from his old adversary, the Tammany machine.

US MAP OF STATES CARRIED

◆ B. HARRISON (REPUBLICAN)
◆ CLEVELAND (DEMOCRAT)

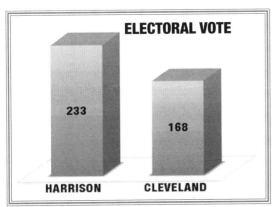

ELECTORAL VOTE

HARRISON 233
CLEVELAND 168

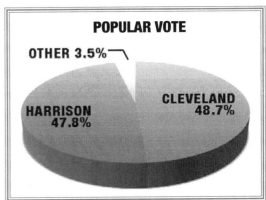

POPULAR VOTE

OTHER 3.5%
HARRISON 47.8%
CLEVELAND 48.7%

STATES	GROVER CLEVELAND		JAMES BLAINE		BENJAMIN BUTLER		JOHN ST. JOHN		TOTAL VOTES
	VOTES	PERCENTAGE	VOTES	PERCENTAGE	VOTES	PERCENTAGE	VOTES	PERCENTAGE	
Alabama	57,177	32.7	117,314	67.0	594	0.3	0	0.0	175,085
Arkansas	59,752	38.0	86,062	54.8	614	0.4	10,630	6.8	157,058
California	124,816	49.7	117,729	46.8	5,761	2.3	0	0.0	251,339
Colorado	50,772	55.2	37,549	40.8	2,182	2.4	1,266	1.4	91,946
Connecticut	74,584	48.4	74,920	48.7	4,234	2.7	240	0.2	153,978
Delaware	12,950	43.5	16,414	55.1	399	1.3	0	0.0	29,764
Florida	26,529	39.9	39,557	59.5	414	0.6	0	0.0	66,500
Georgia	40,499	28.3	100,493	70.3	1,808	1.3	136	0.1	142,936
Illinois	370,475	49.5	348,351	46.6	21,703	2.9	7,134	1.0	747,813
Indiana	263,366	49.0	260,990	48.6	9,939	1.9	2,693	0.5	536,988
Iowa	211,607	52.3	179,876	44.4	3,550	0.9	9,105	2.2	404,694
Kansas	182,845	55.2	102,739	31.0	6,774	2.0	37,838	11.4	331,133
Kentucky	155,138	45.0	183,830	53.3	5,223	1.5	677	0.2	344,868
Louisiana	30,660	26.5	85,032	73.4	160	0.1	39	0.0	115,891
Maine	73,730	57.5	50,472	39.4	2,691	2.1	1,344	1.0	128,253
Maryland	99,986	47.4	106,188	50.3	4,767	2.3	0	0.0	210,941
Massachusetts	183,892	53.4	151,590	44.0	8,701	2.5	0	0.0	344,243
Michigan	236,387	49.7	213,469	44.9	20,945	4.4	4,555	1.0	475,356
Minnesota	142,492	54.1	104,372	39.7	15,201	5.8	1,097	0.4	263,162
Mississippi	30,095	26.0	85,451	73.8	240	0.2	0	0.0	115,786
Missouri	236,252	45.3	261,943	50.2	4,539	0.9	18,625	3.6	521,359
Nebraska	108,417	53.5	80,552	39.8	9,435	4.7	4,226	2.1	202,630
Nevada	7,229	57.5	5,303	42.2	41	0.3	0	0.0	12,573
New Hampshire	45,734	50.4	43,382	47.8	1,596	1.8	0	0.0	90,770
New Jersey	144,347	47.5	151,493	49.9	7,794	2.6	0	0.0	303,801
New York	650,338	49.3	635,965	48.2	30,231	2.3	627	0.0	1,321,270
North Carolina	134,784	47.2	147,902	51.8	2,840	1.0	0	0.0	285,946
Ohio	416,054	49.6	395,456	47.1	24,356	2.9	3,491	0.4	839,357
Oregon	33,291	53.8	26,518	42.8	1,676	2.7	0	0.0	61,889
Pennsylvania	526,091	52.7	446,633	44.8	20,947	2.1	3,873	0.4	997,568
Rhode Island	21,969	53.9	17,530	43.0	1,251	3.1	18	0.0	40,775
South Carolina	13,736	17.2	65,824	82.3	0	0.0	0	0.0	79,997
Tennessee	138,978	45.8	158,699	52.3	5,969	2.0	48	0.0	304,313
Texas	88,604	25.0	232,189	65.5	4,739	1.3	28,880	8.1	363,484
Vermont	45,193	71.2	16,788	26.4	1,460	2.3	0	0.0	63,476
Virginia	150,399	49.5	152,004	50.0	1,684	0.6	0	0.0	304,087
West Virginia	78,171	49.0	78,677	49.3	1,084	0.7	1,508	0.9	159,440
Wisconsin	176,553	49.8	155,232	43.8	14,277	4.0	8,552	2.4	354,614
TOTALS	5,449,825	47.8	5,539,118	48.6	249,492	2.2	146,602	1.3	11,395,705

1888 ELECTION: STATE-BY-STATE RESULTS (CLEVELAND vs. BLAINE vs. BUTLER vs. ST. JOHN)

THE ISSUES — PROTECTIONISM

Should the United States policy employ more or less protectionism?

The DEMOCRATIC CONVENTION

PLACE: Chicago, IL

DATE: June 21 to 23, 1892

NOMINATED: Grover Cleveland, of New Hampshire, for President

NOMINATED: Adlai E. Stevenson, of Illinois, for Vice President

The REPUBLICAN CONVENTION

PLACE: Industrial Exposition Building, Minneapolis, MN

DATE: June 7 to 10, 1892

NOMINATED: Benjamin Harrison, of Indiana, for President

NOMINATED: Whitelaw Reid, of New York, for VP

James Blaine, Harrison's Secretary of State resigned, shortly before the 1892 Republican Convention. Blaine then mounted a last minute campaign to earn the Republican presidential nomination. Blaine's bid was not effective. Harrison received 535 1/4 votes on the first ballot. In that same ballot, Blaine received 182 1/4 votes, and 182 votes were cast for McKinley.

Grover Cleveland, who had narrowly lost his bid for re-election in 1888, wanted to run again in 1892. He had wide support within the party. The major objections to his candidacy came, again, from Tammany Hall in New York. They held a snap state convention and nominated one of their own. Despite not having support from his state delegation, Cleveland easily won the nomination on the first ballot, at a convention held at the "Wigwam".

Grover Cleveland
ELECTED

PRESIDENTIAL CANDIDATES

Grover Cleveland (Democrat)

Benjamin Harrison (Republican)

James Weaver (Populist)

President Cleveland was unanimously renominated for a second term by the delegates of the 1888 Democratic convention. The 1888 Republican Convention nominated Benjamin Harrison, on the eighth ballot. The 1888 election campaign was highly restrained. Neither side actively campaigned. The major focus of the campaign was the issue of tariffs. Benjamin Harrison supported a strong tariff policy. Harrison strongly opposed Cleveland's policy of reducing tariffs. Cleveland fervently favored tariff reduction, having said to his advisors: "What is the point of being elected, or being re-elected, unless you stand for something."

As the sitting President, Cleveland did not campaign at all. Benjamin Harrison, on the other hand, carried on an effective front porch campaign. Harrison gave over 80 campaign speeches from the front porch of his home. The election results were exceptionally close. Cleveland won the popular vote, but lost the electoral vote to Harrison. Cleveland lost New York's crucial 34 votes, as a result of efforts from his old adversary, the Tammany machine.

US MAP OF STATES CARRIED

ELECTION RESULTS

◆ B. HARRISON (Republican)
◆ CLEVELAND (Democrat)
⌐ WEAVER (Populist)

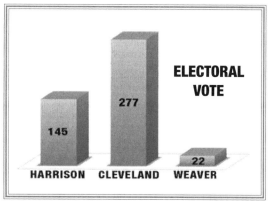

ELECTORAL VOTE

HARRISON 145
CLEVELAND 277
WEAVER 22

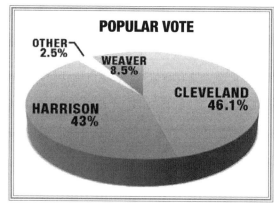

POPULAR VOTE

OTHER 2.5%
WEAVER 8.5%
CLEVELAND 46.1%
HARRISON 43%

STATES	GROVER CLEVELAND		BENJAMIN HARRISON		JAMES WEAVER		JOHN BIDWELL		TOTAL VOTES
	VOTES	PERCENTAGE	VOTES	PERCENTAGE	VOTES	PERCENTAGE	VOTES	PERCENTAGE	
Alabama	138,135	59.4	9,184	3.9	84,984	36.5	240	0.1	232,543
Arkansas	87,834	59.3	47,072	31.8	11,831	8	113	0.1	148,117
California	118,151	43.8	118,027	43.8	25,311	9.4	8,096	3	269,585
Colorado	0	0.0	38,620	41.1	53,584	57.1	1,677	1.8	93,881
Connecticut	82,395	50.1	77,030	46.8	809	0.5	4,026	2.4	164,593
Delaware	18,581	49.9	18,077	48.5	0	0.0	564	1.5	37,235
Florida	30,153	85.0	0	0.0	4,843	13.7	475	1.3	35,567
Georgia	129,446	58.0	48,408	21.7	41,939	18.8	988	0.4	223,961
Idaho	0	0.0	8,599	44.3	10,520	54.2	288	1.5	19,407
Illinois	426,281	48.8	399,308	45.7	22,207	2.5	25,871	3	873,667
Indiana	262,740	47.5	255,615	46.2	22,208	4	13,050	2.4	553,613
Iowa	196,367	44.3	219,795	49.6	20,595	4.6	6,402	1.4	443,159
Kansas	0	0.0	156,134	48.3	162,888	50.3	4,569	1.4	323,591
Kentucky	175,461	51.5	135,462	39.7	23,500	6.9	6,441	1.9	340,864
Louisiana	87,926	76.5	26,963	23.5	0	0.0			118,287
Maine	48,049	41.3	62,936	54.0	2,396	2.1	3,066	2.6	116,013
Maryland	113,866	53.4	92,736	43.5	796	0.4	5,877	2.8	213,275
Massachusetts	176,813	45.2	202,814	51.9	3,210	0.8	7,539	1.9	391,028
Michigan	202,396	43.3	222,708	47.7	20,031	4.3	20,857	4.5	466,917
Minnesota	100,589	37.6	122,736	45.8	30,399	11.3	14,117	5.3	267,461
Mississippi	40,030	76.2	1,398	2.7	10,118	19.3	973	1.9	52,519
Missouri	268,400	49.6	227,646	42.0	41,204	7.6	4,333	0.8	541,583
Montana	17,690	39.8	18,871	42.4	7,338	16.5	562	1.3	44,461
Nebraska	24,956	12.5	87,213	43.6	83,134	41.5	4,902	2.4	200,205
Nevada	703	6.5	2,811	26.0	7,226	66.7	86	0.8	10,826
New Hampshire	42,081	47.1	45,658	51.1	292	0.3	1,297	1.5	89,328
New Jersey	170,987	50.7	156,059	46.2	969	0.3	8,133	2.4	337,485
New York	654,868	49.0	609,350	45.6	16,429	1.2	38,190	2.9	1,336,793
North Carolina	132,951	47.4	100,346	35.8	44,336	15.8	2,637	0.9	280,270
North Dakota 2	0	0.0	17,519	48.5	17,700	49.0	899	2.5	36,118
Ohio	404,115	47.5	405,187	47.7	14,850	1.7	26,012	3.1	850,164
Oregon	14,243	18.2	35,002	44.7	26,875	34.3	2,258	2.9	78,378
Pennsylvania	452,264	45.1	516,011	51.4	8,714	0.9	25,123	2.5	1,003,000
Rhode Island	24,336	45.7	26,975	50.7	228	0.4	1,654	3.1	53,196
South Carolina	54,680	77.6	13,345	18.9	2,407	3.4	0	0.0	70,504
South Dakota	8,894	12.7	34,714	49.5	26,552	37.8	0	0.0	70,513
Tennessee	136,468	51.4	100,537	37.8	23,918	9.0	4,809	1.8	265,732
Texas	236,979	57.7	70,982	17.3	96,649	23.5	2,164	0.5	422,447
Vermont	16,325	29.3	37,992	68.1	42	0.1	1,424	2.6	55,793
Virginia	164,136	56.2	113,098	38.7	12,275	4.2	2,729	0.9	292,238
Washington	29,802	33.9	36,459	41.4	19,165	21.8	2,542	2.9	87,968
West Virginia	84,467	49.4	80,292	46.9	4,167	2.4	2,153	1.3	171,079
Wisconsin	177,325	47.7	171,101	46.1	9,919	2.7	13,136	3.5	371,481
Wyoming	0	0.0	8,454	50.6	7,722	46.2	498	3	16,703
TOTALS	5,554,617	46.0	5,186,793	43.0	1,024,280	8.5	270,979	2.2	12,071,548

1892 ELECTION: STATE-BY-STATE RESULTS (CLEVELAND vs. HARRISON vs. WEAVER vs. BIDWELL)

UNITED STATES
PRESIDENTIAL ELECTION OF 1896

THE ISSUES

GOLD OR SILVER

Should America maintain its Gold Standard, or should a Silver Standard be used as well?

The REPUBLICAN CONVENTION

PLACE: St. Louis, MO

DATE: June 16 to 18, 1896

NOMINATED: William McKinley, of Ohio, for President

NOMINATED: Garret A. Hobart, of New Jersey for VP

The Republicans nominated McKinley on the first ballot. The party also issued a platform that clearly supported the continuation of the Gold Standard.

The DEMOCRATIC CONVENTION

PLACE: Chicago, IL

DATE: July 7 to 11, 1896

NOMINATED: William J. Bryan, of Florida, for President

NOMINATED: Arthur Sewall, of Maine, for Vice President

The 1896 Democratic Convention took place against the background of an economic depression. When the convention opened, Senator David Hill of New York, an opponent of Cleveland's nomination, entered a resolution commending "the honesty, economy, courage and fidelity of the present Democratic National Administration". The resolution was defeated 564 to 357.

Cleveland's support of the Gold Standard was not very popular. Many in the party opposed the Gold Standard. They wanted the standard changed to include the use of silver, as part of the currency. Senator Pitchfork Ben Tillman led the charge for what was called "Free Silver". During the debate over the platform, William Jennings Bryan, a two term congressman from Nebraska, gave a stirring speech in support of free silver. In it Bryan stated "Having behind us the producing masses of this nation and the world, supported by the commercial interests, the laboring interests and the toilers everywhere, we will answer their demand for a Gold Standard by saying to them: You shall not press down upon the brow of labor this crown of thorns; you shall not crucify mankind upon a cross of gold". Bryan brought down the house. The convention quickly adopted a platform in favor of free silver. When it came time to nominate a President, Bryan was selected by the third ballot.

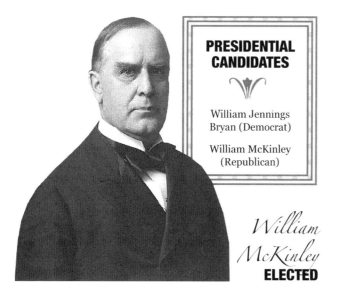

PRESIDENTIAL CANDIDATES

William Jennings Bryan (Democrat)

William McKinley (Republican)

William McKinley
ELECTED

In 1893, one of the most severe economic crises in US history developed. The nation found itself in a deep depression. President Cleveland blamed the depression on the move to accept silver currency. As a result, business confidence was weakened. Cleveland's solution was a repeal of the Sherman Silver Purchase Act. and thus a return to a currency supported only by gold. Repealing the Silver Purchase Act resulted in a tightening of the supply of currency. This only served to worsen the economic situation.

Democrats lost control of both the Senate and the House of Representatives in the 1994 Congressional election. When the party met for their convention in Chicago, the party was ready for a change. William Jennings Bryan gave an electrifying speech and became the party's nominee. The party adopted a platform favoring free sliver. The Populist Party decided to support Bryan. The Populist Party chose not to run a nominee of their own. Republicans nominated the popular Governor of Ohio, William McKinley, on the first ballot. McKinley was backed by Marcus Hanna, a wealthy industrialist, and Chairman of the Republican Party.

The 1896 presidential campaign was marked by contrasts. William Jennings Bryan criss-crossed the country making personal appearances. He was accused of lacking dignity. Bryan answered: "I would rather have it said that I lacked dignity, than that I lacked backbone to meet the enemies of the government who works against its welfare from Wall Street". McKinley stayed home and ran a front porch campaign. Thousands of people came to his home and heard him speak. In the campaign Bryan was depicted as a "radical and a socialist", while McKinley was called a "tool of business". In this election, money played an important role, for the first time, in a political campaign. McKinley raised $3 million (mostly from business interests), compared to $600,000 raised by Bryan. Bryan was able to win almost all of the states of the West. However, Bryan had almost no success in the growing industrial cities of the East. The result of the election showed how the farmers' vote was no longer decisive. By 1896, only 1/3 of Americans lived on farms. It was also clear that the number of Americans living on farms was dropping rapidly. McKinley won the election.

US MAP OF STATES CARRIED

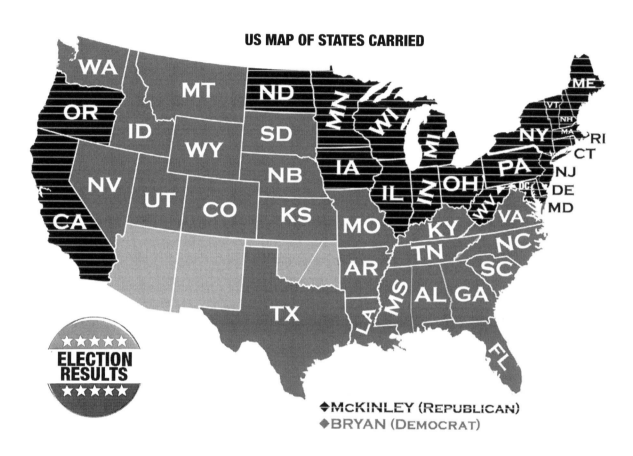

◆ McKINLEY (REPUBLICAN)
◆ BRYAN (DEMOCRAT)

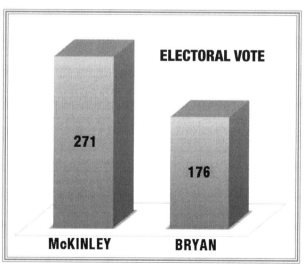

ELECTORAL VOTE

McKINLEY 271
BRYAN 176

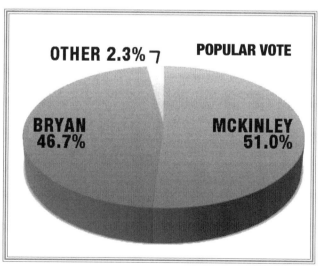

POPULAR VOTE

OTHER 2.3%
BRYAN 46.7%
MCKINLEY 51.0%

STATES	WILLIAM McKINLEY VOTES	WILLIAM McKINLEY PERCENTAGE	WILLIAM J BRYAN VOTES	WILLIAM J BRYAN PERCENTAGE	JOHN PALMER VOTES	JOHN PALMER PERCENTAGE	JOSHUA LEVERING VOTES	JOSHUA LEVERING PERCENTAGE	TOTAL VOTES
Alabama	55,673	28.6	130,298	67.0	6,375	3.3	2,234	1.1	194,580
Arkansas	37,512	25.1	110,103	73.7	0	0.0	889	0.6	149,396
California	146,756	49.1	144,877	48.5	1,730	0.6	2,573	0.9	299,374
Colorado	26,271	13.9	161,005	84.9	1	0.0	1,717	0.9	189,539
Connecticut	110,285	63.2	56,740	32.5	4,336	2.5	1,806	1.0	174,394
Delaware	20,450	53.2	16,574	43.1	966	2.5	466	1.2	31,538
Florida	11,298	24.3	32,756	70.5	1,778	3.8	656	1.4	46,468
Georgia	59,395	36.6	93,885	57.8	3,670	2.3	5,483	3.4	163,309
Idaho	6,324	21.3	23,135	78.1	0	0.0	172	0.6	29,631
Illinois	607,130	55.7	465,593	42.7	6,307	0.6	9,796	0.9	1,090,766
Indiana	323,754	50.8	305,538	48.0	2,145	0.3	3,061	0.5	637,089
Iowa	289,293	55.5	223,744	42.9	4,516	0.9	3,192	0.6	521,550
Kansas	159,484	47.5	173,049	51.5	1,209	0.4	1,723	0.5	336,085
Kentucky	218,171	48.9	217,894	48.9	5,084	1.1	4,779	1.1	445,928
Louisiana	22,037	21.8	77,175	76.4	1,834	1.8	0	0.0	101,046
Maine	80,403	67.9	34,587	29.2	1,867	1.6	1,562	1.3	118,419
Maryland	136,959	54.7	104,150	41.6	2,499	1.0	5,918	2.4	250,249
Massachusetts	278,976	69.5	105,414	26.3	11,749	2.9	2,998	0.7	401,269
Michigan	293,336	53.8	237,164	43.5	6,923	1.3	4,978	0.9	545,583
Minnesota	193,503	56.6	139,735	40.9	3,222	0.9	4,348	1.3	341,762
Mississippi	4,819	6.9	63,355	91.0	1,021	1.5	396	0.6	69,591
Missouri	304,940	45.2	363,667	54.0	2,365	0.4	2,169	0.3	674,032
Montana	10,509	19.7	42,628	79.9	0	0.0	193	0.4	53,330
Nebraska	103,064	46.2	115,007	51.5	2,885	1.3	1,242	0.6	223,181
Nevada	1,938	18.8	8,348	81.2	0	0.0	0	0.0	10,314
New Hampshire	57,444	68.7	21,650	25.9	3,520	4.2	779	0.9	83,670
New Jersey	221,367	59.7	133,675	36.0	6,373	1.7	0	0.0	371,014
New York	819,838	57.6	551,369	38.7	18,950	1.3	16,052	1.1	1,423,876
North Carolina	155,122	46.8	174,408	52.6	578	0.2	635	0.2	331,337
North Dakota	26,335	55.6	20,686	43.6	0	0.0	358	0.8	47,391
Ohio	525,991	51.9	477,497	47.1	1,858	0.2	5,068	0.5	1,014,295
Oregon	48,700	50.0	46,739	48.0	977	1.0	919	0.9	97,335
Pennsylvania	728,300	61.0	433,228	36.3	11,000	0.9	19,274	1.6	1,194,355
Rhode Island	37,437	68.3	14,459	26.4	1,166	2.1	1,160	2.1	54,785
South Carolina	9,313	13.5	58,801	85.3	824	1.2	0	0.0	68,938
South Dakota	41,040	49.5	41,225	49.7	0	0.0	672	0.8	82,937
Tennessee	148,683	46.3	167,168	52.1	1,953	0.6	3,099	1.0	320,903
Texas	163,894	30.3	370,308	68.4	5,022	0.9	1,794	0.3	515,987
Utah	13,491	17.3	64,607	82.7	0	0.0	0	0.0	78,098
Vermont	51,127	80.4	10,367	16.3	1,341	2.1	733	1.2	63,831
Virginia	135,379	45.9	154,708	52.5	2,129	0.7	2,350	0.8	294,674
Washington	39,153	41.8	53,314	57.0	0	0.0	968	1.0	93,583
West Virginia	105,379	52.2	94,480	46.8	678	0.3	1,220	0.6	201,757
Wisconsin	268,135	59.9	165,523	37.0	4,584	1.0	7,507	1.7	447,409
Wyoming	10,072	47.8	10,862	51.6	0	0.0	133	0.6	21,093
TOTALS	7,105,144	51.1	6,370,897	45.8	132,718	1.0	125,118	171,814	13,905,691

1896 ELECTION: STATE-BY-STATE RESULTS (McKINLEY vs. BRYAN vs. PALMER vs. LEVERING)

UNITED STATES
PRESIDENTIAL ELECTION OF 1900

THE ISSUES

OVERSEAS EMPIRE

Should America develop and maintain an empire overseas?

The REPUBLICAN CONVENTION

PLACE: Convention Hall
Philadelphia, PA

DATE: June 19 to 21, 1900

NOMINATED: William McKinley,
of Ohio, for President

NOMINATED: Theodore Roosevelt,
of New York, for VP

Going into the Republican Convention of 1900 there was no question that McKinley would be renominated. The only open question was who would be his vice presidential running mate– since Vice President Hobart died while in office. In fact, there was no question. Since, New York Governor, and war hero, Theodore Roosevelt was the clear choice of the convention body.

The DEMOCRATIC CONVENTION

PLACE: Kansas City, MO

DATE: July 4 to 6, 1900

NOMINATED: William J. Bryan,
of Florida, for President

NOMINATED: Adlai E. Stevenson,
of Illinois, for VP

PRESIDENTIAL CANDIDATES

William Jennings Bryan (Democrat)

William McKinley (Republican)

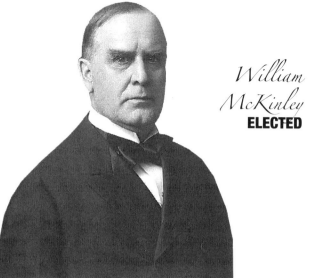

William McKinley
ELECTED

UNITED STATES PRESIDENTIAL Election of 1900

President McKinley was easily renominated at the 1900 Republican Convention, in Philadelphia. The major issue at the convention was who would be the Republican vice presidential candidate. Despite his reluctance to give up the governorship of New York, Theodore Roosevelt accepted the VP nomination. At the Democratic convention, William Jennings Bryan was nominated again as well. The major issue at the Democratic convention was whether to maintain support for the silver plank. Many Democrats thought that with the return of prosperity the Silver Standard was no longer necessary.

The campaign itself was largely a replay of the race in 1896. Bryan campaigned rigorously and McKinley did not venture from the White House. The issue of currency and silver was no longer relevant. Instead the campaign focused on whether the United States should give independence to the territories received in its war with Spain. Bryan called for their immediate independence. Roosevelt, who did most of the campaigning, claimed the United States had a duty to civilize those lands first.

The 1900 election was ultimately decided on the issue of continued prosperity. The Republican's theme was "a full lunch pail". The prosperity of the McKinley era ultimately decided the election. McKinley won this election by an even greater margin than his 1896 election victory.

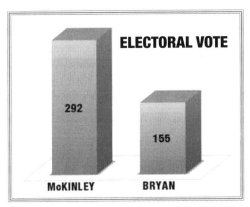

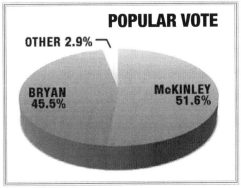

US MAP OF STATES CARRIED

◆McKINLEY (REPUBLICAN)
◆BRYAN (DEMOCRAT)

STATES	WILLIAM McKINLEY		WILLIAM J BRYAN		JOHN WOOLSEY		EUGENE DEBS		TOTAL VOTES
	VOTES	PERCENTAGE	VOTES	PERCENTAGE	VOTES	PERCENTAGE	VOTES	PERCENTAGE	
Alabama	55,634	34.7	96,368	60.1	3,796	2.4	928	0.6	160,477
Arkansas	44,800	35.0	81,242	63.5	584	0.5	0	0.0	127,966
California	164,755	54.5	124,985	41.3	5,087	1.7	7,572	2.5	302,399
Colorado	92,701	42.0	122,705	55.5	3,790	1.7	686	0.3	220,895
Connecticut	102,572	56.9	74,014	41.1	1,617	0.9	1,029	0.6	180,195
Delaware	22,535	53.7	18,852	44.9	546	1.3	56	0.1	41,989
Florida	7,463	18.8	28,273	71.1	2,244	5.7	654	1.6	39,777
Georgia	34,260	28.2	81,180	66.9	1,402	1.2	0	0.0	121,410
Idaho	27,198	47.9	28,260	49.8	857	1.5	0	0.0	56,760
Illinois	597,985	52.8	503,061	44.4	17,626	1.6	9,687	0.9	1,131,898
Indiana	336,063	50.6	309,584	46.6	13,718	2.1	2,374	0.4	664,094
Iowa	307,799	58.0	209,261	39.5	9,502	1.8	2,743	0.5	530,345
Kansas	185,955	52.6	162,601	46.0	3,605	1.0	1,605	0.5	353,766
Kentucky	227,801	48.5	234,889	50.2	2,814	0.6	0	0.0	467,580
Louisiana	14,234	21.0	53,668	79.0	0	0.0	0	0.0	67,906
Maine	66,413	61.7	37,822	35.1	2,585	2.4	878	0.8	107,698
Maryland	136,151	51.5	122,237	46.2	4,574	1.7	900	0.3	264,386
Massachusetts	238,866	57.6	156,997	37.8	6,202	1.5	9,607	2.3	414,804
Michigan	316,014	58.1	211,432	38.9	11,804	2.2	2,820	0.5	543,789
Minnesota	190,461	60.2	112,901	35.7	8,555	2.7	3,065	1.0	316,311
Mississippi	5,707	9.7	51,706	87.6	0	0.0	0	0.0	59,055
Missouri	314,092	45.9	351,922	51.5	5,965	0.9	6,139	0.9	683,658
Montana	25,409	39.8	37,311	58.4	306	0.5	711	1.1	63,856
Nebraska	121,835	50.5	114,013	47.2	3,655	1.5	823	0.3	241,430
Nevada	3,849	37.8	6,347	62.2	0	0.0	0	0.0	10,196
New Hampshire	54,799	59.3	35,489	38.4	1,270	1.4	790	0.9	92,364
New Jersey	221,707	55.3	164,808	41.1	7,183	1.8	4,609	1.1	401,050
New York	822,013	53.1	678,462	43.8	22,077	1.4	12,869	0.8	1,548,043
North Carolina	132,997	45.5	157,733	53.9	990	0.3	0	0.0	292,518
North Dakota	35,898	62.1	20,524	35.5	735	1.3	517	0.9	57,783
Ohio	543,918	52.3	474,882	45.7	10,203	1.0	4,847	0.5	1,040,073
Oregon	46,526	55.2	33,385	39.6	2,536	3.1	1,494	1.8	84,216
Pennsylvania	712,665	60.7	424,232	36.2	27,908	2.4	4,831	0.4	1,173,210
Rhode Island	33,784	59.7	19,812	35.0	1,529	2.7	0	0.0	56,548
South Carolina	3,525	7.0	47,173	93.0	0	0.0	0	0.0	50,698
South Dakota	54,574	56.7	39,538	41.1	1,541	1.6	176	0.2	96,169
Tennessee	123,108	45.0	145,240	53.0	3,844	1.4	346	0.1	273,860
Texas	131,174	30.9	267,945	63.1	2,642	0.6	1,846	0.4	424,334
Utah	47,089	50.6	44,949	48.3	205	0.2	717	0.8	93,071
Vermont	42,569	75.7	12,849	22.9	383	0.7	39	0.1	56,212
Virginia	115,769	43.8	146,079	55.3	2,130	0.8	0	0.0	264,208
Washington	57,455	53.4	44,833	41.7	2,363	2.2	2,006	1.9	107,523
West Virginia	119,829	54.3	98,807	44.8	1,628	0.7	286	0.1	220,796
Wisconsin	265,760	60.1	159,163	36.0	10,027	2.3	7,048	1.6	442,501
Wyoming	14,482	58.6	10,164	41.1	0	0.0	21	0.1	24,708
TOTALS	7,219,193	51.7	6,357,698	45.5	210,028	1.5	94,719	0.7	13,972,525

1900 ELECTION: STATE-BY-STATE RESULTS (McKINLEY vs. BRYAN vs. WOOLSEY vs. DEBS)

UNITED STATES
PRESIDENTIAL ELECTION OF 1904

THE ISSUES

ROOSEVELT THE ACTIVIST

Was Theodore Roosevelt's activist leadership style effective? Was Roosevelt's leadership style admired?

The REPUBLICAN CONVENTION

PLACE: Chicago, IL

DATE: June 21 to 23, 1904

NOMINATED: Theodore Roosevelt, of New York, for President

NOMINATED: Charles W. Fairbanks, of Indiana, for VP

Republicans nominated Theodore Roosevelt by a vote of acclamation at their 1904 convention.

Theodore Roosevelt
ELECTED

The DEMOCRATIC CONVENTION

PLACE: Kansas City, MO

DATE: July 6 to 9, 1904

NOMINATED: Alton B. Parker, of New York, for President

NOMINATED: Henry G. Davis, of West Virginia, for VP

Many at the Democratic convention felt the time had come to drop their support for Free Silver, and return to the support of gold. The discovery of significant deposits of gold eliminated the need to change the Gold Standard. Bryan was extremely vocal, opposing any modification to the current Democratic platform. However, Bryan failed to effect the platform on currency. His hand could be seen in a number of other areas, where the platform called for Philippine independence and direct elections. Bryan attempted to block the nomination of Alton Parker, who was the candidate of New York's Tammany Hall. Despite his opposition, Parker was nominated on the first ballot.

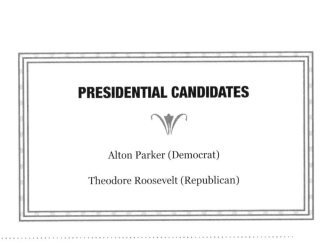

PRESIDENTIAL CANDIDATES

Alton Parker (Democrat)

Theodore Roosevelt (Republican)

UNITED STATES PRESIDENTIAL Election of 1904

Theodore Roosevelt's nomination at the Republican convention, in June of 1904, was without opposition. At their convention, Democrats nominated Alton Parker, of New York, on the first ballot. Parker was unknown outside of New York. For the Vice

Presidential slot, Democrats nominated Henry Davis, an 82 year old businessman. The two candidates differed very little on the issues. As such, the 1904 election centered on the personalities of the two candidates. Teddy Roosevelt, however, was the most popular President in a generation. His "square deal" was immensely popular with voters. Neither candidate bothered to campaign, since the election results were a foregone conclusion. Theodore Roosevelt won the election easily.

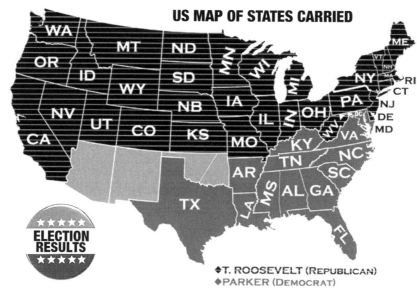

US MAP OF STATES CARRIED

◆ T. ROOSEVELT (REPUBLICAN)
◆ PARKER (DEMOCRAT)

ELECTION RESULTS

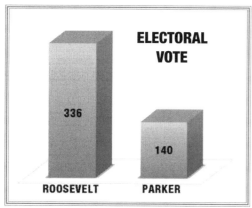

ELECTORAL VOTE

ROOSEVELT 336
PARKER 140

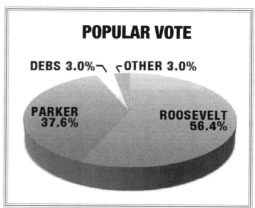

POPULAR VOTE

DEBS 3.0% ⌐ OTHER 3.0%
PARKER 37.6%
ROOSEVELT 56.4%

STATES	THEODORE ROOSEVELT		ALTON PARKER		EUGENE DEBS		SILAS SWALLOW		TOTAL VOTES
	VOTES	PERCENTAGE	VOTES	PERCENTAGE	VOTES	PERCENTAGE	VOTES	PERCENTAGE	
Alabama	22,472	20.7	79,797	73.4	853	0.8	612	0.6	108,785
Arkansas	46,760	40.2	64,434	55.4	1,816	1.6	992	0.9	116,328
California	205,226	61.9	89,294	26.9	29,535	8.9	7,380	2.2	331,768
Colorado	134,661	55.3	100,105	41.1	4,304	1.8	3,438	1.4	243,667
Connecticut	111,089	58.1	72,909	38.1	4,543	2.4	1,506	0.8	191,136
Delaware	23,705	54.1	19,347	44.1	146	0.3	607	1.4	43,856
Florida	8,314	21.5	26,449	68.3	2,337	6	0	0.0	39,302
Georgia	24,004	18.3	83,466	63.7	196	0.1	685	0.5	130,986
Idaho	47,783	65.8	18,480	25.5	4,949	6.8	1,013	1.4	72,577
Illinois	632,645	58.8	327,606	30.4	69,225	6.4	34,770	3.2	1,076,495
Indiana	368,289	54	274,356	40.2	12,023	1.8	23,496	3.4	682,206
Iowa	307,907	63.4	149,141	30.7	14,847	3.1	11,601	2.4	485,703
Kansas	213,455	64.9	86,164	26.2	15,869	4.8	7,306	2.2	329,047
Kentucky	205,457	47.1	217,170	49.8	3,599	0.8	6,603	1.5	435,946
Louisiana	5,205	9.7	47,708	88.5	995	1.8	0	0.0	53,908
Maine	65,432	67.4	27,642	28.5	2,102	2.2	1,510	1.6	96,036
Maryland	109,497	48.8	109,446	48.8	2,247	1	3,034	1.4	224,229
Massachusetts	257,813	57.9	165,746	37.2	13,604	3.1	4,279	1	445,100
Michigan	361,863	69.5	134,163	25.8	8,942	1.7	13,312	2.6	520,443
Minnesota	216,651	74	55,187	18.8	11,692	4	6,253	2.1	292,860
Mississippi	3,280	5.6	53,480	91.1	462	0.8	0	0.0	58,721
Missouri	321,449	49.9	296,312	46	13,009	2	7,191	1.1	643,861
Montana	33,994	53.5	21,816	34.3	5,675	8.9	339	0.5	63,568
Nebraska	138,558	61.4	52,921	23.4	7,412	3.3	6,323	2.8	225,732
Nevada	6,864	56.7	3,982	32.9	925	7.6	0	0.0	12,115
New Hampshire	54,157	60.1	34,071	37.8	1,090	1.2	750	0.8	90,151
New Jersey	245,164	56.7	164,566	38.1	9,587	2.2	6,845	1.6	432,547
New York	859,533	53.1	683,981	42.3	36,883	2.3	20,787	1.3	1,617,765
North Carolina	82,442	39.7	124,091	59.7	124	0.1	342	0.2	207,818
North Dakota	52,595	75.1	14,273	20.4	2,009	2.9	1,137	1.6	70,279
Ohio	600,095	59.7	344,674	34.3	36,260	3.6	19,339	1.9	1,004,395
Oregon	60,309	67.3	17,327	19.3	7,479	8.3	3,795	4.2	89,656
Pennsylvania	840,949	68	337,998	27.3	21,863	1.8	33,717	2.7	1,236,738
Rhode Island	41,605	60.6	24,839	36.2	956	1.4	768	1.1	68,656
South Carolina	2,570	4.6	53,320	95.4	0	0.0	0	0.0	55,890
South Dakota	72,083	71.1	21,969	21.7	3,138	3.1	2,965	2.9	101,395
Tennessee	105,363	43.4	131,653	54.2	1,354	0.6	1,889	0.8	242,750
Texas	51,307	22	167,088	71.5	2,788	1.2	3,933	1.7	233,609
Utah	62,446	61.4	33,413	32.9	5,767	5.7	0	0.0	101,626
Vermont	40,459	78	9,777	18.8	859	1.7	792	1.5	51,888
Virginia	48,180	36.9	80,649	61.8	202	0.2	1,379	1.1	130,410
Washington	101,540	70	28,098	19.4	10,023	6.9	3,229	2.2	145,151
West Virginia	132,620	55.3	100,855	42	1,573	0.7	4,599	1.9	239,986
Wisconsin	280,314	63.2	124,205	28	28,240	6.4	9,872	2.2	443,440
Wyoming	20,489	66.9	8,930	29.2	987	3.2	208	0.7	30,614
TOTALS	7,625,599	56.4	5,083,501	37.6	402,490	3.0	258,596	1.9	13,519,039

1904 ELECTION: STATE-BY-STATE RESULTS (ROOSEVELT vs. PARKER vs. DEBS vs. SWALLOW)

THE ISSUES

EXTENT TO REFORMS

How far should labor and other industrial reforms go?

The REPUBLICAN CONVENTION

PLACE: Chicago, IL

DATE: June 16 to 19, 1908

NOMINATED: William H. Taft, of Ohio, for President

NOMINATED: James S. Sherman, of New York, for VP

Taft, who had been Secretary of War, was Roosevelt's appointed successor. Despite some opposition within the party, Taft was nominated on the first ballot. The convention approved a platform. However, the policies in the platform were more conservative than Roosevelt and other progressive Republicans would have liked.

The DEMOCRATIC CONVENTION

PLACE: Denver, CO

DATE: July 7 to 10, 1908

NOMINATED: William J. Bryan, of Florida, for President

NOMINATED: John W. Kern, of Indiana, for VP

After Parker's dismal showing in the 1904 elections, the Democratic party was ready to turn to the progressive wing of the party, once again. They turned back to William Jennings Bryan to become the nominee. Bryan won the nomination on the first ballot.

William H. Taft

ELECTED

PRESIDENTIAL CANDIDATES

William Jennings Bryan (Democrat)

William Howard Taft (Republican)

William Howard Taft was President Roosevelt's chosen successor. Taft received the nomination on the first ballot. Taft was a reluctant candidate. He felt he had no choice, but to run for office. However, the Republican "Old Guard" nominated one of their own, Congressman James Sherman, to be the Republican Vice Presidential candidate. When the Democrats met at their convention in Denver, the party felt they had not choice but to nominate William Jennings Bryan as their presidential candidate once again. As a result, Bryan received the Democratic nomination on the first ballot.

The 1908 presidential campaign got off to a slow start. William Taft was not an enthusiastic campaigner. Bryan did not seem as driven as he had been in past campaigns. Due to President Roosevelt's continued prodding, Taft became more engaged in the campaign. This was the first time both candidates were actively engaged in the campaign.

The major focus of the campaign was choosing the candidate who could best carry out the vastly popular policies of Theodore Roosevelt. Although Taft was Roosevelt's hand picked successor, Bryan claimed he was more likely to continue Roosevelt's policies. However, Bryan made a major mistake when he called for the socialization of the railroads. Taft won an overwhelming victory.

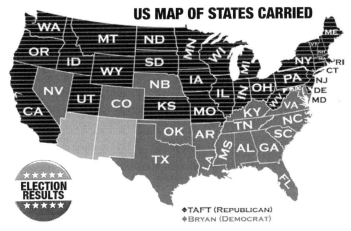

US MAP OF STATES CARRIED

ELECTION RESULTS

◆TAFT (REPUBLICAN)
◆BRYAN (DEMOCRAT)

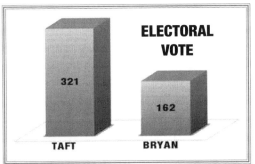

ELECTORAL VOTE

321 TAFT
162 BRYAN

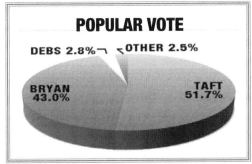

POPULAR VOTE

DEBS 2.8% — OTHER 2.5%
BRYAN 43.0%
TAFT 51.7%

STATES	WILLIAM TAFT		WILLIAM BRYAN		EUGENE DEBS		EUGENE CHAFIN		TOTAL VOTES
	VOTES	PERCENTAGE	VOTES	PERCENTAGE	VOTES	PERCENTAGE	VOTES	PERCENTAGE	
Alabama	25,561	24.3	74,391	70.7	1,450	1.4	690	0.7	105,152
Arkansas	56,684	37.3	87,020	57.3	5,842	3.8	1,026	0.7	151,845
California	214,398	55.5	127,492	33	28,659	7.4	11,770	3	386,625
Colorado	123,693	46.9	126,644	48	7,960	3	5,559	2.1	263,858
Connecticut	112,815	59.4	68,255	35.9	5,113	2.7	2,380	1.3	189,903
Delaware	25,014	52.1	22,055	45.9	239	0.5	670	1.4	48,007
Florida	10,654	21.6	31,104	63	3,747	7.6	1,356	2.7	49,360
Georgia	41,355	31.2	72,350	54.6	584	0.4	1,452	1.1	132,794
Idaho	52,621	54.1	36,162	37.2	6,400	6.6	1,986	2	97,293
Illinois	629,932	54.5	450,810	39	34,711	3	29,364	2.5	1,155,254
Indiana	348,993	48.4	338,262	46.9	13,476	1.9	18,036	2.5	721,117
Iaws	275,210	55.6	200,771	40.6	8,287	1.7	9,837	2	494,770
Kansas	197,316	52.5	161,209	42.9	12,420	3.3	5,030	1.3	376,043
Kentucky	235,711	48	244,092	49.7	4,093	0.8	5,885	1.2	490,719
Louisiana	8,958	11.9	63,568	84.6	2,514	3.3	.		75,117
Maine	66,987	63	35,403	33.3	1,758	1.7	1,487	1.4	106,335
Maryland	116,513	48.8	115,908	48.6	2,323	1	3,302	1.4	238,531
Massachusetts	265,966	58.2	155,533	34	10,778	2.4	4,373	1	456,905
Michigan	333,313	61.9	174,619	32.4	11,527	2.1	16,785	3.1	538,124
Minnesota	195,843	59.3	109,401	33.1	14,472	4.4	10,114	3.1	331,328
Mississippi	4,363	6.5	60,287	90.1	978	1.5			66,904
Missouri	347,203	48.5	346,574	48.4	15,431	2.2	4,209	0.6	715,841
Montana	32,471	46.9	29,511	42.6	5,920	8.6	838	1.2	69,233
Nebraska	126,997	47.6	131,099	49.1	3,524	1.3	5,179	1.9	266,799
Nevada	10,775	43.9	11,212	45.7	2,103	8.6	.		24,526
New Hampshire	53,144	59.3	33,655	37.6	1,299	1.4	905	1	89,595
Now Jersey	265,298	56.8	182,522	39.1	10,249	2.2	4,930	1.1	467,111
Now York	870,070	53.1	667,468	40.7	38,451	2.3	22,667	1.4	1,638,350
North Carolina	114,887	45.5	136,928	54.2	372	0.1	354	0.1	252,554
North Dakota	57,680	61	32,884	34.8	2,421	2.6	1,496	1.6	94,524
Ohio	572,312	51	502,721	44.8	33,795.00	3	11,402	1	1,121,552
Oklahoma	110,473	43.4	122,362	48.1	21,425	8.4	.		254,260
Oregon	62,454	56.5	37,792	34.2	7,322	6.6	2,682	2.4	110,539
Pennsylvania	745,779	58.8	448,782	35.4	33,914	2.7	36,694	2.9	1,267,450
Rhode Island	43,942	60.8	24,706	34.2	1,365	1.9	1,016	1.4	72,317
South Carolina	3,945	5.9	62,288	93.8	100	0.2	.		66,379
South Dakota	67,536	58.8	40,266	35.1	2,846	2.5	4,039	3.5	114,775
Tennessee	117,977	45.9	135,608	52.7	1,870	0.7	301	0.1	257,180
Texas	65,605	22.4	216,662	74	7,779	2.7	1,626	0.6	292,913
Utah	61,165	56.2	42,610	39.2	4,890	4.5	.		108,757
Vermont	39,552	75.1	11,496	21.8	0	0.0	799	1.5	52,680
Virginia	52,572	36.4	82,946	60.5	255	0.2	1,111	0.8	137,065
Washington	106,062	57.8	58,383	31.8	14,177	7.7	4,700	2.6	183,570
West Virginia	137,869	53.4	111,410	43.2	3,679	1.4	5,140	2	258,098
Wisconsin	247,744	54.5	166,662	36.7	28,147	6.2	11,565	2.5	454,438
Wyoming	20,846	55.4	14,918	39.7	1,715	4.6	66	0.2	37,608
TOTALS	7,676,598	51.6	6,406,874	43.0	420,436	2.8	253,428	1.7	14,884,098

1908 ELECTION: STATE-BY-STATE RESULTS (TAFT vs. BRYAN vs. DEBS vs. CHAFIN)

THE ISSUES

CONSERVATISM vs. PROGRESSIVISM vs. LIBERALISM

Which ideology is preferable: Taft's conservatism, Roosevelt's progressivism, or Wilson's liberalism?

The REPUBLICAN CONVENTION

PLACE: Chicago, IL

DATE: June 18 to 22, 1912

NOMINATED: William H. Taft, of Ohio, for President

NOMINATED: James S. Sherman, of NY, for VP

When the Republican party met in Chicago the delegates' loyalties were divided. Roosevelt attempted to remove Taft and win the nomination of his party. Roosevelt won the six primaries that had been held. However, Taft controlled the party machinery. As the convention approached Roosevelt had 411 committed delegates, Taft 201 and LaFollette retained 36 delegates. There were 166 uninstructed delegates. However, there were also 254 contested delegates who were actually Taft delegates. The Republican National Committee allocated the overwhelming majority of the disputed delegates to Taft, before the convention opened. Roosevelt himself broke with tradition and attended the convention. As the convention opened, it became clear Taft had control. Roosevelt's forces tried to elect a convention chairman who was friendly to Roosevelt. They lost their bid in a 558 to 501 vote. After a similar failure to seat a delegation pledged to Roosevelt (instead of one pledged to Taft), Roosevelt concluded that his path back to the White House lay in starting a new party. Roosevelt stopped attempting to block the Taft nomination. Taft was nominated on the first ballot.

The DEMOCRATIC CONVENTION

PLACE: Denver, CO

DATE: July 7 to 10, 1908

NOMINATED: William J. Bryan, of Florida, for President

NOMINATED: John W. Kern, of Indiana, for VP

In 1912 there were three major contenders for the Democratic nomination: House Speaker Champ Clark; Chairman of the House Ways and Means Committee, Congressman, Oscar W. Underwood; and Woodrow Wilson, Governor of New Jersey. 1912 was the first year the Democrats had primaries to select delegates for their convention. Wilson and Clark each won a number of primaries. Clark arrived at the convention with the largest number of delegates pledged to him. When the convention opened, Clark received the support of the Tammany Organization in New York. That support had the effect of turning Bryan, who had been largely neutral, into an opponent of Clark. However, on the first ballot, Clark led with 440 votes (1/4 of the total votes) to Wilson's 324 votes, Harmon's 148 votes, and Underwood's 117 1/4. The remaining votes were scattered. Ballots continued all evening.

On the ninth ballot, the New York delegation changed its vote to support Clark. This gave Clark a majority of the votes. In past conventions that would have been enough to begin a bandwagon for Clark, quickly giving him the 2/3 needed. Instead, this time, the opposition held their ground. Once again, Bryan took center stage, giving a speech castigating Clark for being in the pocket of the privileged class. This solidified the anti-Clark forces, who placed their support behind Wilson. Balloting continued for two days. On the 46th ballot, Wilson achieved 2/3 of the votes and became the Democratic presidential nominee.

When Roosevelt had left the White House in 1908, he was confident that William H. Taft would be a worthy successor. Roosevelt felt assured that President Taft would continue his policies. Upon leaving the White House, Roosevelt sailed to Europe and Africa. Word soon reached him that Taft was abandoning his progressive policies. By the time 1912 arrived Roosevelt was convinced he needed to return to the White House and replace Taft. Roosevelt promptly announced that he would seek to take back the Republican nomination from Taft.

Theodore Roosevelt competed with Taft for the nomination. Roosevelt won 9 out of the ten primaries by large margins. He even beat Taft in Taft's home state. Roosevelt's platform was new nationalism, which included social welfare, direct democracy and federal regulation of business. Roosevelt and his supporters were confident he would win the nomination in Chicago. But the party was controlled by Taft loyalists who steamrolled the convention, insuring that Taft was nominated on the first ballot.

Roosevelt then started a new Progressive party to continue his run for the Presidency. The Democrats were facing a split Republican Party. They knew that if they picked right, they were almost assured the nomination. William Jennings Bryan declined to run. However, Bryan worked very hard behind the scenes to ensure a progressive was nominated. In the end Bryan supported Wilson, who was nominated on the 46th ballot.

Early in the campaign Taft realized he had no chance of winning. As a result, he stopped making campaign appearances. Roosevelt and Wilson campaigned vigorously. Both men were excellent campaigners.

The campaign was interrupted when Roosevelt was almost killed by an assassin, on the evening of October 15th. Although he was shot in the chest, Roosevelt insisted on finishing his speech. The bullet was lodged in his rib close to his lung. Out of respect, all of the presidential candidates took a break from campaigning while Roosevelt recovered. In the end, Woodrow Wilson won the electoral vote by a landslide.

PRESIDENTIAL CANDIDATES

Woodrow Wilson (Democrat)

Theodore Roosevelt (Progressive)

William H. Taft (Republican)

Eugene Debs (Socialist)

Woodrow Wilson
ELECTED

US MAP OF STATES CARRIED

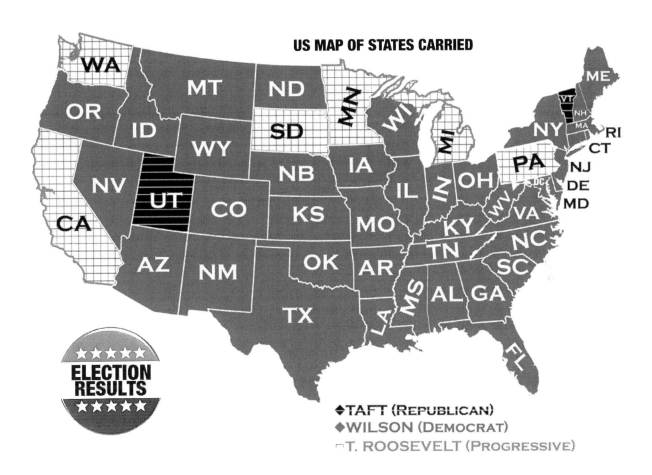

ELECTION RESULTS

◆TAFT (REPUBLICAN)
◆WILSON (DEMOCRAT)
⌐T. ROOSEVELT (PROGRESSIVE)

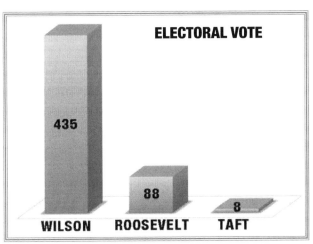

ELECTORAL VOTE

435 — WILSON
88 — ROOSEVELT
8 — TAFT

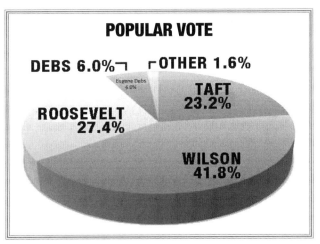

POPULAR VOTE

DEBS 6.0% ⌐OTHER 1.6%
Eugene Debs 6.0%
TAFT 23.2%
ROOSEVELT 27.4%
WILSON 41.8%

STATES	WOODROW WILSON		THEODORE ROOSEVELT		WILLIAM TAFT		EUGENE DEBS		TOTAL VOTES
	VOTES	PERCENTAGE	VOTES	PERCENTAGE	VOTES	PERCENTAGE	VOTES	PERCENTAGE	
Alabama	82,438	69.9	22,680	19.2	9,807	8.3	3,029	2.6	117,959
Arizona	10,324	43.6	6,949	29.3	2,986	12.6	3,163	13.4	23,687
Arkansas	68,814	55.0	21,644	17.3	25,585	20.5	8,153	6.5	125,104
California	283,436	41.8	283,610	41.8	3,847	0.6	79,201	11.7	677,877
Colorado	113,912	42.8	71,752	27.0	58,386	22	16,366	6.2	265,954
Connecticut	74,561	39.2	34,129	17.9	68,324	35.9	10,056	5.3	190,404
Delaware	22,631	46.5	8,886	18.3	15,997	32.9	556	1.1	48,690
Florida	35,343	69.5	4,555	9.0	4,279	8.4	4,806	9.5	51,911
Georgia	93,087	76.6	21,985	18.1	5,191	4.3	1,058	0.9	121,470
Idaho	33,921	32.1	25,527	24.1	32,810	31.0	11,960	11.3	105,754
Illinois	405,048	35.3	386,478	33.7	253,593	22.1	81,278	7.1	1,146,173
Indiana	281,890	43.1	162,007	24.8	151,267	23.1	36,931	5.6	654,474
Iowa	185,322	37.6	161,819	32.9	119,805	24.3	16,967	3.4	492,353
Kansas	143,663	39.3	120,210	32.9	74,845	20.5	26,779	7.3	365,560
Kentucky	219,484	48.5	101,766	22.5	115,510	25.5	11,646	2.6	453,707
Louisiana	60,871	76.8	9,283	11.7	3,833	4.8	5,261	6.6	79,248
Maine	51,113	39.4	48,495	37.4	26,545	20.5	2,541	2.0	129,641
Maryland	112,674	48.6	57,789	24.9	54,956	23.7	3,996	1.7	231,981
Massachusetts	173,408	35.5	142,228	29.1	155,948	32.0	12,616	2.6	488,056
Michigan	150,201	27.4	213,243	38.9	151,434	27.6	23,060	4.2	547,971
Minnesota	106,426	31.8	125,856	37.7	64,334	19.2	27,505	8.2	334,219
Mississippi	57,324	88.9	3,549	5.5	1,560	2.4	2,050	3.2	64,483
Missouri	330,746	47.3	124,375	17.8	207,821	29.7	28,466	4.1	698,566
Montana	28,129	35.0	22,709	28.3	18,575	23.1	10,811	13.5	80,256
Nebraska	109,008	43.7	72,681	29.1	54,226	21.7	10,185	4.1	249,483
Nevada	7,986	39.7	5,620	27.9	3,196	15.9	3,313	16.5	20,115
New Hampshire	34,724	39.5	17,794	20.2	32,927	37.4	1,981	2.3	87,961
New Jersey	178,638	41.2	145,679	33.6	89,066	20.5	15,948	3.7	433,663
New Mexico	20,437	41.9	8,347	17.1	17,164	35.2	2,859	5.9	48,807
New York	655,573	41.3	390,093	24.6	455,487	28.7	63,434	4.0	1,588,315
North Carolina	144,407	59.2	69,135	28.4	29,129	11.9	987	0.4	243,776
North Dakota	29,549	34.2	25,726	29.7	22,990	26.6	6,966	8.1	86,474
Ohio	424,834	41.0	229,807	22.2	278,168	26.8	90,164	8.7	1,037,114
Oklahoma	119,143	47.0	0	0.0	90,726	35.8	41,630	16.4	253,694
Oregon	47,064	34.3	37,600	27.4	34,673	25.3	13,343	9.7	137,040
Pennsylvania	395,637	32.5	444,894	36.5	273,360	22.4	83,614	6.9	1,217,736
Rhode Island	30,412	39.0	16,878	21.7	27,703	35.6	2,049	2.6	77,894
South Carolina	48,355	95.9	1,293	2.6	536	1.1	164	0.3	50,403
South Dakota	48,942	42.1	58,811	50.6	0	0.0	4,664	4.0	116,327
Tennessee	133,021	52.8	54,041	21.5	60,475	24.0	3,564	1.4	251,933
Texas	218,921	72.7	26,715	8.9	28,310	9.4	24,884	8.3	300,961
Utah	36,576	32.6	24,174	21.5	42,013	37.4	8,999	8.0	112,272
Vermont	15,350	24.4	22,129	35.2	23,303	37.1	928	1.5	62,804
Virginia	90,332	65.9	21,776	15.9	23,288	17.0	820	0.6	136,975
Washington	86,840	26.9	113,698	35.2	70,445	21.8	40,134	12.4	322,799
West Virginia	113,097	42.1	79,112	29.4	56,754	21.1	15,248	5.7	268,728
Wisconsin	164,230	41.1	62,448	15.6	130,596	32.7	33,476	8.4	399,975
Wyoming	15,310	36.2	9,232	21.8	14,560	34.4	2,760	6.5	42,283
TOTALS	6,294,326	41.8	4,120,207	27.4	3,486,343	23.2	900,370	6.0	15,043,029

1912 ELECTION: STATE-BY-STATE RESULTS (WILSON vs. ROOSEVELT vs. TAFT vs. DEBS)

UNITED STATES
PRESIDENTIAL ELECTION OF 1916

THE ISSUES

WORLD WAR I

Who would keep America out of the "Great War"?

The REPUBLICAN CONVENTION

PLACE: Chicago, IL

DATE: June 7 to 10, 1916

NOMINATED: Charles E. Hughes, of New York, for President

NOMINATED: Charles W Fairbanks, of Indiana, for VP

Going into the convention Supreme Court Justice Charles Evan Hughes was the clear Republican frontrunner. Roosevelt supporters hoped he could be renominated. Though after two ballots, in which favorite sons blocked Hughes from getting the nomination, Roosevelt supporters gave their support to Hughes. Charles Hughes was nominated on the third ballot.

The DEMOCRATIC CONVENTION

PLACE: Baltimore, MD

DATE: June 14 to 16, 1916

NOMINATED: Woodrow Wilson, of New Jersey, for President

NOMINATED: Thomas R. Marshall, of Indiana, for VP

President Woodrow Wilson was renominated, with only one vote in opposition. The most famous line was stated by convention chairman, Senator Ollie James, of Kentucky. James stated: "Who would say that we can afford to to swap horses while crossing a bloody stream".

Woodrow Wilson

ELECTED

PRESIDENTIAL CANDIDATES

Woodrow Wilson (Democrat)

Charles Evans Hughes (Republican)

Wilson was renominated without opposition at the 1916 Democratic convention held in St. Louis, in June 1916. Former President Roosevelt tried to obtain the Republican nomination. However, too many in the party refused to forgive him for opposing Taft in 1912. Instead, the Republicans nominated Charles Evans Hughes of New York.

Wilson had achieved many of his progressive goals. By 1912, the major issue on most voters minds was the war in Europe. The Democrats' theme was "He kept us out of war". Wilson claimed it was his policies that both defended American rights and kept the US out of the war. Furthermore, Democrats claimed that if Hughes were to win, the US would be drawn into the war. Republicans claimed that Wilson had not protected the neutral rights of the United States. Many political analysts predicted a victory for Hughes.

On election night, when both Wilson and Hughes went to sleep, it appeared Hughes had indeed won. Late editions of several New York papers carried the headline: "President-Elect Hughes". The upset took place overnight, when Wilson carried California by 3,000 votes.

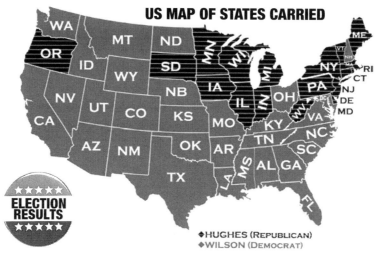

US MAP OF STATES CARRIED

♦HUGHES (REPUBLICAN)
♦WILSON (DEMOCRAT)

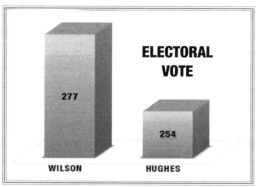

ELECTORAL VOTE

277 WILSON
254 HUGHES

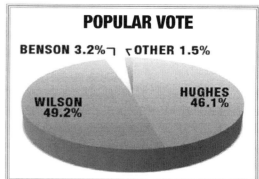

POPULAR VOTE

BENSON 3.2% ⌐ ⌐OTHER 1.5%

WILSON 49.2%

HUGHES 46.1%

STATES	WOODROW WILSON		CHARLES HUGHES		ALLAN BENSON		J. FRANK HANLY		TOTAL VOTES
	VOTES	PERCENTAGE	VOTES	PERCENTAGE	VOTES	PERCENTAGE	VOTES	PERCENTAGE	
Alabama	99,409	75.6	28,809	21.9	1,925	1.5	999	0.8	131,142
Arizona	33,170	57.2	20,522	35.4	3,174	5.5	1,153	2.0	58,019
Arkansas	112,186	66.6	47,148	28.0	6,999	4.2	2,015	1.2	168,348
California	465,936	46.6	462,516	46.3	42,8898	4.3	27,713	2.8	999,250
Colorado	178,816	60.5	102,308	34.8	10,049	3.4	2,793	0.9	294,375
Connecticut	99,786	46.7	106,514	49.8	5,179	2.4	1,789	0.8	213,874
Delaware	24,753	47.8	26,011	50.2	480	0.9	566	1.1	51,810
Florida	55,984	69.3	14,611	18.1	5,353	6.6	4,786	5.9	80,734
Georgia	125,845	79.3	11,225	7.1	967	0.6	0	0.0	158,690
Idaho	70,054	52.0	55,368	41.1	8,066	6.0	1,127	0.8	134,615
Illinois	950,229	43.3	1,152,549	52.6	61,394	2.8	26,047	1.2	2,192,707
Indiana	334,063	46.5	341,005	47.4	21,860	3.0	16,368	2.3	718,853
Iowa	221,699	42.7	280,439	54.1	10,976	2.1	3,371	0.6	518,738
Kansas	314,588	49.9	277,658	44.1	24,685	3.9	12,882	2.0	629,813
Kentucky	269,990	51.9	241,854	46.5	4,734	0.9	3,039	0.6	520,078
Louisiana	79,875	85.9	6,466	7.0	284	0.3	0	0.0	92,974
Maine	64,033	47.0	69,508	51.0	2,177	1.6	596	0.4	136,314
Maryland	138,359	52.8	117,347	44.8	2,674	1.0	2,903	1.1	262,039
Massachusetts	247,885	46.6	268,784	50.5	11,058	2.1	2,993	0.6	531,822
Michigan	283,993	43.9	337,952	52.2	16,012	2.5	8,085	1.2	646,873
Minnesota	179,155	46.2	179,544	46.3	20,117	5.2	7,793	2.0	387,367
Mississippi	80,422	92.8	4,253	4.9	1,484	1.7	0	0.0	86,679
Missouri	398,032	50.6	369,339	46.9	14,612	1.9	3,887	0.5	786,773
Montana	101,104	56.8	66,933	37.6	9,634	5.4	0	0.0	178,009
Nebraska	158,827	55.3	117,771	41.0	7,141	2.5	2,952	1.0	287,315
Nevada	17,776	53.4	12,127	36.4	3,065	9.2	346	1.0	33,314
New Hampshire	43,781	49.1	43,725	49.1	1,318	1.5	303	0.3	89,127
New Jersey	211,018	42.7	268,982	54.4	10,405	2.1	3,182	0.6	494,442
New Mexico	33,693	50.4	31,097	46.5	1,977	3.0	112	0.2	66,879
New York	759,426	44.5	879,238	51.5	45,944	2.7	19,031	1.1	1,706,305
North Carolina	168,383	58.1	120,890	41.7	509	0.2	55	0.0	289,837
North Dakota	55,206	47.8	53,471	46.3	5,716	5.0	997	0.9	115,390
Ohio	604,161	51.9	514,753	44.2	38,092	3.3	8,085	0.7	1,165,091
Oklahoma	148,123	50.7	97,233	33.3	45,091	15.4	1,646	0.6	292,327
Oregon	120,087	45.9	126,813	48.5	9,711	3.7	4,729	1.8	261,650
Pennsylvania	521,784	40.2	703,823	54.3	42,638	3.3	28,525	2.2	1,297,189
Rhode Island	40,394	46.0	44,858	51.1	1,914	2.2	470	0.5	87,816
South Carolina	61,845	96.7	1,550	2.4	135	0.2	0	0.0	63,950
South Dakota	59,191	45.9	6,4,217	49.8	3,760	2.9	1,774	1.4	128,942
Tennessee	153,280	56.3	116,223	42.7	2,542	0.9	145	0.1	272,190
Texas	286,514	76.9	64,999	17.5	18,969	5.1	1,985	0.5	372,467
Utah	84,145	58.8	54,137	37.8	4,460	3.1	149	0.1	143,145
Vermont	22,708	35.2	40,250	62.4	798	1.2	709	1.1	64,475
Virginia	102,825	66.8	49,358	32.1	1,060	0.7	683	0.4	153,993
Washington	183,388	48.1	167,208	43.9	22,800	6.0	6,868	1.8	380,994
West Virginia	140,403	48.5	143,124	49.4	6,144	2.1	0	0.0	289,671
Wisconsin	191,363	42.8	220,822	49.4	27,631	6.2	7,318	1.6	447,134
Wyoming	28,376	54.7	21,698	41.8	1,459	2.8	373	0.7	51,906
TOTALS	9,126,063	49.2	8,547,039	46.1	590,110	3.2	221,293	1.2	18,535,445

1916 ELECTION: STATE-BY-STATE RESULTS (WILSON vs. HUGHES vs. BENSON vs. HANLY)

THE ISSUES

LEAGUE OF NATIONS

Should the United States join the League of Nations?

The DEMOCRATIC CONVENTION

PLACE: Civic Auditorium
San Francisco, California

DATE: June 28 to July 6, 1920

NOMINATED: James M. Cox,
of Ohio, for President

NOMINATED: Franklin D. Roosevelt,
of New York, for VP

The Democrats opened their convention with no clear choice for President. President Wilson was ill and would not going to run for another term. The convention looked at and rejected both Secretary of the Treasury William McAdoo and Attorney General Mitchell Palmer. On the 44th ballot, the convention turned to Governor James Cox of Ohio. Cox, in turn, selected Franklin D. Roosevelt, then Secretary of the Navy as his running-mate. At that point, Roosevelt's only elected office had been State Senator.

The REPUBLICAN CONVENTION

PLACE: Chicago, IL

DATE: June 8 to 12, 1920

NOMINATED: Warren G. Harding,
of Ohio, for President

NOMINATED: Calvin Coolidge,
of Massachusetts, for VP

The Republicans entered 1920 with no front-runner as their Presidential nominee. Four candidates competed for the Republican nomination. General Leonard Wood, Governor Frank O. Lowden, Senator Hiram Johnson, and Senator Warren G. Harding. In the first ballot, Wood and Lowden deadlocked, with 300 votes each. Harding trailed the others, with only sixty votes. It took until the tenth ballot, but Harding broke the deadlock, and won the nomination.

PRESIDENTIAL CANDIDATES

Warren Harding (Republican)

James M. Cox (Democrat)

Warren Harding
ELECTED

By the end of the Wilson Presidency the American people were clearly ready for a change. The Republican convention met in Chicago. There were no front-runners going into the convention. The convention was deadlocked between General Leonard Wood and Governor Frank Lowden. Finally, the convention turned to Warren Harding. Harding was an obscure Senator. After the tenth ballot, the party bosses decided Harding was the best candidate.

The Democrats nominated James Cox for the Presidency, and Franklin Roosevelt for the Vice Presidency. The 1920 election campaign was primarily a referendum on the Wilson presidency and the League of Nations. Cox fully supported the League of Nations, while Harding did not make his position clear. Harding supported prohibition and Cox opposed it. Cox ran a vigorous campaign, while Harding ran mostly a front porch campaign. Cox's efforts and the efforts of his hard campaigning vice presidential candidate had little effect. The weariness of the nation determined election in favor of Harding, who obtained an overwhelming victory.

US MAP OF STATES CARRIED

◆HARDING (REPUBLICAN)
◆COX (DEMOCRAT)

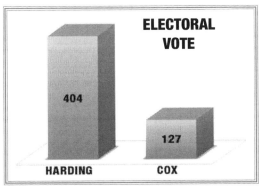

ELECTORAL VOTE

404 HARDING
127 COX

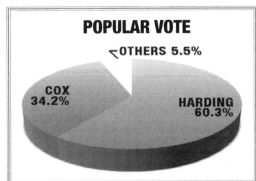

POPULAR VOTE

OTHERS 5.5%
COX 34.2%
HARDING 60.3%

STATES	WARREN HARDING		JAMES COX		EUGENE DEBS		PARLEY CHRISTENSEN		TOTAL VOTES
	VOTES	PERCENTAGE	VOTES	PERCENTAGE	VOTES	PERCENTAGE	VOTES	PERCENTAGE	
Alabama	74,719	31.9	156,064	66.7	2,402	1.0	0	0.0	233,951
Arizona	37,016	55.4	29,546	44.2	222	0.3	15	0.0	66,803
Arkansas	72,316	39.3	106,427	57.9	5,128	2.8	0	0.0	183,637
California	624,992	66.2	229,191	24.3	64,076	6.8	0	0.0	943,463
Colorado	173,248	59.3	104,936	35.9	8,046	2.8	3,016	1.0	292,053
Connecticut	229,238	62.7	120,721	33	10,350	2.8	1,947	0.5	365,518
Delaware	52,858	55.7	39,911	42.1	988	1.0	93	0.1	94,875
Florida	44,853	30.8	90,515	62.1	5,189	3.6	0	0.0	145,684
Georgia	42,981	28.7	106,112	71.0	465	0.3	0	0.0	149,558
Idaho	91,351	66.1	46,930	33.9	0	0.0	0	0.0	138,359
Illinois	1,420,480	67.8	534,395	25.5	74,747	3.6	49,630	2.4	2,094,714
Indiana	696,370	55.1	511,364	40.5	24,713	2.0	16,499	1.3	1,262,974
Iowa	634,674	70.9	227,804	25.5	16,981	1.9	10,321	1.2	894,959
Kansas	369,268	64.8	185,464	32.5	15,511	2.7	0	0.0	570,274
Kentucky	452,480	49.3	456,497	49.7	6,409	0.7	0	0.0	918,636
Louisiana	38,539	30.5	87,519	69.2	0	0.0	0	0.0	126,397
Maine	136,355	68.9	58,961	29.8	2,214	1.1	0	0.0	197,840
Maryland	236,117	55.1	180,626	42.2	8,876	2.1	1,645	0.4	428,443
Massachusetts	681,153	68.5	276,691	27.8	32,267	3.2	0	0.0	993,718
Michigan	762,865	72.8	233,450	22.3	28,947	2.8	10,480	1.0	1,048,411
Minnesota	519,421	70.6	142,994	19.4	56,106	7.6	0	0.0	735,838
Mississippi	11,576	14.1	69,136	84.0	1,639	2.0	0	0.0	82,351
Missouri	727,252	54.6	574,699	43.1	20,342	1.5	3,108	0.2	1,332,140
Montana	109,430	61.1	57,372	32.1	0	0.0	12,204	6.8	179,006
Nebraska	247,498	64.7	119,608	31.3	9,600	2.5	0	0.0	382,743
Nevada	15,479	56.9	9,851	36.2	1,864	6.9	0	0.0	27,194
New Hampshire	95,196	59.8	62,662	39.4	1,234	0.8	0	0.0	159,092
New Jersey	615,333	67.6	258,761	28.4	27,385	3.0	2,264	0.2	910,251
New Mexico	57,634	54.7	46,668	44.3	2	0.0	1,104	1.0	105,412
New York	1,871,167	64.6	781,238	27.0	203,201	7.0	18,413	0.6	2,898,513
North Carolina	232,819	43.2	305,367	56.7	446	0.1	0	0.0	538,649
North Dakota	160,082	77.8	37,422	18.2	8,282	4.0	0	0.0	205,786
Ohio	1,182,022	58.5	780,037	38.6	57,147	2.8	0	0.0	2,021,653
Oklahoma	243,840	50.2	216,122	44.5	25,716	5.3	0	0.0	485,678
Oregon	143,592	60.2	80,019	33.5	9,801	4.1	0	0.0	238,522
Pennsylvania	1,218,215	65.8	503,202	27.2	70,021	3.8	15,642	0.8	1,851,248
Rhode Island	107,463	64.0	55,062	32.8	4,351	2.6	0	0.0	167,981
South Carolina	2,610	3.9	64,170	96.1	28	0	0	0.0	66,808
South Dakota	110,692	60.7	35,938	19.7	0	0.0	34,707	19.0	182,237
Tennessee	219,229	51.2	206,558	48.3	2,249	0.5	0	0.0	428,036
Texas	114,658	23.6	287,920	59.2	8,124	1.7	0	0.0	486,109
Utah	81,555	55.9	56,639	38.8	3,159	2.2	4,475	3.1	145,828
Vermont	68,212	75.8	20,919	23.3	0	0.0	0	0.0	89,961
Virginia	87,456	37.9	141,670	61.3	808	0.3	240	0.1	231,000
Washington	223,137	56.0	84,298	21.1	8,913	2.2	77,246	19.4	398,715
West Virginia	282,007	55.3	220,785	43.3	5,618	1.1	0	0.0	509,936
Wisconsin	498,576	71.1	113,422	16.2	80,635	11.5	0	0.0	701,281
Wyoming	35,091	62.4	17,429	31.0	1,288	2.3	2,180	3.9	56,253
TOTALS	16,151,916	60.3	9,134,074	34.1	915,511	3.4	265,235	1.0	26,768,457

1920 ELECTION: STATE-BY-STATE RESULTS (HARDING vs. COX vs. DEBS vs. CHRISTENSEN)

THE ISSUES

PROSPERITY vs. CORRUPTION

Could Coolidge maintain prosperity in America, without continuing the corruption of the Harding Administration?

The REPUBLICAN CONVENTION

PLACE: Cleveland, OH

DATE: June 10 to 12, 1924

NOMINATED: Calvin Coolidge, of Massachusetts, for President

NOMINATED: Charles G. Dawes, of Illinois, for VP

By the time the Republican party met in Cleveland, President Coolidge had successfully established himself as the party leader. Coolidge was nominated without opposition. The theme of the 1920 Republican convention was: "stay cool with Coolidge."

PRESIDENTIAL CANDIDATES

Calvin Coolidge
(Republican)

John W. Davis
(Democrat)

Robert M.
LaFollette
(Progressive)

The DEMOCRATIC CONVENTION

PLACE: New York, NY

DATE: June 24 to July 9, 1924

NOMINATED: John W. Davis, of New York, for President

NOMINATED: Charles W. Bryan, of Nebraska, for VP

The Democratic Convention of the 1924 revealed a party severely split on a number of important issues. The largest issues that divided the party were the Klu Klux Clan and Prohibition. Eastern and urban voters strongly opposed the Clan. Southern, westerners and rural voters either supported the Clan or were silent on the topic. Opponents to the Clan attempted to have the convention pass a resolution condemning the organization. However, that initiative failed by one vote. The nominees being considered, also reflected the ideological splits in the party. Governor Al Smith, of New York, was the clear choice of the Eastern urban voters. William McAdoo, who supported Prohibition, was a favorite of the West. McAdoo was hurt by being indirectly tied to the scandals of the Harding Administration. Smith's Catholicism was seen as a major impediment to his nomination.

The Democratic Convention, which was broadcast live on national radio, was deadlocked between the two contestants. Through nine long days and 103 ballots, the Democrats fought on. By then, the Congress selected John Davis, a Wall Street lawyer to be the party's standard bearer.

Calvin Coolidge

ELECTED

UNITED STATES PRESIDENTIAL Election of 1924

Coolidge was renominated on the first ballot of the Republican Convention, in Cleveland. This convention was the first convention to be broadcast on radio. Coolidge's opponent was John Davis, of West Virginia. Davis was a compromise candidate. He was selected after the Democratic convention in New York was deadlocked for over 100 ballots. Robert LaFollete, of Wisconsin, ran as a candidate of the Progressive party.

The Republican's most successful campaign slogan was "Keep Cool With Coolidge". Coolidge did very little campaigning. The death of his son further curtailed his activities. Davis campaigned vigorously, attacking the inactivity of Coolidge. LaFollette also campaigned vigorously, promoting the Progressive platform, that called for far-reaching reforms.

The discovery of the criminal actions of members of Warren Harding's administration did not affect Coolidge's support. Opposition to Coolidge was divided between Democrats and the Progressives.

With America enjoying prosperity, Calvin Coolidge went on to enjoy an overwhelming election victory.

US MAP OF STATES CARRIED

ELECTION RESULTS

◆COOLIDGE (REPUBLICAN)
◆DAVIS (DEMOCRAT)
─LAFOLLETTE (PROGRESSIVE)

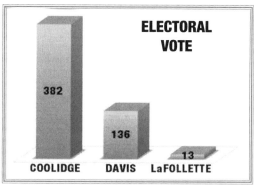

ELECTORAL VOTE

382 COOLIDGE
136 DAVIS
13 LaFOLLETTE

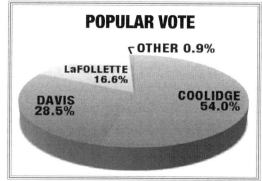

POPULAR VOTE

OTHER 0.9%
LaFOLLETTE 16.6%
DAVIS 28.5%
COOLIDGE 54.0%

STATES	CALVIN COOLIDGE		JOHN DAVIS		ROBERT La FOLLETTE		HERMAN FARIS		TOTAL VOTES
	VOTES	PERCENTAGE	VOTES	PERCENTAGE	VOTES	PERCENTAGE	VOTES	PERCENTAGE	
Alabama	42,823	26.0	113,138	68.8	8,040	4.9	538	0.3	166,593
Arizona	30,516	41.3	26,235	35.5	17,210	23.3	0	0.0	73,961
Arkansas	40,583	29.3	84,790	61.2	13,167	9.5	0	0.0	138,540
California	733,250	57.2	105,514	8.2	424,649	33.1	18,365	1.4	1,281,778
Colorado	195,171	57.0	75,238	22.0	69,946	20.4	966	0.3	342,261
Connecticut	246,322	61.5	110,184	27.5	42,416	10.6	0	0.0	400,396
Delaware	52,441	57.7	33,445	36.8	4,979	5.5	0	0.0	90,885
Florida	30,633	28.1	62,083	56.9	8,625	7.9	5,498	5.0	109,158
Georgia	30,300	18.2	123,262	74.0	12,687	7.6	231	0.1	166,635
Idaho	69,791	47.3	23,951	16.2	53,948	36.5	0	0.0	147,690
Illinois	1,453,321	58.8	576,975	23.4	432,027	17.5	2,367	0.1	2,470,067
Indiana	703,042	55.3	492,245	38.7	71,700	5.6	4,416	0.3	1,272,390
Iowa	537,458	55.0	160,382	16.4	274,448	28.1	0	0.0	976,770
Kansas	407,671	61.5	156,320	23.6	98,461	14.9	0	0.0	662,456
Kentucky	396,758	48.8	375,593	46.2	38,465	4.7	0	0.0	816,070
Louisiana	24,670	20.2	93,218	76.4	-		0	0.0	121,951
Maine	138,440	72.0	41,964	21.8	11,382	5.9	0	0.0	192,192
Maryland	162,414	45.3	148,072	41.3	47,157	13.1	0	0.0	358,630
Massachusetts	703,476	62.3	280,831	24.9	141,225	12.5	0	0.0	1,129,837
Michigan	874,631	75.4	152,359	13.1	122,014	10.5	6,085	0.5	1,160,419
Minnesota	420,759	51.2	55,913	6.8	339,192	41.3	0	0.0	822,146
Mississippi	8,494	7.6	100,474	69.4	3,474	3.1	0	0.0	112,442
Missouri	648,488	49.5	574,962	43.9	83,996	6.4	1,418	0.1	1,310,095
Montana	74,138	42.5	33,805	19.4	66,124	37.9	0	0.0	174,425
Nebraska	218,985	47.2	137,299	29.6	105,681	22.8	1,594	0.3	463,559
Nevada	11,243	41.8	5,909	21.9	9,769	36.3	0	0.0	26,921
New Hampshire	98,575	59.8	57,201	34.7	8,993	5.5	0	0.0	164,769
New Jersey	676,277	62.2	298,043	27.4	109,028	10	1,660	0.2	1,088,054
New Mexico	54,745	48.5	48,542	43.0	9,543	8.5	0	0.0	112,830
New York	1,820,058	55.8	950,796	29.1	474,913	14.6	0	0.0	3,263,939
North Carolina	190,754	39.6	284,190	59.0	6,651	1.4	13	0.0	481,608
North Dakota	94,931	47.7	13,858	7.0	89,922	45.2	0	0.0	199,081
Ohio	1,176,130	58.3	477,887	23.7	358,008	17.8	0	0.0	2,016,296
Oklahoma	225,756	42.8	255,798	48.5	46,274	8.8	0	0.0	527,928
Oregon	142,579	51.0	67,589	24.2	68,403	24.5	0	0.0	279,488
Pennsylvania	1,401,481	65.3	409,192	19.1	307,567	14.3	9,779	0.5	2,144,850
Rhode Island	125,286	59.6	76,606	36.5	7,628	3.6	0	0.0	210,115
South Carolina	1,123	2.2	49,008	96.6	623	1.2	0	0.0	50,755
South Dakota	101,299	49.7	27,214	13.3	75,355	37	0	0.0	203,868
Tennessee	130,831	43.5	159,339	52.9	10,666	3.5	94	0.0	301,030
Texas	130,794	19.9	483,381	73.6	42,879	6.5	0	0.0	657,054
Utah	77,327	49.3	47,001	29.9	32,662	20.8	0	0.0	156,990
Vermont	80,498	78.2	16,124	15.7	5,964	5.8	326	0.3	102,917
Virginia	73,328	32.8	139,717	62.5	10,369	4.6	0	0.0	223,603
Washington	220,224	52.2	42,842	10.2	150,727	35.8	0	0.0	421,549
West Virginia	288,635	49.5	257,232	44.1	36,723	6.3	0	0.0	583,662
Wisconsin	311,614	37.1	68,115	8.1	453,678	54	2,918	0.3	840,827
Wyoming	41,858	52.4	12,868	16.1	25,174	31.5	0	0.0	79,900
TOTALS	15,724,310	54.0	8,386,532	28.8	4,827,184	16.6	56,268	0.2	29,099,380

1924 ELECTION: STATE-BY-STATE RESULTS (COOLIDGE vs. DAVIS vs. La FOLLETTE vs. FARIS)

THE ISSUES

PROSPERITY!

Which candidate would be best able to lead America towards continued prosperity?

The REPUBLICAN CONVENTION

PLACE: Kansas City, MO

DATE: June 12 to 15, 1928

NOMINATED: Herbert Hoover, of California, for President

NOMINATED: Charles Curtis, of Kansas, for VP

Hoover was the most well known member of the Coolidge Administration. He was the clear front runner for the Republican nomination. Hoover won most of the primaries. As the convention neared, Hoover had 400 delegates of the 545 needed to win the nomination. He was selected on the first ballot.

The DEMOCRATIC CONVENTION

PLACE: Houston, TX

DATE: June 26 to 28, 1928

NOMINATED: Alfred E. Smith, of New York, for President

NOMINATED: Charles W. Bryan, of Nebraska, for VP

The Democrats learned their lessons from the 1924 convention. The divisiveness of the 1924 Democratic Convention proved to be a disaster for the party. Democratic delegates arrived in Houston almost completely united in their support for Smith. No major fights were allowed to take place over the Ku Klux Clan or over Prohibition. Smith received 7241/2 votes on the first ballot. This was only ten votes short of the required two thirds. Ohio quickly switched its vote from its favorite son to Smith. Others states followed Ohio's lead, giving Smith all but 55 1/2 votes.

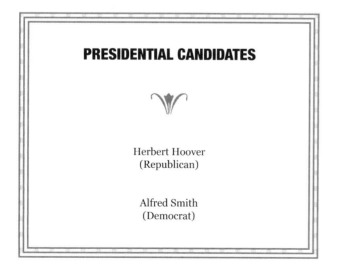

PRESIDENTIAL CANDIDATES

Herbert Hoover
(Republican)

Alfred Smith
(Democrat)

Herbert Hoover
ELECTED

When President Coolidge announced he would not seek another term the road was open for a new Republican nominee. Herbert Hoover was nominated on the first ballot at the Republican convention in Kansas City. after World War I, Hoover was the food administrator for Europe and Secretary of Commerce in the Harding and Coolidge Administrations. In his acceptance speech Hoover stated that: "We in America today are nearer to the final triumph over poverty than ever before in the history of this land... We shall soon with the help of God be in sight of the day when poverty will be banished from this land."

Alfred Smith was nominated by the Democrats on the second ballot, at their convention in Houston. Smith was the first Roman Catholic to run for the presidency.

The major issues in the 1928 campaign were religion and prohibition. Attacks were made against Smith, claiming that if elected, he would make Catholicism the national religion. Smith campaigned against prohibition, while Hoover supported its continuation. One of the slogans used by Hoover campaigners was "A chicken in every pot and a car in every garage."

This was the first campaign in which radio played an important role. While Smith was a better campaigner in person, Hoover presented himself more effectively on radio. The combination of the continued prosperity, combined with a country that was not yet ready to elect a Catholic President insured that Hoover, went on to an overwhelming victory.

In 1927, President Coolidge was extremely popular. The expectation was that Coolidge would run for re-election. It was also expected would easily win. Coolidge, however, had other plans. On August 2, 1927, Coolidge held a press conference where he handed our cards that stated: " I do not choose to run for President in 1928.

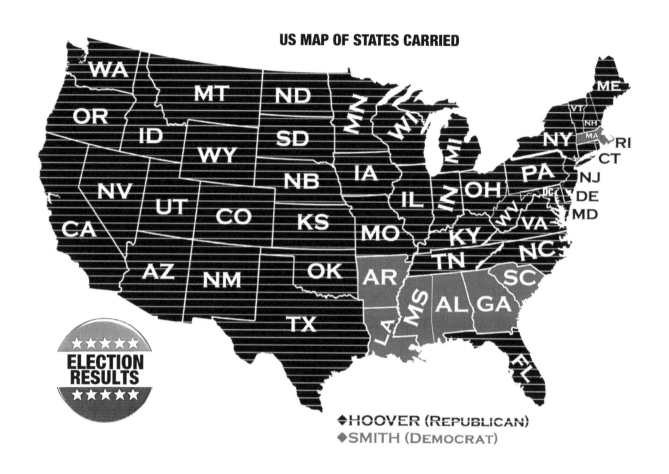

US MAP OF STATES CARRIED

ELECTION RESULTS

◆HOOVER (REPUBLICAN)
◆SMITH (DEMOCRAT)

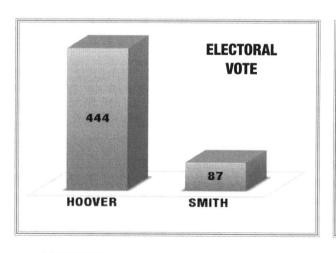

ELECTORAL VOTE

444

87

HOOVER   SMITH

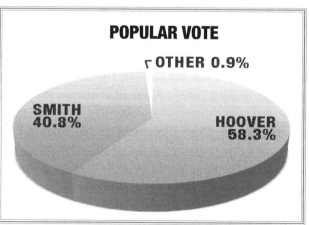

POPULAR VOTE

OTHER 0.9%

SMITH
40.8%

HOOVER
58.3%

STATES	HERBERT HOOVER		ALFRED SMITH		NORMAN THOMAS		WILLIAM FOSTER		TOTAL VOTES
	VOTES	PERCENTAGE	VOTES	PERCENTAGE	VOTES	PERCENTAGE	VOTES	PERCENTAGE	
Alabama	120,725	48.5	127,796	51.3	460	0.2	0	0.0	248,981
Arizona	52,533	57.6	38,537	42.2	0	0.0	184	0.2	91,254
Arkansas	77,784	39.3	119,196	60.3	429	0.2	317	0.2	197,726
California	1,162,323	64.7	614,365	34.2	19,595	1.1	0	0.0	1,796,656
Colorado	253,872	64.7	133,131	33.9	3,472	0.9	675	0.2	392,242
Connecticut	296,641	53.6	252,085	45.6	3,029	0.5	738	0.1	553,118
Delaware	68,860	65.8	35,354	33.8	329	0.3	59	0.1	104,602
Florida	145,860	57.9	101,764	40.4	4,036	1.6	3,704	1.5	253,672
Georgia	101,800	44.0	129,604	56.0	124	0.1	64	0.0	231,592
Idaho	97,322	64.2	52,926	34.9	1,308	0.8	0	0.0	154,230
Illinois	1,769,141	56.9	1,313,817	42.3	19,138	0.6	3,581	0.1	3,107,489
Indiana	848,290	59.7	562,691	39.6	3,871	0.3	321	0.0	1,421,314
Iowa	623,570	61.8	379,011	37.6	2,960	0.3	328	0.0	1,009,189
Kansas	513,672	72.0	193,003	27.1	6,205	0.9	320	0.0	713,200
Kentucky	558,064	59.3	381,070	40.5	783	0.1	288	0.0	940,521
Louisiana	51,160	23.7	164,655	76.3	0	0.0	0	0.0	215,833
Maine	179,923	68.6	81,179	31.0	1,068	0.4	0	0.0	262,170
Maryland	301,479	57.1	223,626	42.3	1,701	0.3	636	0.1	528,348
Massachusetts	775,566	49.2	792,758	50.2	6,262	0.4	2,461	0.2	1,577,823
Michigan	965,396	70.4	396,762	28.9	3,516	0.3	2,881	0.2	1,372,082
Minnesota	560,977	57.8	396,451	40.8	6,774	0.7	4,853	0.5	970,976
Mississippi	27,030	17.8	124,538	82.2	0	0.0	0	0.3	151,568
Missouri	834,080	55.6	662,684	44.2	3,739	0.2	0	0.0	1,500,845
Montana	113,300	58.4	78,578	40.5	1,667	0.9	563	0.1	194,108
Nebraska	345,745	63.2	197,950	36.2	3,433	0.6	0	0.0	547,128
Nevada	18,327	56.5	14,090	43.5	0	0.0	0	0.0	32,417
New Hampshire	115,404	58.7	80,715	41.0	465	0.2	173	0.1	196,757
New Jersey	926,050	59.8	616,517	39.8	4,897	0.3	1,257	0.1	1,549,381
New Mexico	69,708	59.0	48,211	40.8	0	0.0	158	0.1	118,077
New York	2,193,344	49.8	2,089,863	47.4	107,332	2.4	10,876	0.2	4,405,626
North Carolina	348,923	54.9	286,227	45.1	0	0.0	0	0.0	635,150
North Dakota	131,419	54.8	106,648	44.5	936	0.4	842	0.4	239,845
Ohio	1,627,546	64.9	864,210	34.5	8,683	0.3	2,836	0.1	2,508,346
Oklahoma	394,046	63.7	219,174	35.4	3,924	0.6	0	0.0	618,427
Oregon	205,341	64.2	109,223	34.1	2,720	0.9	1,094	0.3	319,942
Pennsylvania	2,055,382	65.2	1,067,586	33.9	18,647	0.6	4,726	0.2	3,150,612
Rhode Island	117,522	49.5	118,973	50.2	0	0.0	283	0.1	237,194
South Carolina	5,858	8.5	62,700	91.4	47	0.1	0	0.0	68,605
South Dakota	157,603	60.2	102,660	39.2	443	0.2	224	0.1	261,857
Tennessee	195,388	55.3	157,143	44.5	567	0.2	94	0.0	353,192
Texas	372,324	51.9	344,542	48.0	722	0.1	209	0.0	708,999
Utah	94,618	53.6	80,985	45.9	954	0.5	46	0.0	176,603
Vermont	90,404	66.9	44,440	32.9	0	0.0	0	0.0	135,191
Virginia	164,609	53.9	140,146	45.9	249	0.1	179	0.1	305,364
Washington	335,844	67.1	156,772	31.3	2,615	0.5	1,541	0.3	500,840
West Virginia	375,551	58.4	263,784	41.0	1,313	0.2	401	0.1	642,752
Wisconsin	544,205	53.5	450,259	44.3	18,213	1.8	1,528	0.2	1,016,831
Wyoming	52,748	63.7	29,299	35.4	788	1.0	0	0.0	82,835
TOTALS	21,432,823	58.2	15,004,336	40.8	267,414	0.7	48,440	0.1	36,801,510

1928 ELECTION: STATE-BY-STATE RESULTS (HOOVER vs. SMITH vs. THOMAS vs. FOSTER)

UNITED STATES
PRESIDENTIAL ELECTION OF 1932

THE ISSUES ECONOMIC DEPRESSION

Could Franklin D. Roosevelt bring about new economic programs to save America?

The REPUBLICAN CONVENTION

PLACE: Chicago, IL

DATE: June 14 to 16, 1932

NOMINATED: Herbert Hoover, of California, for President

NOMINATED: Charles Curtis, of Kansas, for VP

While the Republicans who met in Chicago, in June, were not enthusiastic about renominating Hoover, there were no credible challengers. As such, Hoover was renominated without opposition. The Republican platform praised Hoover and pledged to maintain a balanced budget.

PRESIDENTIAL CANDIDATES

Herbert Hoover
(Republican)

Franklin D. Roosevelt
(Democrat)

The DEMOCRATIC CONVENTION

PLACE: Chicago, IL

DATE: June 27 to July 2, 1932

NOMINATED: Franklin Delano Roosevelt, of New York, for President

NOMINATED: John Nance Gardner, of Texas,, for VP

The Democratic Convention opened with the majority of delegated pledged to Franklin Delano Roosevelt. FDR won most of the primaries he faced against Al Smith, whom he had replaced as Governor. There was, however, significant opposition to Roosevelt among those who believed he was too liberal. On the first ballot Roosevelt received 666 1/4 votes, 102 less than the two thirds majority needed for the nomination. Two more ballots were held the same night, but to no avail. Roosevelt still could not muster the two thirds needed. Overnight Roosevelt supporters succeeded in convincing both the California and Texas delegations to support Roosevelt. The next day, William McAdoo, the head of the California delegation rose and stated: "California came here to choose the next President of the United States. She did not come here to deadlock this convention, or engage in another disastrous contest like that of 1924". With that, McAdoo announced that California would support Roosevelt. FDR ended up with 945 of the conventions delegates. Roosevelt broke previous traditions, by flying to Chicago to accept the party's nomination.

Franklin Delano Roosevelt
ELECTED

ON THIS ... ELECTION

Franklin Roosevelt's overwhelming victory in his 1930 re-election campaign for Governor set the stage for his bid for the Presidency. Roosevelt and his aids immediately began to maneuver behind the scenes to gain Roosevelt the Democratic presidential nomination. Louis Howe worked on the inside, while Jim Farely traveled the country attempting to garner support for Roosevelt. Franklin was the early favorite, but due to the Democratic convention rules that a candidate needed to receive 2/3 of the votes at the convention, a mere lead was not enough.

On March 15, Governor Roosevelt officially announced he was running for the Presidency. As the convention approached, Roosevelt clearly had the lead. His opponents included Al Smith, and John Garner of Texas. The key to securing a convention victory was winning the nomination on one of the first ballots. On June 30, the first votes were cast for the nomination. Roosevelt received 666 (1/2), Smith received 203 (3/4), and Garner received 90 (1/4.) It was an impressive showing for Roosevelt. However, FDR wast still 104 votes shy of the 2/3 needed to receive the nomination. Finally, on the fourth ballot, after Garner was offered the vice presidential candidacy, Roosevelt won the presidential nomination. The next day, in a break with tradition, Roosevelt flew to Chicago to accept the nomination.

Roosevelt engaged in a vigorous campaign, attacking the policies of the Hoover administration. The onset of the economic depression made the Republican position almost untenable. The Republicans had taken credit for the country's economic prosperity. Now, it was hard to evade responsibility for the economic depression. Roosevelt's one area of weakness was the corruption of New York's Tammany political organization. Charges of corruption had been brought against New York City's Mayor, James Walker. Roosevelt personally conducted the hearing. FDR gained important support by virtue of his resourceful handling of this investigation.

The campaign took place against the background of the great economic depression. Roosevelt campaigned feverishly to prove that, despite his disability, he could vigorously undertake the position of United States President. At first, Hoover had planned to stay in the White House working during the crisis, but Roosevelt's ads brought Hoover out on the campaign trail. Hoover tried to depict Roosevelt as an extremist who would bring the country to ruin. Hoover's dour campaigning, compared to Roosevelt's more positive upbeat approach, worked against him. With 1/4 of work force unemployed, Roosevelt won an overwhelming victory.

US MAP OF STATES CARRIED

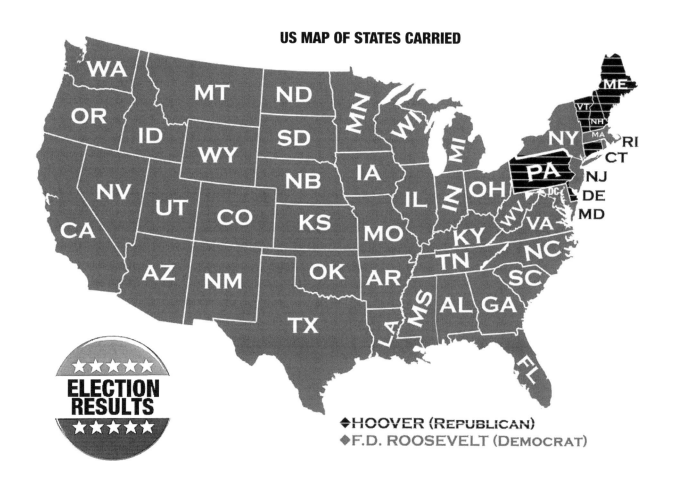

◆HOOVER (REPUBLICAN)
◆F.D. ROOSEVELT (DEMOCRAT)

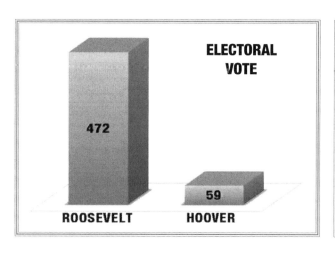

ELECTORAL VOTE

472 ROOSEVELT

59 HOOVER

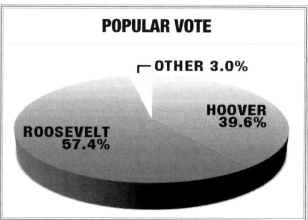

POPULAR VOTE

OTHER 3.0%

HOOVER 39.6%

ROOSEVELT 57.4%

STATES	FRANKLIN D. ROOSEVELT		HERBERT HOOVER		NORMAN THOMAS		WILLIAM FOSTER		TOTAL VOTES
	VOTES	PERCENTAGE	VOTES	PERCENTAGE	VOTES	PERCENTAGE	VOTES	PERCENTAGE	
Alabama	207,910	84.8	34,675	14.1	2,030	0.8	675	0.3	245,303
Arizona	79,264	67.0	36,104	30.5	2,618	2.2	256	0.2	118,251
Arkansas	186,829	86.3	27,465	12.7	1,166	0.5	157	0.1	216,569
California	1,324,157	58.4	847,902	37.4	63,299	2.8	1,023	0.0	2,266,972
Colorado	250,877	54.8	189,617	41.4	13,591	3.0	787	0.2	457,696
Connecticut	281,632	47.4	288,420	48.5	20,480	3.4	1,364	0.2	594,183
Delaware	54,319	48.1	57,073	50.6	1,376	1.2	133	0.1	112,901
Florida	206,307	74.5	69,170	25.0	775	0.3	0	0.0	276,973
Georgia	234,118	91.6	19,863	7.8	461	0.2	23	0.0	255,590
Idaho	109,479	58.7	71,312	38.2	526	0.3	491	0.3	186,520
Illinois	1,882,304	55.2	1,432,756	42.0	67,258	2.0	15,582	0.5	4,407,926
Indiana	862,054	54.7	677,184	42.9	21,388	1.4	2,187	0.1	1,576,927
Iowa	598,019	57.7	414,433	40.0	20,467	2.0	559	0.1	1,036,687
Kansas	424,204	53.6	349,498	44.1	18,276	2.3	0	0.0	791,978
Kentucky	580,574	59.1	394,716	40.2	3,853	0.4	271	0.0	983,059
Louisiana	249,418	92.8	18,853	7.0	0	0.0	0	0.0	268,804
Maine	128,907	43.2	166,631	55.8	2,489	0.8	162	0.1	298,444
Maryland	314,314	61.5	184,184	36.0	10,489	2.1	1,031	0.2	511,054
Massachusetts	800,148	50.6	736,959	46.6	34,305	2.2	4,821	0.3	1,580,114
Michigan	871,700	52.4	739,894	44.4	39,205	2.4	9,318	0.6	1,664,765
Minnesota	600,806	59.9	363,959	36.3	25,476	2.5	6,101	0.6	1,002,843
Mississippi	140,168	96.0	5,180	3.5	686	0.5	0	0.0	146,034
Missouri	1,025,406	63.7	564,713	35.1	16,374	1.0	568	0.0	1,609,894
Montana	127,286	58.8	78,078	36.1	7,891	3.6	1,775	0.8	216,479
Nebraska	359,082	63.0	201,177	35.3	9,876	1.7	0	0.0	570,135
Nevada	28,756	69.4	12,674	30.6	0	0.0	0	0.0	41,430
New Hampshire	100,680	49.0	103,629	50.4	947	0.5	264	0.1	205,520
New Jersey	806,630	49.5	775,684	47.6	42,998	2.6	2,915	0.2	1,630,063
New Mexico	95,089	62.7	54,217	35.8	1,776	1.2	135	0.1	151,606
New York	2,534,959	54.1	1,937,963	41.3	177,397	3.8	27,956	0.6	4,688,614
North Carolina	497,566	69.9	208,344	29.3	5,588	0.8	0	0.0	711,498
North Dakota	178,350	69.6	71,772	28.0	3,521	1.4	830	0.3	256,290
Ohio	1,301,695	49.9	1,227,319	47.0	64,094	2.5	7,231	0.3	2,609,728
Oklahoma	516,468	73.3	188,165	26.7	0	0.0	0	0.0	704,633
Oregon	213,871	58.0	136,019	36.9	15,540	4.2	1,681	0.5	368,751
Pennsylvania	1,295,948	45.3	1,453,540	50.8	91,119	3.2	5,658	0.2	2,859,021
Rhode Island	146,604	55.1	115,266	43.3	3,138	1.2	546	0.2	266,170
South Carolina	102,347	98.0	1,978	1.9	82	0.1	0	0.0	104,407
South Dakota	183,515	63.6	99,212	34.4	1,551	0.5	364	0.1	288,438
Tennessee	259,473	66.5	126,752	32.5	1,796	0.5	254	0.1	390,273
Texas	760,348	88.1	97,959	11.3	4,450	0.5	207	0.0	863,406
Utah	116,750	56.5	84,795	41.0	4,087	2.0	946	0.5	206,578
Vermont	56,266	41.1	78,984	57.7	1,533	1.1	195	0.1	136,980
Virginia	203,979	68.5	89,637	30.1	2,382	0.8	86	0.0	297,942
Washington	353,260	57.5	208,645	33.9	17,080	2.8	2,972	0.5	614,814
West Virginia	405,124	54.5	330,731	44.5	5,133	0.7	444	0.1	743,774
Wisconsin	707,410	63.5	347,741	31.2	53,379	4.8	3,105	0.3	1,114,814
Wyoming	54,370	56.1	39,583	40.8	2,829	2.9	180	0.2	96,962
TOTALS	22,818,740	57.4	15,760,425	39.6	884,685	2.2	103,253	0.3	39,747,783

1932 ELECTION: STATE-BY-STATE RESULTS (FDROOSEVELT vs. HOOVER vs. THOMAS vs. FOSTER)

UNITED STATES
PRESIDENTIAL ELECTION OF 1936

THE ISSUES

GOVERNMENT POWER

Had Franklin Roosevelt gone too far in extending government powers?

The REPUBLICAN CONVENTION

PLACE: Cleveland, OH

DATE: June 9 to 12, 1936

NOMINATED: Alf M. Landon, of Kansas, for President

NOMINATED: Frank Knox, of Illinois, for VP

Alf Landon, the Governor of Kansas, was the only serious contender for the Republican nomination in 1936. Landon was nominated on the first ballot. The Republican convention supported a number of the popular New Deal programs, such as Social Security.

The DEMOCRATIC CONVENTION

PLACE: Philadelphia, PA

DATE: June 23 to 27, 1936

NOMINATED: Franklin Delano Roosevelt, of New York, for President

NOMINATED: John Nance Gardner, of Texas, for VP

The 1936 Democratic convention renominated, the exceptionally popular, Franklin D. Roosevelt without any opposition.

Franklin Delano Roosevelt
ELECTED

PRESIDENTIAL CANDIDATES

Franklin Delano Roosevelt (Democrat)

Alfred Mossman Landon (Republican)

UNITED STATES PRESIDENTIAL Election of 1936

The 1936 Democratic convention voted overwhelmingly to renominate Roosevelt as their presidential nominee. The convention eliminated the rule requiring 2/3 of the delegates to vote in favor of a candidate to receive the Presidential nomination. This simplified the future selection of presidential candidates.

The Republicans met in Cleveland in 1936. They nominated Alfred "Alf" Landon, of Kansas. Landon attacked the Roosevelt administration's New Deal, while supporting some of its goals. The Republicans enjoyed support from businesses and from most newspapers. Businesses opposed the larger role that government undertook, as a result of the policies of the Roosevelt administration.

Roosevelt became an active campaigner. He took to the road and airways in October. Roosevelt proved he had no peer, as a politician. Landon, on the other hand, proved to be a lackluster candidate. The Republicans became desperate and claimed Social Security, which was schedule to go into effect in 1937, was a fraud. Roosevelt gave a rousing defense of Social Security a few days before the election.

Roosevelt won the election by an overwhelming majority of votes. By doing so, Roosevelt cemented a major realignment in American politics.

US MAP OF STATES CARRIED

ELECTION RESULTS

◆LANDON (REPUBLICAN)
◆F.D. ROOSEVELT (DEMOCRAT)

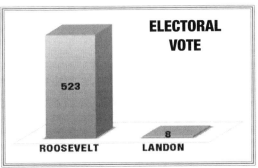

ELECTORAL VOTE

523 ROOSEVELT

8 LANDON

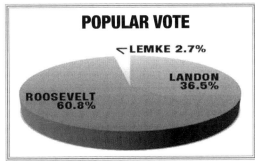

POPULAR VOTE

LEMKE 2.7%
LANDON 36.5%
ROOSEVELT 60.8%

STATES	FRANKLIN D. ROOSEVELT		ALFRED LANDON		WILLIAM LEMKE		NORMAN THOMAS		TOTAL VOTES
	VOTES	PERCENTAGE	VOTES	PERCENTAGE	VOTES	PERCENTAGE	VOTES	PERCENTAGE	
Alabama	238,196	86.4	35,358	12.8	551	0.2	242	0.1	275,744
Arizona	86,722	69.8	33,433	26.9	3,307	2.7	317	0.3	124,163
Arkansas	146,765	81.8	32,049	17.9	4	0.0	446	0.2	179,431
California	1,766,836	67.0	836,431	31.7	0	0.0	11,331	0.4	2,638,882
Colorado	295,021	60.4	181,267	37.1	9,962	2.0	1,594	0.3	488,685
Connecticut	382,129	55.3	278,685	40.3	21,805	3.2	5,683	0.8	690,723
Delaware	69,702	54.6	57,236	44.9	442	0.3	172	0.1	127,603
Florida	249,117	76.1	78,248	23.9	0	0.0	0	0.0	327,436
Georgia	255,363	87.1	36,943	12.6	136	0.0	68	0.0	293,170
Idaho	125,683	63.0	66,256	33.2	7,678	3.8	0	0.0	199,617
Illinois	2,282,999	57.7	1,570,393	39.7	89,439	2.3	7,530	0.2	3,956,522
Indiana	934,974	56.6	691,570	41.9	19,407	1.2	3,856	0.2	1,650,897
Iowa	621,756	54.4	487,977	42.7	29,687	2.6	1,373	0.1	1,142,737
Kansas	464,520	53.7	397,727	46	494	0.1	2,766	0.3	865,507
Kentucky	541,944	58.5	369,702	39.9	12,501	1.3	627	0.1	926,214
Louisiana	292,894	88.8	36,791	11.2	0	0.0	0	0.0	329,778
Maine	126,333	41.5	168,823	55.5	7,581	2.5	783	0.3	304,240
Maryland	389,612	62.3	231,435	37	0	0.0	1,629	0.3	624,896
Massachusetts	942,716	51.2	768,613	41.8	118,639	6.4	5,111	0.3	1,840,357
Michigan	1,016,794	56.3	699,733	38.8	75,795	4.2	8,208	0.5	1,805,098
Minnesota	698,811	61.8	350,461	31	74,296	6.6	2,872	0.3	1,129,975
Mississippi	157,333	97.0	4,467	2.8	0	0.0	342	0.2	162,142
Missouri	1,111,043	60.8	697,891	38.2	14,630	0.8	3,454	0.2	1,828,635
Montana	159,690	69.3	63,598	27.6	5,539	2.4	1,066	0.5	230,502
Nebraska	347,445	57.1	247,731	40.7	12,847	2.1	0	0.0	608,023
Nevada	31,925	72.8	11,923	27.2	0	0.0	0	0.0	43,838
New Hampshire	108,460	49.7	104,642	48	4,819	2.2	0	0.0	218,114
New Jersey	1,083,850	59.5	720,322	39.6	9,407	0.5	3,931	0.2	1,820,437
New Mexico	106,037	62.7	61,727	36.5	924	0.5	343	0.2	169,135
New York	3,293,222	58.8	2,180,670	39	0	0.0	86,897	1.6	5,596,398
North Carolina	616,141	73.4	223,294	26.6	2	0.0	21	0.0	839,475
North Dakota	163,148	59.6	72,751	26.6	36,708	13.4	552	0.2	273,716
Ohio	1,747,140	58.0	1,127,855	37.4	132,212	4.4	167	0.0	3,012,660
Oklahoma	501,069	66.8	245,122	32.7	0	0.0	2,221	0.3	749,740
Oregon	266,733	64.4	122,706	29.6	21,831	5.3	2,143	0.5	414,021
Pennsylvania	2,353,788	56.9	1,690,300	40.8	67,467	1.6	14,375	0.3	4,138,105
Rhode Island	164,338	53.0	125,031	40.3	19,569	6.3	0	0.0	310,278
South Carolina	113,791	98.6	1,646	1.4	0	0.0	0	0.0	115,437
South Dakota	160,137	54.0	125,977	42.5	10,338	3.5	0	0.0	296,452
Tennessee	328,083	68.8	147,055	30.8	296	0.1	687	0.1	475,533
Texas	739,952	87.1	104,661	12.3	3,187	0.4	1,075	0.1	843,482
Utah	150,248	69.3	64,555	29.8	1,121	0.5	432	0.2	216,679
Vermont	62,124	43.2	81,023	56.4	0	0.0	0	0.0	143,689
Virginia	234,980	70.2	98,336	29.4	233	0.1	313	0.1	334,590
Washington	459,579	66.4	206,892	29.9	17,463	2.5	3,496	0.5	692,338
West Virginia	502,582	60.6	325,358	39.2	0	0.0	832	0.1	829,945
Wisconsin	802,984	63.8	380,828	30.3	60,297	4.8	10,626	0.8	1,258,560
Wyoming	62,624	60.6	38,739	37.5	1,653	1.6	200	0.2	103,382
TOTALS	27,750,866	60.8	16,679,683	36.5	892,361	2.0	187,781	0.4	45,656,991

1936 ELECTION: STATE-BY-STATE RESULTS (FDROOSEVELT vs. LANDON vs. LEMKE vs. THOMAS)

THE ISSUES — WAR OR PEACE

Who could best keep America out of World War II? Would Franklin Delano Roosevelt be permitted to run for a third term?

The REPUBLICAN CONVENTION

PLACE: Cleveland, OH

DATE: June 24 to 28, 1940

NOMINATED: Wendell L. Willkie, of Indiana, for President

NOMINATED: Charles L. McNary, of Oregon, for VP

The Republican convention of 1940 resulted in one of the largest upsets in election convention history. In early 1940, the leading candidates for the Republican nomination were: Senator Robert Taft and Thomas E. Dewey, the New York District Attorney. As the international situation became worse, with the fall of France, both Taft and Dewey were considered by many as too isolationist. Wendell Wilkie's candidacy was promoted. Wilkie, who was best known as a utility executive, and had opposed Roosevelt's TVA. Wilkie was an outspoken supporter of American support for the Allies. When the time came for the balloting, Dewey led on the first three ballots. However, the galleries demanded Wilkie. On the fourth ballot, Wilkie took the lead. Wendell Wilkie clinched the nomination on the fourth ballot.

PRESIDENTIAL CANDIDATES

Franklin Delano Roosevelt (Democrat)

Wendell Wilkie (Republican)

The DEMOCRATIC CONVENTION

PLACE: Chicago Stadium Chicago, Cook County, Illinois

DATE: July 15 to 18, 1940

NOMINATED: Franklin Delano Roosevelt, of New York, for President

NOMINATED: Henry Wallace, of Iowa, for VP

For much of the time leading up to the 1940 Democratic convention, Roosevelt had to play it cool. He had to appear ambivalent as to whether he was planning to uphold the two term tradition established by Washington, or if he would choose to run again. A week before the convention Roosevelt made it known that the worsening war situation, (i.e. France had just been overrun), made him feel he should run again. At the convention, a seemingly spontaneous demonstration in support of Roosevelt made his nomination inevitable. FDR was nominated on the first ballot, with 946 votes. The Vice Presidential nomination was more contested. Roosevelt made in known he wished to have Henry Wallace nominated as his running mate. There was a great deal of opposition to Wallace. Some of the objections were clearly a reaction to the feeling Roosevelt had manipulated his renomination. Eleanor Roosevelt flew to the convention and gave a strong speech in favor of Wallace. Ultimately, Wallace was nominated with 626 votes.

Franklin Delano Roosevelt

ELECTED

UNITED STATES PRESIDENTIAL Election of 1940

As the election of 1940 approached, the question arose as to whether Roosevelt would break with American tradition and run for a third term. The start of the war in Europe, in September 1939, persuaded Roosevelt to seek a third term. Roosevelt made it clear he was available for a draft by the Democratic party. The delegates at the Democratic convention chose to do just that.

The Republicans met in Philadelphia in June. There were three leading contenders for the Republican nomination. However, none of these leading candidates won. Instead, the party picked a political novice, Wendell Willkie. Wilkie was a Wall Street novice. Though he was charismatic and colorful.

The Republican party had been strongly isolationist. However, Willkie abandoned his party's position. He came out strongly against Hitler, and in support of the extension of the draft. The one issue on which Willkie attacked Roosevelt was for breaking the tradition of "no third term". In October Roosevelt announced the Lend Lease Act, a plan to turn over 50 destroyers and other military supplies to Britain. Wilkie supported the action, but attacked Roosevelt for not obtaining Congressional support for his actions.

For most of the campaign FDR did not actively campaign. Finally, immediately prior to the election, President Roosevelt did come out and defend his policies. Despite the fact that 78% of the newspapers endorsed Wilkie, Roosevelt carried all of the large cities, except for Cincinnati.

US MAP OF STATES CARRIED

ELECTION RESULTS

◆WILKIE (Republican)
◆F.D. ROOSEVELT (Democrat)

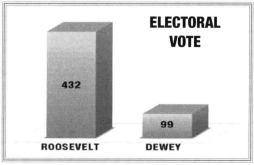

ELECTORAL VOTE

432 ROOSEVELT
99 DEWEY

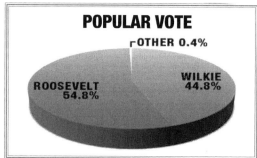

POPULAR VOTE

OTHER 0.4%
ROOSEVELT 54.8%
WILKIE 44.8%

STATES	FRANKLIN D. ROOSEVELT		WENDELL WILKIE		NORMAN THOMAS		ROGER BABSON		TOTAL VOTES
	VOTES	PERCENTAGE	VOTES	PERCENTAGE	VOTES	PERCENTAGE	VOTES	PERCENTAGE	
Alabama	250,726	85.2	42,184	14.3	100	0.0	700	0.2	294,219
Arizona	95,267	63.5	54,030	36	0	0.0	742	0.5	150,039
Arkansas	157,213	78.4	42,122	21	301	0.2	793	0.4	200,429
California	1,877,618	57.4	1,351,419	41.3	16,506	0.5	9,400	0.3	3,268,791
Colorado	265,554	48.4	279,576	50.9	1,899	0.3	1,597	0.3	549,004
Connecticut	417,621	53.4	361,819	46.3	0	0.0	0	0.0	781,502
Delaware	74,599	54.7	61,440	45.1	115	0.1	220	0.2	136,374
Florida	359,334	74	126,158	26	0	0.0	0	0.0	485,640
Georgia	265,194	84.8	46,495	14.9	0	0.0	983	0.3	312,686
Idaho	127,842	54.4	106,553	45.3	497	0.2	0	0.0	235,168
Illinois	2,149,934	51	2,047,240	48.5	10,914	0.3	9,190	0.2	4,217,935
Indiana	874,063	49	899,466	50.5	2,075	0.1	6,437	0.4	1,782,747
Iowa	578,802	47.6	632,370	52	0	0.0	2,284	0.2	1,215,432
Kansas	364,725	42.4	489,169	56.9	2,347	0.3	4,056	0.5	860,297
Kentucky	557,322	57.4	410,384	42.3	1,014	0.1	1,443	0.1	970,163
Louisiana	319,751	85.9	52,446	14.1	0	0.0	0	0.0	372,305
Maine	156,478	48.8	163,951	51.1	0	0.0	0	0.0	320,840
Maryland	384,546	58.3	269,534	40.8	4,093	0.6	0	0.0	660,104
Massachusetts	1,076,522	53.1	939,700	46.4	4,091	0.2	1,370	0.1	2,026,993
Michigan	1,032,991	49.5	1,039,917	49.9	7,593	0.4	1,795	0.1	2,085,929
Minnesota	644,196	51.5	596,274	47.7	5,454	0.4	0	0.0	1,251,188
Mississippi	168,267	95.7	7,364	4.2	193	0.1	0	0.0	175,824
Missouri	958,476	52.3	871,009	47.5	2,226	0.1	1,809	0.1	1,833,729
Montana	145,698	58.8	99,579	40.2	1,443	0.6	664	0.3	247,873
Nebraska	263,677	42.8	352,201	57.2	0	0.0	0	0.0	615,878
Nevada	31,945	60.1	21,229	39.9	0	0.0	0	0.0	53,174
New Hampshire	125,292	53.2	110,127	46.8	0	0.0	0	0.0	235,419
New Jersey	1,016,808	51.5	945,475	47.9	2,433	0.1	873	0.0	1,972,552
New Mexico	103,699	56.6	79,315	43.3	144	0.1	100	0.1	183,258
New York	3,251,918	51.6	3,027,478	48	18,950	0.3	3,250	0.1	6,301,596
North Carolina	609,015	74	213,633	26	0	0.0	0	0.0	822,648
North Dakota	124,036	44.2	154,590	55.1	1,279	0.5	325	0.1	280,775
Ohio	1,733,139	52.2	1,586,773	47.8	0	0.0	0	0.0	3,319,912
Oklahoma	474,313	57.4	348,872	42.2	0	0.0	3,027	0.4	826,212
Oregon	258,415	53.7	219,555	45.6	398	0.1	154	0.0	481,240
Pennsylvania	2,171,035	53.2	1,889,848	46.3	10,967	0.3	0	0.0	4,078,714
Rhode Island	182,181	56.7	138,654	43.2	0	0.0	74	0.0	321,152
South Carolina	95,470	95.6	4,360	4.4	0	0.0	0	0.0	99,830
South Dakota	131,362	42.6	177,065	57.4	0	0.0	0	0.0	308,427
Tennessee	351,601	67.3	169,153	32.4	463	0.1	1,606	0.3	522,823
Texas	909,974	80.9	212,692	18.9	723	0.1	925	0.1	1,041,168
Utah	154,277	62.3	93,151	37.6	200	0.1	0	0.0	247,819
Vermont	64,269	44.9	78,371	54.8	0	0.0	0	0.0	143,062
Virginia	235,961	68.1	109,363	31.6	282	0.1	882	0.3	346,608
Washington	462,145	58.2	322,123	40.6	4,586	0.6	1,686	0.2	793,833
West Virginia	495,662	57.1	372,414	42.9	0	0.0	0	0.0	868,076
Wisconsin	704,821	50.1	679,206	48.3	15,071	1.1	2,148	0.2	1,405,522
Wyoming	59,287	52.8	52,633	46.9	148	0.1	172	0.2	112,240
TOTALS	27,343,218	54.7	22,334,940	44.8	116,510	0.2	58,705	0.1	49,817,149

1940 ELECTION: STATE-BY-STATE RESULTS (FDROOSEVELT vs. WILKIE vs. THOMAS vs. BABSON)

THE ISSUES

ROOSEVELT, AGAIN?

Was Franklin Delano Roosevelt too tired to serve for an unprecedented fourth term?

The REPUBLICAN CONVENTION

PLACE: Chicago, IL

DATE: June 26 to 28, 1944

NOMINATED: Thomas E. Dewey, of New York, for President

NOMINATED: John W. Bricker, of Ohio, for VP

Wendell Willkie, who had been the 1940 Republican nominee competed to be the 1944 nominee. Though after coming in third in the Wisconsin primary, it was clear Willkie did not have support among the Republican base. When the convention opened, the front runner was Thomas Dewey. Dewey received the nomination on the first ballot.

The DEMOCRATIC CONVENTION

PLACE: Chicago Stadium Chicago, Cook County, Illinois

DATE: July 19 to 21, 1944

NOMINATED: Franklin Delano Roosevelt, of New York, for President

NOMINATED: Harry S. Truman, of Missouri, for VP

With the United States fully engaged in WWII, there was no question that Franklin Roosevelt would seek, and receive the nomination once again. The question remained, who would run for Vice President. The current Vice President, Henry Wallace, inspired significant opposition. Roosevelt decided to replace Wallace with Senator Harry Truman. Truman's victory was not won easily. In the first ballot, he received only five vote more than Wallace. Quickly, however, support for Truman grew. In the end, Truman secured the nomination.

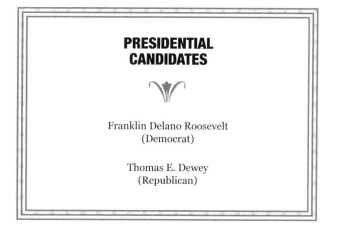

PRESIDENTIAL CANDIDATES

Franklin Delano Roosevelt
(Democrat)

Thomas E. Dewey
(Republican)

Franklin Delano Roosevelt

ELECTED

Roosevelt began his campaign in October. The most memorable moment of the campaign came when the Republicans attacked Roosevelt for using a Navy destroyer to retrieve his dog, who was left behind in the Aleutian Islands. Roosevelt responded by saying: "These Republican leaders have not been content with attacks on me, or my wife, or on my sons. No, not content with that, they now include my little dog, Fala. Well, of course, I don't resent attacks and my family doesn't resent attacks, but Fala does resent them." His speech galvanized Roosevelt supporters. Roosevelt campaigned vigorously to show he was still up to the job. The 1944 election was the closest one for Roosevelt. However, once again, he won.

In the midst of the war, there was no question that Roosevelt would be renominated. Though Vice President Wallace had become quite unpopular in the Democratic party. As a result, President Roosevelt was forced to replace Henry Wallace with Senator Harry Truman as his 1944 vice presidential running mate.

The Republicans nominated Thomas Dewey at the their convention in Chicago. For the first time the Republican platform totally abandoned its traditional opposition to involvement in foreign treaties. It supported the United States' participation in post war organizations.

With a war going on, Dewey did not attack the Roosevelt's policies. On the other hand, he indirectly questioned President Roosevelt's abilities to continue, by continually referring to FDR as the "tired old man."

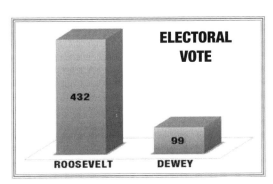

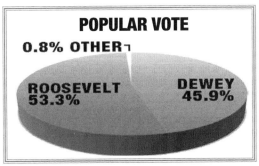

STATES	FRANKLIN D. ROOSEVELT		THOMAS DEWEY		NORMAN THOMAS		CLAUDE WATSON		TOTAL VOTES
	VOTES	PERCENTAGE	VOTES	PERCENTAGE	VOTES	PERCENTAGE	VOTES	PERCENTAGE	
Alabama	198,918	81.3	44,540	18.2	190	0.1	1,095	0.4	244,743
Arizona	80,926	58.8	56,287	40.9	0	0.0	421	0.3	137,634
Arkansas	148,965	70	63,551	29.8	438	0.2	0	0.0	212,954
California	1,988,564	56.5	1,512,965	43	2,515	0.1	14,770	0.4	3,520,875
Colorado	234,331	46.4	268,731	53.2	1,977	0.4	0	0.0	505,039
Connecticut	435,146	52.3	390,527	46.9	5,097	0.6	0	0.0	831,990
Delaware	68,166	54.4	56,747	45.3	154	0.1	294	0.2	125,161
Florida	339,377	70.3	143,215	29.7	0	0.0	0	0.0	482,803
Georgia	268,187	81.7	59,900	18.3	6	0.0	36	0.0	328,129
Idaho	107,399	51.6	100,137	48.1	282	0.1	503	0.2	208,321
Illinois	2,079,479	51.5	1,939,314	48	180	0.0	7,411	0.2	4,036,061
Indiana	781,403	46.7	875,891	52.4	2,223	0.1	12,574	0.8	1,672,091
Iowa	499,876	47.5	547,267	52	1,511	0.1	3,752	0.4	1,052,599
Kansas	287,458	39.2	442,096	60.2	1,613	0.2	2,609	0.4	733,776
Kentucky	472,589	54.5	392,448	45.2	535	0.1	2,023	0.2	867,924
Louisiana	281,564	80.6	67,750	19.4	0	0.0	0	0.0	349,383
Maine	140,631	47.4	155,434	52.4	0	0.0	0	0.0	296,400
Maryland	315,490	51.9	292,949	48.1	0	0.0	0	0.0	608,439
Massachusetts	1,035,296	52.8	921,350	47	0	0.0	973	0.0	1,960,665
Michigan	1,106,899	50.2	1,084,423	49.2	4,598	0.2	6,503	0.3	2,205,223
Minnesota	589,864	52.4	527,416	46.9	5,048	0.4	0	0.0	1,125,504
Mississippi	168,621	93.6	11,613	6.4	0	0.0	0	0.0	180,234
Missouri	807,356	51.4	761,175	48.4	1,751	0.1	1,195	0.1	1,571,697
Montana	112,556	54.3	93,163	44.9	1,296	0.6	340	0.2	207,355
Nebraska	233,246	41.4	329,880	58.6	0	0.0	0	0.0	563,126
Nevada	29,623	54.6	24,611	45.4	0	0.0	0	0.0	54,234
New Hampshire	119,663	52.1	109,916	47.9	46	0.0	0	0.0	229,625
New Jersey	987,874	50.3	961,335	49	3,358	0.2	4,255	0.2	1,963,761
New Mexico	81,389	53.5	70,688	46.4	0	0.0	148	0.1	152,225
New York	3,304,238	52.3	2,987,647	47.3	10,553	0.2	0	0.0	6,316,790
North Carolina	527,399	66.7	263,155	33.3	0	0.0	0	0.0	790,554
North Dakota	100,144	45.5	118,535	53.8	954	0.4	549	0.2	220,182
Ohio	1,570,763	49.8	1,582,293	50.2	0	0.0	0	0.0	3,153,056
Oklahoma	401,549	55.6	319,424	44.2	0	0.0	1,663	0.2	722,636
Oregon	248,635	51.8	225,365	46.9	3,785	0.8	2,362	0.5	480,147
Pennsylvania	1,940,479	51.1	1,835,054	48.4	11,721	0.3	5,750	0.2	3,794,793
Rhode Island	175,356	58.6	123,487	41.3	0	0.0	433	0.1	299,276
South Carolina	90,601	87.6	4,617	4.5	0	0.0	365	0.4	103,382
South Dakota	96,711	41.7	135,365	58.3	0	0.0	0	0.0	232,076
Tennessee	308,707	60.4	200,311	39.2	792	0.2	882	0.2	510,692
Texas	821,605	71.4	191,423	16.6	594	0.1	1,018	0.1	1,150,334
Utah	150,088	60.4	97,891	39.4	340	0.1	0	0.0	248,319
Vermont	53,820	42.9	71,527	57.1	0	0.0	0	0.0	125,361
Virginia	242,276	62.4	145,243	37.4	417	0.1	459	0.1	388,485
Washington	486,774	56.8	361,689	42.2	3,824	0.4	2,396	0.3	856,328
West Virginia	392,777	54.9	322,819	45.1	0	0.0	0	0.0	715,596
Wisconsin	650,413	48.6	674,532	50.4	13,205	1.0	0	0.0	1,339,152
Wyoming	49,419	48.8	51,921	51.2	0	0.0	0	0.0	101,340
TOTALS	25,612,610	53.4	22,021,053	45.9	79,003	0.2	0.2	0.2	47,976,670

1944 ELECTION: STATE-BY-STATE RESULTS (FDROOSEVELT vs. DEWEY vs. THOMAS vs. WATSON)

THE ISSUES

PROSPERITY & THE COLD WAR

What was the best way to confront the Soviet Union regarding the cold war? Who could best bring back peacetime prosperity to America?

The DEMOCRATIC CONVENTION

PLACE: Chicago Stadium Chicago, Illinois Municipal Auditorium

DATE: July 12 to 14, 1948

NOMINATED: Harry S. Truman, of Missouri, for President

NOMINATED: Alben R. Barkley, of Kentucky, for VP

The REPUBLICAN CONVENTION

PLACE: Municipal Auditorium Philadelphia, PA

DATE: June 21 to 25, 1948

NOMINATED: Thomas E. Dewey, of New York, for President

NOMINATED: Earl Warren, of California, for VP

In 1948 there were three serious candidates for the Republican nomination: Robert Taft, Harold Stassen, and Thomas Dewey. Stassen stumbled in a primary debate. When the convention, opened only Taft and Dewey were serious contenders. Dewey won the nomination on the third ballot.

The Democratic party was unenthusiastic about nominating Harry Truman in 1948. Some members of the party attempted to get General Eisenhower to agree to be drafted for a presidential run. When Eisenhower refused, the party rallied around Truman. The most notable event at the convention was the controversy over states' rights and integration. Southern delegates wanted a very strong platform in support of individual state rights. When the convention body refused to support South's platform initiatives, some of the Southern delegates walked out of the convention.

Harry S. Truman

ELECTED

PRESIDENTIAL CANDIDATES

Harry S. Truman (Democrat)

Thomas E. Dewey (Republican)

Strom Thurmond (Dixiecrat)

As the 1948 elections approached, President Truman was not popular. In April 1944, one poll showed Truman with only 36% of the population approving of his performance as President. He was attacked by the Republicans with slogans, such as "To Err is Truman" and "Had Enough".

When the Democrats met in Philadelphia they reluctantly nominated Truman on the first ballot of the convention, despite his clear lack of popularity. Mayor Herbert Humphrey, of Minneapolis, pushed for a strong civil rights platform for the Democratic party. Humphrey's civil rights platform was adopted. As a result, many of the Southern delegates chose to leave the convention. The Republicans renominated Thomas Dewey, the governor of New York, as their nominee. Strom Thurmond of South Carolina ran as a candidate of the Dixiecraft party (a break away party made up of disgruntled Southern Democrats). Henry Wallace ran as a candidate of the Progressives, on a platform that opposed the Marshall Plan, and was more conciliatory to the Soviet Union.

The campaign began with Truman as the underdog. In his acceptance speech Truman stated: "I'm going to fight hard. I'm going to give 'em hell" So he did. He began a coast-to-coast train campaign, in which he covered 22,000 miles and gave ten speeches a day. It became known as the "whistle stop" campaign. In contrast, Dewey tried to run a more relaxed campaign, one more suited for the incumbent than for a challenger.

As the campaign drew to an close, pundits wrote Truman off, despite growing support for him. The night of the election newspapers gave the victory to Dewey. The next morning the stunning extent of the Truman's victory became clear. Truman had won 24 million votes to Dewey's 22 million.

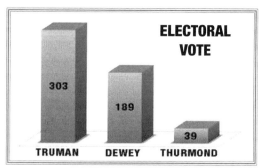

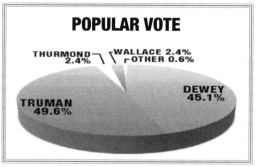

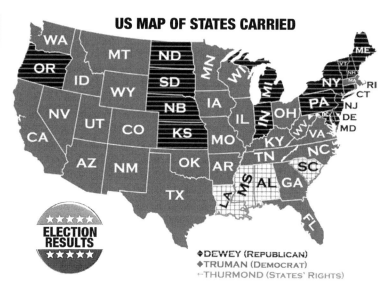

STATES	HARRY TRUMAN		THOMAS DEWEY		J STROM THURMOND		HENRY WALLACE		TOTAL VOTES
	VOTES	PERCENTAGE	VOTES	PERCENTAGE	VOTES	PERCENTAGE	VOTES	PERCENTAGE	
Alabama	0	0.0	40,930	19.0	171,443	79.7	1,522	0.7	214,980
Arizona	95,251	53.8	77,597	43.8	0	0.0	3,310	1.9	177,065
Arkansas	149,659	61.7	50,959	21.0	40,068	16.5	751	0.3	242,475
California	1,913,134	47.6	1,895,269	471	1,228		190,381	4.7	4,021,538
Colorado	267,288	51.9	239,714	46.5	0	0.0	6,115	1.2	515,237
Connecticut	423,297	47.9	437,754	49.5	0	0.0	13,713	1.6	883,518
Delaware	67,813	48.8	69,588	50.0	0	0.0	1,050	0.8	139,073
Florida	281,988	48.8	194,280	33.6	89,755	15.5	11,620	2.0	577,643
Georgia	254,646	60.8	76,691	1&3	85,135	20.3	1,636	0.4	413,844
Idaho	107,370	50.0	101,514	47.3	0	0.0	4,972	2.3	214,816
Illinois	1,994,715	50.1	1,961,103	49.2	0	0.0	0	0.0	3,984,046
Indiana	807,831	48.8	821,079	49.6	0	0.0	9,649	0.6	1,656,212
Iowa	522,380	50.3	494,018	47.6	0	0.0	12,125	1.2	1,038,264
Kansas	351,902	44.6	423,039	53.6	0	0.0	4,603	0.6	788,819
Kentucky	466,756	56.7	341,210	41.5	10,411	1.3	1,567	0.2	822,658
Louisiana	136,344	32.7	72,657	17.5	204,290	49.1	3,035	0.7	416,336
Maine	111,916	42.3	150,234	56.7	0	0.0	1,884	0.7	264,787
Maryland	286,521	48.0	294,814	49.4	2,489	0.4	9,983	1.7	596,748
Massachusetts	1,151,788	54.7	909,370	43.2	0	0.0	38,157	1.8	2,107,146
Michigan	1,003,448	47.6	1,038,595	49.2	0	0.0	46,515	2.2	2,109,609
Minnesota	692,966	57.2	483,617	39.9	0	0.0	27,866	2.3	1,212,226
Mississippi	19,384	10.1	5,043	2.6	167,538	87.2	225	0.1	192,190
Missouri	917,315	58.1	655,039	41.5	0	0.0	3,998	0.3	1,578,628
Montana	119,071	53.1	96,770	43.1	0	0.0	7,313	3.3	224,278
Nebraska	224,165	45.8	264,774	54.2	0	0.0	0	0.0	488,940
Nevada	31,291	50.4	29,357	47.3	0	0.0	1,469	2.4	62,117
New Hampshire	107,995	46.7	121,299	52.4	7		1,970	0.9	231,440
New Jersey	895,455	45.9	981,124	50.3	0	0.0	42,683	2.2	1,949,555
New Mexico	105,464	56.4	80,303	42.9	0	0.0	1,037	0.6	187,063
New York	2,780,204	45.0	2,841,163	46.0	0	0.0	509,559	8.2	6,177,337
North Carolina	459,070	58.0	258,572	32.7	69,652	8.8	3,915	0.5	791,209
North Dakota	95,812	43.4	115,139	52.2	374	0.2	8,391	3.8	220,716
Ohio	1,452,791	49.5	1,445,684	49.2	0	0.0	37,596	1.3	2,936,071
Oklahoma	452,782	62.7	268,817	37.3	0	0.0	0	0.0	721,599
Oregon	243,147	46.4	260,904	49.8	0	0.0	14,978	2.9	524,080
Pennsylvania	1,752,426	46.9	1,902,197	50.9	0	0.0	55,161	1.5	3,735,348
Rhode Island	188,736	57.6	135,787	41.4	0	0.0	2,619	0.8	327,702
South Carolina	34,423	24.1	5,386	3.8	102,607	72	154	0.1	142,571
South Dakota	117,653	47.0	129,651	51.8	0	0.0	2,801	1.1	250,105
Tennessee	270,402	49.1	202,914	36.9	73,815	13.4	1,864	0.3	550,283
Texas	824,235	66.0	303,467	24.3	113,920	9.1	3,918	0.3	1,147,245
Utah	149,151	54.0	124,402	45.0	0	0.0	2,679	1.0	276,306
Vermont	45,557	36.9	75,926	61.5	0	0.0	1,279	1.0	123,382
Virginia	200,786	47.9	172,070	41.0	43,393	10.4	2,047	0.5	419,256
Washington	476,165	52.6	386,314	42.7	0	0.0	31,692	3.5	905,058
West Virginia	429,188	57.3	316,251	42.2	0	0.0	3,311	0.4	748,750
Wisconsin	647,310	50.7	590,959	46.3	0	0.0	25,282	2.0	1,276,800
Wyoming	52,354	51.6	47,947	47.3	0	0.0	931	0.9	101,425
TOTALS	24,105,810	49.5	21,970,064	45.1	1,169,114	2.4	1,157,172	2.4	48,691,494

1948 ELECTION: STATE-BY-STATE RESULTS (TRUMAN vs. DEWEY vs. THURMOND vs. WALLACE)

THE ISSUES

KOREAN WAR/COLD WAR

Who could best bring the Korean War to an end? How should the US confront the Soviets?

The REPUBLICAN CONVENTION

PLACE: Municipal Auditorium Philadelphia, PA

DATE: July 7 to 11, 1952

NOMINATED: Dwight D. Eisenhower, of New York, for President

NOMINATED: Richard M. Nixon, of California, for VP

General Eisenhower entered the Presidential race late. By the time Eisenhower got on board, Robert Taft had won many of the early primaries. Eisenhower rapidly came close to reaching parity in delegates with Taft. Though Taft's delegates still outnumbered Eisenhower's delegates. As a result, the Eisenhower campaign resorted to challenging the credentials of some of Taft's delegates. They ran a public relations campaign whose theme painted Taft as an old politician who made back room deals, compared to the new statesmanship offered by Eisenhower. These challenges succeeded. Eisenhower was only nine delegates short on the first vote. By the second vote, Eisenhower secured enough delegates to win the Republican nominations.

PRESIDENTIAL CANDIDATES

Adlai Stevenson (Democrat)

Dwight D. Eisenhower (Republican)

The DEMOCRATIC CONVENTION

PLACE: Chicago Stadium Chicago, Illinois Municipal Auditorium

DATE: July 19 to 21, 1952

NOMINATED: Adlai Stevenson, of New York, for President

NOMINATED: John J. Sparkman, of Alabama, for VP

President Truman decided he did not want to run again, much to the relief of many Democrats. Senator Kefauver actively sought the nomination. Kefauver entered the convention with significant support due to his primary victories. Truman, however, opposed Kefauver. He worked on Governor Stevenson, of Illinois, to accept the nomination. Once the convention opened, Stevenson agreed to be nominated. On the first ballot Kefauver led, with 340 delegates. Stevenson received 273 delegates. The rest of the delegates were scattered among favorite sons. Stevenson secured the nomination by the third ballot.

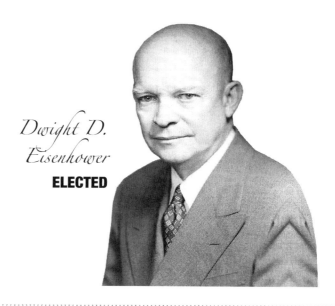

Dwight D. Eisenhower

ELECTED

General Dwight D. Eisenhower was actively courted by both the Republican and Democratic parties. However, Eisenhower, was a Republican at heart. He agreed to run as the Republican nominee for the "good of the nation." Senator Robert Taft, of Ohio, opposed Eisenhower for the nomination. Taft represented the old "isolationist wing" of the Republican Party. Taft won more of the primaries than Eisenhower. Yet, General Eisenhower was nominated on the first ballot at the 1952 Republican convention in Chicago.

It was initially believed that President Truman would run for reelection. Though after he was defeated in the New Hampshire Primary, Truman withdrew his candidacy. He chose to support Governor Adlai Stevenson, of Illinois, for the Democratic nomination. At the Democratic convention in Chicago Stevenson was elected on the third ballot.

Eisenhower took the high road in the campaign. He left the job of leveling attacks to his Vice Presidential candidate Richard Nixon. The Republicans accused the Democrats of "K1C2"– Korea, Communism and Corruption. Nixon, himself, was almost dropped from the campaign. The pressure began after he was accused of maintaining an $18,000 slush fund. Nixon went on national TV, in a speech later known as "The 'Checkers' speech". The speech was named after Nixon's dog, "Checkers", whom he referred to in his speech. Most of the responses to this speech were very favorable to Nixon. This enabled Nixon to keep his position on the Republican ticket.

Toward the end of the campaign, Eisenhower promised to go to Korea and end the impasse of the war. The country voted overwhelmingly for Eisenhower.

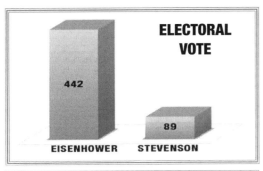

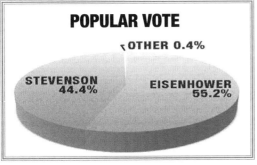

US MAP OF STATES CARRIED

◆EISENHOWER (REPUBLICAN)
◆STEVENSON (DEMOCRAT)

STATES	DWIGHT EISENHOWER		ADLAI STEVENSON		VINCENT HALLINAN		STUART HAMBLEN		TOTAL VOTES
	VOTES	PERCENTAGE	VOTES	PERCENTAGE	VOTES	PERCENTAGE	VOTES	PERCENTAGE	
Alabama	149,231	35.0	275,075	64.6	0	0.0	1,814	0.4	426,120
Arizona	152,042	58.3	108,528	41.7	0	0.0	0	0.0	260,570
Arkansas	177,155	43.8	226,300	55.9	0	0.0	886	0.2	404,800
California	2,897,310	56.3	2,197,548	42.7	24,106	0.5	15,653	0.3	5,141,849
Colorado	379,782	60.3	245,504	39.0	1,919	0.3	0	0.0	630,103
Connecticut	611,012	55.7	481,649	43.9	1,466	0.1	0	0.0	1,096,911
Delaware	90,059	51.8	83,315	47.9	155	0.1	234	0.1	174,025
Florida	544,036	55.0	444,950	45.0	0	0.0	0	0.0	989,337
Georgia	198,961	30.3	456,823	69.7	0	0.0	0	0.0	655,785
Idaho	180,707	65.4	95,081	34.4	443	0.2	0	0.0	276,254
Illinois	2,457,327	54.8	2,013,920	44.9	0	0.0	0	0.0	4,481,058
Indiana	1,136,259	58.1	801,530	41.0	1,085	0.1	15,335	0.8	1,955,049
Iowa	808,906	63.8	451,513	35.6	5,085	0.4	2,882	0.2	1,268,773
Kansas	616,302	68.8	273,296	30.5	0	0.0	6,038	0.7	896,166
Kentucky	495,029	49.8	495,729	49.9	336	0.0	1,161	0.1	993,148
Louisiana	306,925	47.1	345,027	52.9	0	0.0	0	0.0	651,952
Maine	232,353	66.0	118,806	33.8	332	0.1	0	0.0	351,786
Maryland	499,424	55.4	395,337	43.8	7,313	0.8	0	0.0	902,074
Massachusetts	1,292,325	54.2	1,083,525	45.5	4,636	0.2	886	0.0	2,383,398
Michigan	1,551,529	55.4	1,230,657	44.0	3,922	0.1	10,331	0.4	2,798,592
Minnesota	763,211	55.3	608,458	44.1	2,666	0.2	2,147	0.2	1,379,483
Mississippi	112,966	39.6	172,566	60.4	0	0.0	0	0.0	285,532
Missouri	959,429	50.7	929,830	49.1	987	0.1	885	0.0	1,892,062
Montana	157,394	59.4	106,213	40.1	723	0.3	548	0.2	265,037
Nebraska	421,603	69.2	188,057	30.8	0	0.0	0	0.0	609,660
Nevada	50,502	61.4	31,688	38.6	0	0.0	0	0.0	82,190
New Hampshire	166,287	60.9	106,663	39.1	0	0.0	0	0.0	272,950
New Jersey	1,373,613	56.8	1,015,902	42.0	5,589	0.2	989	0.0	2,418,554
New Mexico	132,170	55.4	105,661	44.3	225	0.1	297	0.1	238,608
New York	3,952,813	55.5	3,104,601	43.6	64,211	0.9	0	0.0	7,128,239
North Carolina	558,107	46.1	652,803	53.9	0	0.0	0	0.0	1,210,910
North Dakota	191,712	71.0	76,694	28.4	344	0.1	302	0.1	270,127
Ohio	2,100,391	56.8	1,600,367	43.2	0	0.0	0	0.0	3,700,758
Oklahoma	518,045	54.6	430,939	45.4	0	0.0	0	0.0	948,984
Oregon	420,815	60.5	270,579	38.9	3,665	0.5	0	0.0	695,059
Pennsylvania	2,415,789	52.7	2,146,269	46.9	4,222	0.1	8,951	0.2	4,580,969
Rhode Island	210,935	50.9	203,293	49.0	187	0.0	0	0.0	414,498
South Carolina	168,082	49.3	173,004	50.7	0	0.0	1	0.0	341,087
South Dakota	203,857	69.3	90,426	30.7	0	0.0	0	0.0	294,283
Tennessee	446,147	50.0	443,710	49.7	885	0.1	1,432	0.2	892,553
Texas	1,102,878	53.1	969,228	46.7	294	0.0	1,983	0.1	2,075,946
Utah	194,190	58.9	135,364	41.1	0	0.0	0	0.0	329,554
Vermont	109,717	71.5	43,355	28.2	282	0.2	0	0.0	153,557
Virginia	349,037	56.3	268,677	43.4	311	0.1	0	0.0	619,689
Washington	599,107	54.3	492,845	44.7	2,460	0.2	0	0.0	1,102,708
West Virginia	419,970	48.1	453,578	51.9	0	0.0	0	0.0	873,548
Wisconsin	979,744	61.0	622,175	38.7	2,174	0.1	0	0.0	1,607,370
Wyoming	81,049	62.7	47,934	37.1	0	0.0	194	0.2	129,253
TOTALS	33,777,945	54.9	27,314,992	44.4	140,023	0.2	72,949	0.1	61,550,918

1952 ELECTION: STATE-BY-STATE RESULTS (EISENHOWER vs. STEVENSON vs. HALLINAN vs. HAMBLEN)

UNITED STATES
PRESIDENTIAL ELECTION OF 1956

THE ISSUES

HEALTH OF THE PRESIDENT

Was Dwight D. Eisenhower healthy enough to serve as President of the United States for a second term?

The REPUBLICAN CONVENTION

PLACE: Cow Palace, San Francisco, CA

DATE: August 20 to 23, 1956

NOMINATED: Dwight D. Eisenhower, of New York, for President

NOMINATED: Richard M. Nixon, of California, for VP

President Eisenhower was renominated by acclamation at the 1956 Republican convention.

The DEMOCRATIC CONVENTION

PLACE: Chicago, Illinois

DATE: August 13 to 17, 1956

NOMINATED: Adlai Stevenson, of New York, for President

NOMINATED: Estes Kefauver, of Tennessee, for Vice President

With President's Eisenhower's popularity high, there were few who wished to challenge him, for the Democratic nomination. Stevenson however, wanted another chance to run against the President. Eisenhower suffered a heart attack. His health was in some doubt, Averall Hariman decided to challenge Stevenson. Despite support from Truman, Harriman was unable to mount a credible challenge. Stevenson was elected on the first ballot.

The real drama at the 1956 Democratic convention was the selection of a Vice Presidential nominee. Going into the convention there was talk of selecting Senator John F. Kennedy as Stevenson's vice presidential running mate. Instead, Stevenson decided to open the selection to the convention body in an open vote. Kennedy came close, but fell short in to secure the nomination on the first ballot. Kefauver then came from behind to win the prize.

Dwight D. Eisenhower
ELECTED

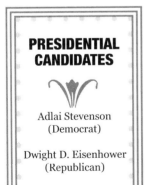

PRESIDENTIAL CANDIDATES

Adlai Stevenson
(Democrat)

Dwight D. Eisenhower
(Republican)

At the 1956 Democratic convention, in Chicago, the delegates renominated Adlai Stevenson. The only drama at the convention occurred when Stevenson opened up to the convention body to decide on his Vice Presidential running mate. John F. Kennedy opposed the veteran Senator Estes Kefauver for the nomination. Senator Kefauver won.

Stevenson faced almost insurmountable odds, in opposing the very popular incumbent President. Stevenson attempted to contrast his vigor, with Eisenhower's health problems. Stevenson made proposals regarding benefits for senior citizens, health, education, natural resources, and economic policies. He also called for the end of the draft and the creation of a professional army. Stevenson further called for a Test Ban Treaty on Atomic weapons with the Soviet Union. Stevenson's efforts were totally unsuccessful. Eisenhower won a landslide victory.

With the 1956 elections approaching, the major question was whether President Eisenhower would run for a second term. He had suffered a heart attack in 1955. In February, Eisenhower announced his decision to seek a second term. He was immediately nominated for re-election by the Republicans in San Francisco. The only question was whether Nixon would remain on the ticket. Eisenhower decided in favor of keeping Nixon on as his running mate.

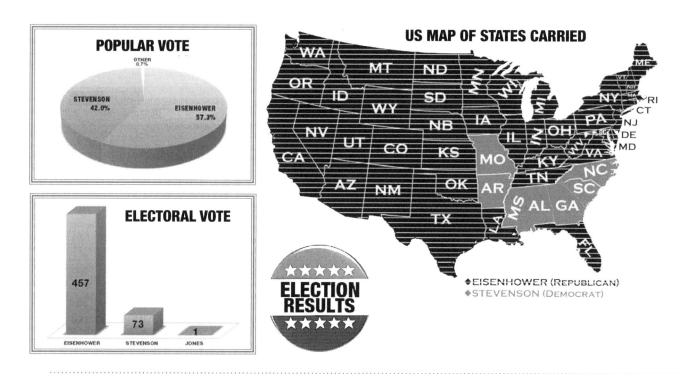

POPULAR VOTE

OTHER 0.7%

STEVENSON 42.0%

EISENHOWER 57.3%

ELECTORAL VOTE

457 — EISENHOWER
73 — STEVENSON
1 — JONES

ELECTION RESULTS

US MAP OF STATES CARRIED

◆EISENHOWER (REPUBLICAN)
◆STEVENSON (DEMOCRAT)

STATES	DWIGHT EISENHOWER		ADLAI STEVENSON		T. COLEMAN ANDREWS		ERIC HASS		TOTAL VOTES
	VOTES	PERCENTAGE	VOTES	PERCENTAGE	VOTES	PERCENTAGE	VOTES	PERCENTAGE	
Alabama	195,694	39.4	280,844	56.5	0	0.0	0	0.0	496,861
Arizona	176,990	61	112,880	38.9	303	0.1	0	0.0	290,173
Arkansas	186,287	45.8	213,277	52.5	7,008	1.7	0	0.0	406,572
California	3,027,668	55.4	2,420,135	44.3	6,087	0.1	300	0.0	5,466,355
Colorado	394,479	60	257,997	39.3	759	0.1	3,308	0.5	657,074
Connecticut	711,837	63.7	405,079	36.3	0	0.0	0	0.0	1,117,121
Delaware	98,057	55.1	79,421	44.6	0	0.0	110	0.1	177,988
Florida	643,849	57.2	480,371	42.7	0	0.0	0	0.0	1,125,762
Georgia	222,778	33.3	444,688	66.4	2,096	0.3	0	0.0	669,655
Idaho	166,979	61.2	105,868	38.8	126	0.0	0	0.0	272,989
Illinois	2,623,327	59.5	1,775,682	40.3	0	0.0	8,342	0.2	4,407,407
Indiana	1,182,811	59.9	783,908	39.7	0	0.0	1,334	0.1	1,974,607
Iowa	729,187	59. 1	501,858	40.7	3,202	0.3	125	0.0	1,234,564
Kansas	566,878	65.4	296,317	34.2	0	0.0	0	0.0	866,243
Kentucky	572,192	54.3	476,453	45.2	0	0.0	358	0.0	1,053,805
Louisiana	329,047	53.3	243,977	39.5	0	0.0	0	0.0	617,544
Maine	249,238	70.9	102,468	29.1	0	0.0	0	0.0	351,706
Maryland	559,738	60	372,613	39.9	0	0.0	0	0.0	932,827
Massachusetts	1,393,197	59.3	948,190	40.4	0	0.0	5,573	0.2	2,348,506
Michigan	1,713,647	55.6	1,359,898	44.1	0	0.0	0	0.0	3,080,468
Minnesota	719,302	53.7	617,525	46.1	0	0.0	2,080	0.2	1,340,005
Mississippi	60,685	24.5	144,453	58.2	0	0.0	0	0.0	248,104
Missouri	914,289	49.9	918,273	50.1	0	0.0	0	0.0	1,832,562
Montana	154,933	57.1	116,238	42.9	0	0.0	0	0.0	271,171
Nebraska	378,108	65.5	199,029	34.5	0	0.0	0	0.0	577,137
Nevada	56,049	58	40,640	42	0	0.0	0	0.0	96,689
New Hampshire	176,519	66.1	90,364	33.8	111	0.0	0	0.0	266,994
New Jersey	1,606,942	64.7	850,337	34.2	5,317	0.2	6,736	0.3	2,484,312
New Mexico	146,788	57.8	106,098	41.8	364	0.1	69	0.0	253,926
New York	4,345,506	61.2	2,747,944	38.7	1,027	0.0	150	0.0	7,095,971
North Carolina	575,062	49.3	590,530	50.7	0	0.0	0	0.0	1,165,592
North Dakota	156,766	61.7	96,742	38.1	483	0.2	0	0.0	253,991
Ohio	2,262,610	61.1	1,439,655	38.9	0	0.0	0	0.0	3,702,265
Oklahoma	473,769	55.1	385,581	44.9	0	0.0	0	0.0	859,350
Oregon	406,393	55.2	329,204	44.7	0	0.0	0	0.0	736,132
Pennsylvania	2,585,252	56.5	1,981,769	43.3	0	0.0	7,447	0.2	4,576,503
Rhode Island	225,819	58.3	161,790	41.7	0	0.0	0	0.0	387,609
South Carolina	75,700	25.2	136,372	45.4	2	0.0	0	0.0	300,583
South Dakota	171,569	58.4	122,288	41.6	0	0.0	0	0.0	291,857
Tennessee	462,288	49.2	456,507	48.6	19,820	2.1	0	0.0	939,404
Texas	1,080,619	55.3	859,958	44	14,591	0.7	0	0.0	1,955,168
Utah	215,631	64.6	118,364	35.4	0	0.0	0	0.0	333,995
Vermont	110,390	72.2	42,549	27.8	0	0.0	0	0.0	152,978
Virginia	386,459	55.4	267,760	38.4	42,964	6.2	351	0.1	697,978
Washington	620,430	53.9	523,002	45.4	0	0.0	7,457	0.6	1,150,889
West Virginia	449,297	54.1	381,534	45.9	0	0.0	0	0.0	830,831
Wisconsin	954,844	61.6	586,768	37.8	6,918	0.4	710	0.0	1,550,558
Wyoming	74,573	60.1	49,554	39.9	0	0.0	0	0.0	124,127
TOTALS	**35,590,472**	**57.4**	**26,022,752**	**42.0**	**111,178**	**0.2**	**44,450**	**0.1**	**62,026,908**

1956 ELECTION: STATE-BY-STATE RESULTS (EISENHOWER vs. STEVENSON vs. ANDREWS vs. HASS)

THE ISSUES

MISSILE GAP AND ECONOMIC PROSPERITY

Who was responsible for the Russia's seeming possession of more missiles? What steps would get the economy moving again?

The DEMOCRATIC CONVENTION

PLACE: Los Angeles, California

DATE: July 11 to 15, 1960

NOMINATED: John F. Kennedy, of Massachusetts, for President

NOMINATED: Lyndon B. Johnson, of Texas, for Vice President

Senator Kennedy worked tirelessly to receive the Democratic presidential nomination, starting from the time of the 1956 election. Kennedy had won the majority of the primaries. Just before the convention, Senator Johnson, the Majority Leader of the Senate announced his intention to seek the nomination. Kennedy entered the convention with the majority of the delegates pledged to vote for him. Kennedy's supporters worked relentlessly to ensure the delegates stayed committed to JFK. Their hard work paid off. Kennedy won the nomination on the first ballot. Then, Kennedy made a surprise selection of Lyndon Johnson as his Vice Presidential running mate.

1960 represented the end of an era. While Kennedy did win on the first ballot, when the convention opened his victory was not an assured thing. 1960 represented the last time there was true drama at a Democratic convention. Since 1960, the outcomes of the conventions have been known in advance.

The REPUBLICAN CONVENTION

PLACE: Chicago, Illinois

DATE: July 25 to 28, 1960

NOMINATED: Richard M. Nixon, of California, for President

NOMINATED: Henry Cabot Lodge, of Massachusetts, for Vice President

By the time the Republican convention opened, Richard Nixon had no opponents for the presidential nomination. The highlight of the convention was the speech delivered by Barry Goldwater, removing himself from the race. In the speech, Goldwater called on the Conservatives to take back the party.

PRESIDENTIAL CANDIDATES

John F. Kennedy (Democrat)

Richard M. Nixon (Republican)

John F. Kennedy
ELECTED

Senator Kennedy entered seven primaries and won all seven primaries he entered. His victory in West Virginia was particularly important. West Virginia had almost no Catholic voters. JFK's victory there showed he could win anywhere. Kennedy went into the Democratic convention of Los Angeles as the clear front runner. His superb campaign organization guaranteed him the victory on the convention hall. In his acceptance speech Kennedy stated: "We stand today on the verge on a new frontier; the frontier of the 1960's; a frontier of unknown opportunities and perils; a frontier of unfulfilled hopes and threats."Vice President Richard Nixon was nominated by the Republicans in Chicago.

Kennedy campaigned on the theme of getting the country moving again. He assailed the "missile gap" with the Russians, and denounced the Eisenhower administration for allowing a Communist regime to come to power in Cuba. Nixon criticized Kennedy for his lack of experience. However, Nixon forbade his staff from bringing up the question of Kennedy's religion (JFK was Catholic). Despite that fact, Kennedy's religion remained an issue. The final analysis of the election showed that Kennedy's religion ended up helping him more than it hurt him.

The 1960 presidential campaign included the first televised debates. Kennedy was declared the winner in their first debate by those who saw him on TV, (though not by those who heard on the radio). This gave Kennedy an edge. When Reverend Martin Luther King, Jr. was arrested in Atlanta, Kennedy called to offer his sympathy. This garnered Kennedy substantial Black support. Towards the end of the race, President Eisenhower began to campaign actively for Nixon, but it was too late. The 1960 presidential election was predicted to be a very close race, and it truly was.

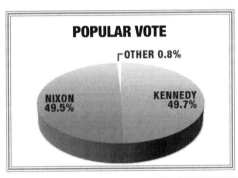

POPULAR VOTE

OTHER 0.8%

NIXON 49.5%

KENNEDY 49.7%

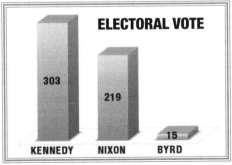

ELECTORAL VOTE

303 KENNEDY

219 NIXON

15 BYRD

US MAP OF STATES CARRIED

◆NIXON (REPUBLICAN)
◆KENNEDY (DEMOCRAT)
−BYRD (INDEPENDANT)

ELECTION RESULTS

STATES	JOHN F. KENNEDY		RICHARD M. NIXON		ERIC HASS		TOTAL VOTES
	VOTES	PERCENTAGE	VOTES	PERCENTAGE	VOTES	PERCENTAGE	
Alabama	324,050	56.8	237,981	41.7	0	0.0	570,225
Alaska	29,809	49.1	30,953	50.9	0	0.0	60,762
Arizona	176,781	44.4	221,241	55.5	469	0.1	398,491
Arkansas	215,049	50.2	184,508	43.1	0	0.0	428,509
California	3,224,099	49.6	3,259,722	50.1	1,051	0.0	6,506,578
Colorado	330,629	44.9	402,242	54.6	2,803	0.4	736,236
Connecticut	657,055	53.7	565,813	46.3	0	0.0	1,222,883
Delaware	99,590	50.6	96,373	49.0	82		196,683
Florida	748,700	48.5	795,476	51.5	0	0.0	1,544,176
Georgia	458,638	62.5	274,472	37.4	0	0.0	733,349
Hawaii	92,410	50.0	92,295	50.0	0	0.0	184,705
Idaho	138,853	46.2	161,597	53.8	0	0.0	300,450
Illinois	2,377,846	50	2,368,988	49.8	10,560	0.2	4,757,409
Indiana	952,358	44.6	1,175,120	55.0	1,136	0.1	2,135,360
Iowa	550,565	43.2	722,381	56.7	230	0.0	1,273,810
Kansas	363,213	39.1	561,474	60.4	0	0.0	928,825
Kentucky	521,855	46.4	602,607	53.6	0	0.0	1,124,462
Louisiana	407,339	50.4	230,980	28.6	0	0.0	807,891
Maine	181,159	43.0	240,608	57.0	0	0.0	421,767
Maryland	565,808	53.6	489,538	46.4	0	0.0	1,055,349
Massachusetts	1,487,174	60.2	976,750	39.6	3,892	0.2	2,469,480
Michigan	1,687,269	50.9	1,620,428	48.8	1,718	0.1	3,318,097
Minnesota	779,933	50.6	757,915	49.2	962	0.1	1,541,887
Mississippi	108,362	36.3	73,561	24.7	0	0.0	298,171
Missouri	972,201	50.3	962,221	49.7	0	0.0	1,934,422
Montana	134,891	48.6	141,841	51.1	0	0.0	277,579
Nebraska	232,542	37.9	380,553	62.1	0	0.0	613,095
Nevada	54,880	51.2	52,387	48.8	0	0.0	107,267
New Hampshire	137,772	46.6	157,989	53.4	0	0.0	295,761
New Jersey	1,385,415	50.0	1,363,324	49.2	4,262	0.2	2,773,111
New Mexico	156,027	50.2	153,733	49.4	570	0.2	311,107
New York	3,830,085	52.5	3,446,419	47.3	0	0.0	7,291,079
North Carolina	713,136	52.1	655,420	47.9	0	0.0	1,368,556
North Dakota	123,963	44.5	154,310	55.4	0	0.0	278,431
Ohio	1,944,248	46.7	2,217,611	53.3	0	0.0	4,161,859
Oklahoma	370,111	41.0	533,039	59.0	0	0.0	903,150
Oregon	367,402	47.3	408,060	52.6	0	0.0	776,421
Pennsylvania	2,556,282	51.1	2,439,956	48.7	7,185	0.1	5,006,541
Rhode Island	258,032	63.6	147,502	36.4	0	0.0	405,535
South Carolina	198,129	51.2	188,558	48.8	0	0.0	386,688
South Dakota	128,070	41.8	178,417	58.2	0	0.0	306,487
Tennessee	481,453	45.8	556,577	52.9	0	0.0	1,051,792
Texas	1,167,567	50.5	1,121,310	48.5	0	0.0	2,311,084
Utah	169,248	45.2	205,361	54.8	0	0.0	374,709
Vermont	69,186	41.3	98,131	58.6	0	0.0	167,324
Virginia	362,327	47	404,521	52.4	397	0.1	771,449
Washington	599,298	48.3	629,273	50.7	10,895	0.9	1,241,572
West Virginia	441,786	52.7	395,995	47.3	0	0.0	837,781
Wisconsin	830,805	48.0	895,175	51.8	1,310	0.1	1,729,082
Wyoming	63,331	45.0	77,451	55.0	0	0.0	140,782
TOTALS	34,226,731	49.7	34,108,157	49.5	47,522	0.1	68,838,219

1960 ELECTION: STATE-BY-STATE RESULTS (KENNEDY vs. NIXON vs. HASS)

UNITED STATES
PRESIDENTIAL ELECTION OF 1964

THE ISSUES **FIGHTING COMMUNISM**

Who was best equipped to combat communism? Was Goldwater too dangerous to be President of the United States?

The DEMOCRATIC CONVENTION

PLACE: Atlantic City, NJ

DATE: August 24 to 27, 1964

NOMINATED: Lyndon B. Johnson, of Texas, for President

NOMINATED: Hubert Humphrey, of Minnesota, for Vice President

The 1964 Democratic convention nominated President Johnson and his choice for running mate Senator Hubert Humphrey by a vote of acclamation.

The REPUBLICAN CONVENTION

PLACE: Cow Palace, San Francisco, CA

DATE: July 13 to 16, 1964

NOMINATED: Barry M. Goldwater, of Arizona, for President

NOMINATED: Hubert Humphrey, of Minnesota, for Vice President

Barry Goldwater clinched the Republican nomination long before the convention. Goldwater supporters had strong control over the convention. When Nelson Rockefeller attempted to add a statement to the plank denouncing extremism, it was defeated.

PRESIDENTIAL CANDIDATES

Lyndon B. Johnson
(Democrat)

Barry Goldwater
(Republican)

Lyndon B. Johnson
ELECTED

President Johnson was nominated for re-election by acclamation at the Democratic convention in Atlantic City. Senator Goldwater ran for the Republican nomination, He was opposed by Nelson Rockefeller. However, Johnson was nominated on the first ballot.

Goldwater promised "a choice, and not an echo." Goldwater suggested the use of tactical nuclear weapons in Vietnam, if necessary. He also called for deep cuts in the social programs. Goldwater opposed much of the civil rights legislation. He suggested that Social Security become voluntary, and that the Tennessee Valley Authority be sold. Johnson campaigned on a platform of continued social programs, and limited involvement in Vietnam.

The election of 1964 was the first election, since 1932, that was fought over true issues. This election brought ideology into Americans politics. The Democrats claimed that Goldwater's policies were dangerous and that he would lead the US into war. The Democratic slogans included: "In Your Guts, You Know He is Nuts".

The Johnson campaign ran a very devastating ad, featuring a little girl and an atomic bomb. The advertisement only ran once, yet this ad seemed to frame the election.

President Johnson won the election by a landslide.

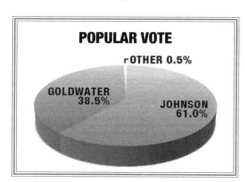

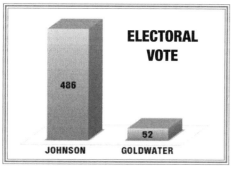

STATES	LYNDON JOHNSON VOTES	LYNDON JOHNSON PERCENTAGE	BARRY GOLDWATER VOTES	BARRY GOLDWATER PERCENTAGE	ERIC HASS VOTES	ERIC HASS PERCENTAGE	CLIFTON DeBERRY VOTES	CLIFTON DeBERRY PERCENTAGE	TOTAL VOTES
Alabama	210,205	30.5	479,085	69.5	0	0.0	0	0.0	689,818
Alaska	44,329	65.9	22,930	34.1	0	0.0	0	0.0	67,259
Arizona	237,753	49.5	242,535	50.4	482	0.1	0	0.0	480,770
Arkansas	314,197	56.1	243,264	43.4	0	0.0	0	0.0	560,426
California	4,171,877	59.1	1,879,108	40.8	489	0.0	378	0.0	7,057,586
Colorado	476,024	61.3	296,767	38.2	302	0.0	2,537	0.3	776,986
Connecticut	826,269	67.8	390,996	32.1	0	0.0	0	0.0	1,218,578
Delaware	122,704	60.9	78,078	38.8	113	0.1	0	0.0	201,320
Florida	948,540	51.1	905,941	48.9	0	0.0	0	0.0	1,854,481
Georgia	522,556	45.9	616,584	54.1	0	0.0	0	0.0	1,139,335
Hawaii	163,249	78.8	44,022	21.2	0	0.0	0	0.0	207,271
Idaho	148,920	50.9	143,557	49.1	0	0.0	0	0.0	292,477
Illinois	2,796,833	59.5	1,905,946	40.5	0	0.0	0	0.0	4,702,841
Indiana	1,170,848	56	911,118	43.6	1,374	0.1	0	0.0	2,091,606
Iowa	733,030	61.9	449,148	37.9	182	0.0	159	0.0	1,184,539
Kansas	464,028	54.1	386,579	45.1	1,901	0.2	0	0.0	857,901
Kentucky	669,659	64	372,977	35.7	0	0.0	0	0.0	1,046,105
Louisiana	387,068	43.2	509,225	56.8	0	0.0	0	0.0	896,293
Maine	262,264	68.8	118,701	31.2	0	0.0	0	0.0	380,965
Maryland	730,912	65.5	385,495	34.5	0	0.0	0	0.0	1,116,457
Massachusetts	1,786,422	76.2	549,727	23.4	4,755	0.2	0	0.0	2,344,798
Michigan	2,136,615	66.7	1,060,152	33.1	1,704	0.1	3,817	0.1	3,203,102
Minnesota	991,117	63.8	559,624	36	2,544	0.2	1,177	0.1	1,554,462
Mississippi	52,618	12.9	356,528	87.1	0	0.0	0	0.0	409,146
Missouri	1,164,344	64	653,535	36	0	0.0	0	0.0	1,817,879
Montana	164,246	58.9	113,032	40.6	0	0.0	332	0.1	278,628
Nebraska	307,307	52.6	276,847	47.4	0	0.0	0	0.0	584,154
Nevada	79,339	58.6	56,094	41.4	0	0.0	0	0.0	135,433
New Hampshire	184,064	63.9	104,029	36.1	0	0.0	0	0.0	288,093
New Jersey	1,868,231	65.6	964,174	33.9	7,075	0.2	8,183	0.3	2,847,663
New Mexico	194,015	59	132,838	40.4	1,217	0.4	0	0.0	328,645
New York	4,913,102	68.6	2,243,559	31.3	6,118	0.1	3,228	0.0	7,166,275
North Carolina	800,139	56.2	624,844	43.8	0	0.0	0	0.0	1,424,983
North Dakota	149,784	58	108,207	41.9	0	0.0	224	0.1	258,389
Ohio	2,498,331	62.9	1,470,865	37.1	0	0.0	0	0.0	3,969,196
Oklahoma	519,834	55.7	412,665	44.3	0	0.0	0	0.0	932,499
Oregon	501,017	63.7	282,779	36	0	0.0	0	0.0	786,305
Pennsylvania	3,130,954	64.9	1,673,657	34.7	5,092	0.1	10,456	0.2	4,822,690
Rhode Island	315,463	80.9	74,615	19.1	0	0.0	0	0.0	390,091
South Carolina	215,723	41.1	309,048	58.9	0	0.0	0	0.0	524,779
South Dakota	163,010	55.6	130,108	44.4	0	0.0	0	0.0	293,118
Tennessee	634,947	55.5	508,965	44.5	0	0.0	0	0.0	1,143,946
Texas	1,663,185	63.3	958,566	36.5	0	0.0	0	0.0	2,626,811
Utah	219,628	54.7	181,785	45.3	0	0.0	0	0.0	401,413
Vermont	108,127	66.3	54,942	33.7	0	0.0	0	0.0	163,089
Virginia	558,038	53.5	481,334	46.2	2,895	0.3	0	0.0	1,042,267
Washington	779,881	62	470,366	37.4	7,772	0.6	537	0.0	1,258,556
West Virginia	538,087	67.9	253,953	32.1	0	0.0	0	0.0	792,040
Wisconsin	1,050,424	62.1	638,495	37.7	1,204	0.1	1,692	0.0	1,691,815
Wyoming	80,718	56.6	61,998	43.4	0	0.0	0	0.0	142,716
District of Columbia	169,796	85.5	28,801	14.5	0	0.0	0	0.0	198,597
TOTALS	43,129,566	61.1	27,178,168	38.5	45,219	0.1	32,720	0.0	70,644,592

1964 ELECTION: STATE-BY-STATE RESULTS (JOHNSON vs. GOLDWATER vs. HASS vs. DeBERRY)

UNITED STATES
PRESIDENTIAL ELECTION OF 1968

THE ISSUES VIETNAM WAR

Who could best put an end to the Vietnam War and bring all American soldiers home?

The DEMOCRATIC CONVENTION

PLACE: Chicago, IL

DATE: August 26 to 29, 1968

NOMINATED: Hubert Humphrey, of Minnesota, for President

NOMINATED: Edmund Muskie, of Maine, for Vice President

The Democratic convention was marked by two major issues. However, there was no conflict regarding who would be the Presidential nominee. When the convention opened Humphrey's lead in delegates was too large for any other candidate to receive the nomination. The first issue was the question of the convention plank on the Vietnam War. Two very different planks were entered; one supporting the Administration's position and the second calling for an end to bombing, with a phased withdrawal of troops. The Administration's plank was adopted by a vote of 1,527 to 1,041. The failure of the anti-war plank increased the level of demonstrations in the streets. The Chicago police reacted to the anti-war demonstrations with a brutality unseen in many years, (The brutality certainly rivaled anything seen before on television). Delegates were appalled, as scenes of violence on the streets were shown at the convention. Senator Ribicoff of Connecticut placed Senator McGovern's name before the convention and stated: "With George McGovern as president we would not have 'Gestapo' tactics in the streets of Chicago."

The REPUBLICAN CONVENTION

PLACE: Miami Beach, FL

DATE: August 5 to 8, 1968

NOMINATED: Richard M. Nixon, of California, for President

NOMINATED: Spiro T. Agnew, of Maryland, for Vice President

Richard Nixon was nominated on the first ballot of the Republican convention, despite a late minute challenge by California Governor, Ronald Reagan. Nixon surprised the convention with his choice of Spiro Agnew as his Vice Presidential running mate.

PRESIDENTIAL CANDIDATES

Hubert Humphrey (Democrat)

Richard Nixon (Republican)

George Wallace (American Independant)

Richard Nixon
ELECTED

Richard Nixon entered the Republican convention as the front runner. He won the nomination on the first ballot. In his acceptance speech Nixon stated: "When the strongest nation in the world can be tied down for four years in a war in Vietnam, with no end in sight; when the richest nation in the world cannot manage its economy; when the nation with the greatest tradition of the rule of law is plagued by unprecedented racial violence; when the President of the United States cannot travel abroad, or to any major city at home, then it's time for new leadership for the United States."

The Democrats went through a grueling primary campaign. Eugene McCarthy, an early opponent of the war in Vietnam, almost upset President Johnson in the New Hampshire primary. This convinced Johnson not to run for re-election. At that point, Vice President Humphrey announced his candidacy for the nomination. A primary battle followed, with Robert Kennedy pulling in the lead, until his assassination. With Kennedy gone, Humphrey was able to sew up the Democratic nomination. Humphrey was nominated on the first ballot, at a tumultuous convention in Chicago. The rioting, and the police actions outside the convention hall, dominated the news coverage, and did not get the Humphrey campaign off to a good start.

Nixon began the campaign as the front runner, with a clear lead. He campaigned against rising crime. He claimed he would restore "law and order". Nixon also instituted the Southern policy, taking advantage of Southern voters' resentments at civil rights legislation passed by the Johnson administration. Nixon successfully received support from what had been a solidly Democratic South. Toward the end of the campaign, as Humphrey became more critical of Johnson's handling of the war, the lead narrowed. However, the lead did not narrow enough to stop a Nixon victory.

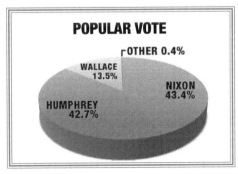

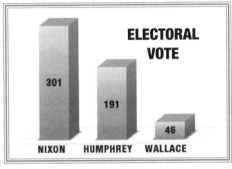

STATES	RICHARD NIXON		HUBERT HUMPHREY		GEORGE WALLACE		HENNING BLOMEN		TOTAL VOTES
	VOTES	PERCENTAGE	VOTES	PERCENTAGE	VOTES	PERCENTAGE	VOTES	PERCENTAGE	
Alabama	146,923	14	196,579	18.7	691,425	65.9	0	0.0	1,049,922
Alaska	37,600	45.3	35,411	42.6	10,024	12.1	0	0.0	83,035
Arizona	266,721	54.8	170,514	35	46,573	9.6	75	0.0	486,936
Arkansas	190,759	30.8	188,228	30.4	240,982	38.9	0	0.0	819,969
California	3,467,664	47.8	3,244,318	44.7	487,270	6.7	341	0.0	7,251,587
Colorado	409,345	50.5	335,174	41.3	60,813	7.5	3,016	0.4	811,199
Connecticut	556,721	44.3	621,561	49.5	76,650	6.1	0	0.0	1,256,232
Delaware	96,714	45.1	89,194	41.6	28,459	13.3	0	0.0	214,367
Florida	886,804	40.5	676,794	30.9	624,207	28.5	0	0.0	2,187,805
Georgia	380,111	30.4	334,440	26.7	535,550	42.8	0	0.0	1,250,266
Hawaii	91,425	38.7	141,324	59.8	3,469	1.5	0	0.0	236,218
Idaho	165,369	56.8	89,273	30.7	36,541	12.5	0	0.0	291,183
Illinois	2,174,774	47.1	2,039,814	44.2	390,958	8.5	13,878	0.3	4,619,749
Indiana	1,067,885	50.3	806,659	38	243,108	11.4	0	0.0	2,123,597
Iowa	619,106	53	476,699	40.8	66,422	5.7	241	0.0	1,167,931
Kansas	478,674	54.8	302,996	34.7	88,921	10.2	0	0.0	872,783
Kentucky	462,411	43.8	397,541	37.6	193,098	18.3	0	0.0	1,055,893
Louisiana	257,535	23.5	309,615	28.2	530,300	48.3	0	0.0	1,097,450
Maine	169,254	43.1	217,312	55.3	6,370	1.6	0	0.0	392,936
Maryland	517,995	41.9	538,310	43.6	178,734	14.5	0	0.0	1,235,039
Massachusetts	766,844	32.9	1,469,218	63	87,088	3.7	6,180	0.3	2,331,752
Michigan	1,370,665	41.5	1,593,082	48.2	331,968	10	1,762	0.1	3,306,250
Minnesota	658,643	41.5	857,738	54	68,931	4.3	285	0.0	1,588,506
Mississippi	88,516	13.5	150,644	23	415,349	63.5	0	0.0	654,509
Missouri	811,932	44.9	791,444	43.7	206,126	11.4	0	0.0	1,809,502
Montana	138,835	50.6	114,117	41.6	20,015	7.3	0	0.0	274,404
Nebraska	321,163	59.8	170,784	31.8	44,904	8.4	0	0.0	536,851
Nevada	73,188	47.5	60,598	39.3	20,432	13.2	0	0.0	154,218
New Hampshire	154,903	52.1	130,589	43.9	11,173	3.8	0	0.0	297,298
New Jersey	1,325,467	46.1	1,264,206	44	262,187	9.1	6,784	0.2	2,875,395
New Mexico	169,692	51.8	130,081	39.7	25,737	7.9	0	0.0	327,350
New York	3,007,932	44.3	3,378,470	49.7	358,864	5.3	8,432	0.1	6,791,688
North Carolina	627,192	39.5	464,113	29.2	496,188	31.3	0	0.0	1,587,493
North Dakota	138,669	55.9	94,769	38.2	14,244	5.7	0	0.0	247,682
Ohio	1,791,014	45.2	1,700,586	42.9	467,495	11.8	120	0.0	3,959,698
Oklahoma	449,697	47.7	301,658	32	191,731	20.3	0	0.0	943,086
Oregon	408,433	49.8	358,866	43.8	49,683	6.1	0	0.0	819,622
Pennsylvania	2,090,017	44	2,259,405	47.6	378,582	8	4,977	0.1	4,747,928
Rhode Island	122,359	31.8	246,518	64	15,678	4.1	0	0.0	385,000
South Carolina	254,062	38.1	197,486	29.6	215,430	32.3	0	0.0	666,978
South Dakota	149,841	53.3	118,023	42	13,400	4.8	0	0.0	281,264
Tennessee	472,592	37.8	351,233	28.1	424,792	34	0	0.0	1,248,617
Texas	1,227,844	39.9	1,266,804	41.1	584,269	19	0	0.0	3,079,216
Utah	238,728	56.5	156,665	37.1	26,906	6.4	0	0.0	422,568
Vermont	85,142	52.8	70,255	43.5	5,104	3.2	0	0.0	161,404
Virginia	590,319	43.4	442,387	32.5	321,833	23.6	4,671	0.3	1,361,491
Washington	588,510	45.1	616,037	47.2	96,990	7.4	488	0.0	1,304,281
West Virginia	307,555	40.8	374,091	49.6	72,560	9.6	0	0.0	754,206
Wisconsin	809,997	47.9	748,804	44.3	127,835	7.6	1,338	0.1	1,691,538
Wyoming	70,927	55.8	45,173	35.5	11,105	8.7	0	0.0	127,205
District of Columbia	31,012	18.2	139,566	81.8	0	0.0	0	0.0	170,578
TOTALS	31,785,480	43.4	31,275,166	42.7	9,906,473	13.5	52,588	0.1	73,211,875

1968 ELECTION: STATE-BY-STATE RESULTS (NIXON vs. HUMPHREY vs. WALLACE vs. BLOMEN)

THE ISSUES

ENDING THE VIETNAM WAR

Should the United States pull all of its troops out of Vietnam immediately?

The REPUBLICAN CONVENTION

PLACE: Miami Beach, FL

DATE: August 21 to 23, 1972

NOMINATED: Richard M. Nixon,
of California, for President

NOMINATED: Spiro T. Agnew,
of Maryland, for Vice President

Richard Nixon was renominated without opposition.

The DEMOCRATIC CONVENTION

PLACE: Miami, FL

DATE: July 10 to 13, 1972

NOMINATED: George McGovern,
of South Dakota, for President

NOMINATED: Sargent Shriver,
of Maryland, for Vice President

McGovern entered the convention with enough delegates to ensure his victory. A last minute movement to stop McGovern developed, with Humphrey as its leader. The opponents concentrated on challenging the credentials of some of the McGovern delegations. When that failed, McGovern went on to be nominated on the first vote of the convention.

PRESIDENTIAL CANDIDATES

George McGovern (Democrat)

Richard Nixon (Republican)

UNITED STATES PRESIDENTIAL Election of 1972

President Nixon was renominated by the Republican Convention, with only token opposition. Nixon stated in his acceptance speech: "It has become fashionable in recent years to point out what is wrong with the American system. The critics contend that it is unfair, so corrupt, so unjust that we should tear it down and substitute something else in its place. I totally disagree, I believe in the American system."

Senator George McGovern was nominated after a long series of primary battles. As a result, Senators Muskie and Humphrey withdrew from the campaign. Both Senators were considered more moderate than McGovern. McGovern received the Democratic nomination on the first ballot. However, the McGovern campaign began on a sour note, when it was discovered that his Vice Presidential running mate, Senator Thomas Eagan, had received electroshock treatment for depression. Eagan resigned. He was replaced by Sargent Shriver on the ticket.

The Republicans successfully depicted Senator McGovern as a radical leftist. McGovern was unable to shake that depiction. Thus, regardless of the charges that McGovern made, most Americans paid little attention to him. Nixon made few campaign appearances. Nixon also refused to debate McGovern.

As part of the 1972 campaign "CREEP" (Committee for the Reelection of the President) engaged in illegal fundraising. Members of CREEP were arrested during a break-in of the Democratic National Committee offices. That break-in, which took place in the Watergate Complex, led to the Affair that eventually led to the resignation of President Nixon. The break-in, however, had no impact on the election. Two weeks before the election Secretary of State Kissinger announced that "peace was at hand". The result lead to one of the most one-sided elections in American history.

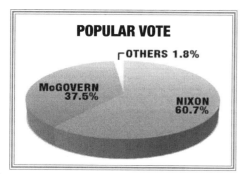

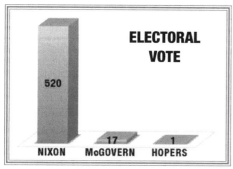

STATES	RICHARD NIXON		GEORGE McGOVERN		JOHN SCHMITZ		BENJAMIN SPOCK		TOTAL VOTES
	VOTES	PERCENTAGE	VOTES	PERCENTAGE	VOTES	PERCENTAGE	VOTES	PERCENTAGE	
Alabama	728,701	72.4	256,923	25.5	11,928	1.2	0	0.0	1,006,111
Alaska	55,349	58.1	32,967	34.6	6,903	7.2	0	0.0	95,219
Arizona	402,812	64.7	198,540	31.9	21,208	3.4	0	0.0	622,926
Arkansas	448,541	68.9	199,892	30.7	2,887	0.4	0	0.0	651,320
California	4,602,096	55	3,475,847	41.5	232,554	2.8	55,167	0.7	8,367,862
Colorado	597,189	62.6	329,980	34.6	17,269	1.8	2,403	0.3	953,884
Connecticut	810,763	58.6	555,498	40.1	17,239	1.2	0	0.0	1,384,277
Delaware	140,357	59.6	92,283	39.2	2,638	1.1	0	0.0	235,516
Florida	1,857,759	71.9	718,117	27.8	0	0.0	0	0.0	2,583,283
Georgia	881,496	75	289,529	24.6	812	0.1	0	0.0	1,174,772
Hawaii	168,865	62.5	101,409	37.5	0	0.0	0	0.0	270,274
Idaho	199,384	64.2	80,826	26	28,869	9.3	903	0.3	310,379
Illinois	2,788,179	59	1,913,472	40.5	2,471	0.1	0	0.0	4,723,236
Indiana	1,405,154	66.1	708,568	33.3	0	0.0	4,544	0.2	2,125,529
Iowa	706,207	57.6	496,206	40.5	22,056	1.8	0	0.0	1,225,944
Kansas	619,812	67.7	270,287	29.5	21,808	2.4	0	0.0	916,095
Kentucky	676,446	63.4	371,159	34.8	17,627	1.7	1,118	0.1	1,067,499
Louisiana	686,852	65.3	298,142	28.4	52,099	5.0	0	0.0	1,051,491
Maine	256,458	61.5	160,584	38.5	0	0.0	0	0.0	417,042
Maryland	829,305	61.3	505,781	37.4	18,726	1.4	0	0.0	1,353,812
Massachusetts	1,112,078	45.2	1,332,540	54.2	2,877	0.1	101	0.0	2,458,756
Michigan	1,961,721	56.2	1,459,435	41.8	63,321	1.8	0	0.0	3,489,727
Minnesota	898,269	51.6	802,346	46.1	31,407	1.8	2,805	0.2	1,741,652
Mississippi	505,125	78.2	126,782	19.6	11,598	1.8	0	0.0	645,963
Missouri	1,153,852	62.2	697,147	37.6	0	0.0	0	0.0	1,855,803
Montana	183,976	57.9	120,197	37.8	13,430	4.2	0	0.0	317,603
Nebraska	406,298	70.5	169,991	29.5	0	0.0	0	0.0	576,289
Nevada	115,750	63.7	66,016	36.3	0	0.0	0	0.0	181,766
New Hampshire	213,724	64	116,435	34.9	3,386	1.0	0	0.0	334,055
New Jersey	1,845,502	61.6	1,102,211	36.8	34,378	1.1	5,355	0.2	2,997,229
New Mexico	235,606	61	141,084	36.5	8,767	2.3	0	0.0	386,241
New York	4,192,778	58.5	2,951,084	41.2	0	0.0	0	0.0	7,165,919
North Carolina	1,054,889	69.5	438,705	28.9	25,018	1.6	0	0.0	1,518,612
North Dakota	174,109	62.1	100,384	35.8	5,646	2.0	0	0.0	280,514
Ohio	2,441,827	59.6	1,558,889	38.1	80,067	2.0	0	0.0	4,094,787
Oklahoma	759,025	73.7	247,147	24	23,728	2.3	0	0.0	1,029,900
Oregon	486,686	52.4	392,760	42.3	46,211	5.0	0	0.0	927,946
Pennsylvania	2,714,521	59.1	1,796,951	39.1	70,593	1.5	0	0.0	4,592,106
Rhode Island	220,383	53	194,645	46.8	25	0.0	5	0.0	415,808
South Carolina	477,044	70.8	186,824	27.7	10,075	1.5	0	0.0	673,960
South Dakota	166,476	54.2	139,945	45.5	0	0.0	0	0.0	307,415
Tennessee	813,147	67.7	357,293	29.7	30,373	2.5	0	0.0	1,201,182
Texas	2,298,896	66.2	1,154,289	33.3	6,039	0.2	0	0.0	3,471,281
Utah	323,643	67.6	126,284	26.4	28,549	6.0	0	0.0	478,476
Vermont	117,149	62.7	68,174	36.5	0	0.0	1,010	0.5	186,947
Virginia	988,493	67.8	438,887	30.1	19,721	1.4	0	0.0	1,457,019
Washington	837,135	56.9	568,334	38.6	58,906	4.0	2,644	0.2	1,470,847
West Virginia	484,964	63.6	277,435	36.4	0	0.0	0	0.0	762,399
Wisconsin	989,430	53.4	810,174	43.7	47,525	2.6	2,701	0.1	1,852,890
Wyoming	100,464	69	44,358	30.5	748	0.5	0	0.0	145,570
District of Columbia	35,226	21.6	127,627	78.1	0	0.0	0	0.0	163,421
TOTALS	47,169,911	60.7	29,170,383	37.5	1,099,482	1.4	78,756	0.1	77,718,554

1972 ELECTION: STATE-BY-STATE RESULTS (NIXON vs. McGOVERN vs. SCHMITZ vs. SPOCK)

THE ISSUES

TIME FOR A CHANGE

After the illegal activities of the Nixon Administration was it time for a Washington outsider?

The REPUBLICAN CONVENTION

PLACE: Kansas City, MO

DATE: August 16 to 20, 1976

NOMINATED: Gerald R. Ford, of Michigan, for President

NOMINATED: Bob Dole, of Kansas, for Vice President

The DEMOCRATIC CONVENTION

PLACE: New York, NY

DATE: July 12- July 16 1976

NOMINATED: Jimmy Carter, of Georgia, for President

NOMINATED: Walter Mondale, of Minnesota, for Vice President

The 1976 Democratic convention was rather routine. Jimmy Carter won the nomination on the first ballot. Carter had selected Walter Mondale as his vice presidential running mate in advance.

President Ford withstood a challenge for the Republican Presidential nomination from California's Governor Reagan. Gerald Ford won on the first ballot, with 1,187 votes to 1,070 votes for Ronald Reagan. Ford agreed to adopt many of Reagan's platform positions.

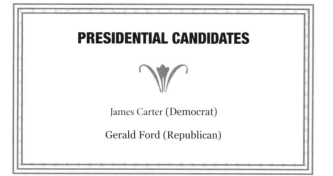

PRESIDENTIAL CANDIDATES

James Carter (Democrat)

Gerald Ford (Republican)

James E. Carter
ELECTED

The forced resignations, separately, of both President Nixon and Vice President Agnew left President Ford the first President ever not elected to national office. Ford did not have the support that most incumbent Presidents enjoyed. The rising right-wing of the party was especially unhappy with Ford, and Governor Reagan of California, chose to challenge Ford for the Republican Presidential nomination.

Reagan challenged Ford in all of the primaries. Ford and Reagan arrived at the convention with nearly the same number of delegates. Ford, however, managed to carry the convention on the first ballot. The convention accepted Ford after he agreed to nominate Senator Dole, of Kansas, as his Vice Presidential running mate. Dole was favored by the right-wing of the party.

The Republican platform, however, reflected the views of the Reaganites: increased defense spending, retention of the Panama canal, opposition to busing and abortion. The Democratic nominee, Governor Carter, of Georgia, was an almost total unknown. Carter started out early and campaigned in each and every primary. Eventually, Carter won so many delegates that he was totally unbeatable.

The 1976 general election campaign began with Ford trailing by over 30 points. Ford challenged Carter to a series of debates. Ford performed well during the first debate and managed to cut Carter's lead by 10 points. In the second debate, Ford made a major mistake by saying that Eastern Europe was free from Soviet domination. This campaign also included the first debates between vice presidential candidates, pitting Dole against Mondale. Mondale came off as the winner of that debate.

Jimmy Carter got into trouble after giving a Playboy interview in which he talked candidly about "desire in his heart". Carter campaigned as an outsider intent on cleaning up Washington. Carter won the election by a very narrow margin over Ford, thanks to his support from the South, labor, blacks and white ethnics.

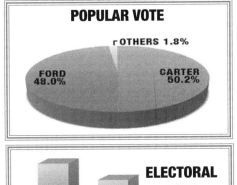

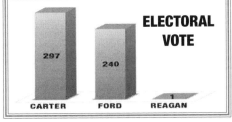

STATES	JIMMY CARTER		GERALD FORD		EUGENE McCARTHY		ROGER MacBRIDE		TOTAL VOTES
	VOTES	PERCENTAGE	VOTES	PERCENTAGE	VOTES	PERCENTAGE	VOTES	PERCENTAGE	
Alabama	659,170	55.7	504,070	42.6	99	0.0	1,481	0.1	1,182,850
Alaska	44,058	35.7	71,555	57.9	0	0.0	6,785	5.5	123,574
Arizona	295,602	39.8	418,642	56.4	19,229	2.6	7,647	1.0	742,719
Arkansas	498,604	65	267,903	34.9	639	0.1	0	0.0	767,535
California	3,742,284	47.6	3,882,244	49.3	58,412	0.7	56,388	0.7	7,867,117
Colorado	460,353	42.6	584,367	54	26,107	2.4	5,330	0.5	1,081,554
Connecticut	647,895	46.9	719,261	52.1	3,759	0.3	209	0.0	1,381,526
Delaware	122,596	52	109,831	46.6	2,437	1.0	0	0.0	235,834
Florida	1,636,000	51.9	1,469,531	46.6	23,643	0.8	103	0.0	3,150,631
Georgia	979,409	66.7	483,743	33	991	0.1	175	0.0	1,467,458
Hawaii	147,375	50.6	140,003	48.1	0	0.0	3,923	1.3	291,301
Idaho	126,549	36.8	204,151	59.3	1,194	0.3	3,558	1.0	344,071
Illinois	2,271,295	48.1	2,364,269	50.1	55,939	1.2	8,057	0.2	4,718,914
Indiana	1,014,714	45.7	1,183,958	53.3	0	0.0	0	0.0	2,220,362
Iowa	619,931	48.5	632,863	49.5	20,051	1.6	1,452	0.1	1,279,306
Kansas	430,421	44.9	502,752	52.5	13,185	1.4	3,242	0.3	957,845
Kentucky	615,717	52.8	531,852	45.6	6,837	0.6	814	0.1	1,167,142
Louisiana	661,365	51.7	587,446	46	6,588	0.5	3,325	0.3	1,278,439
Maine	232,279	48.1	236,320	48.9	10,874	2.3	11	0.0	483,216
Maryland	759,612	52.8	672,661	46.7	4,541	0.3	255	0.0	1,439,897
Massachusetts	1,429,475	56.1	1,030,276	40.4	65,637	2.6	135	0.0	2,547,558
Michigan	1,696,714	46.4	1,893,742	51.8	47,905	1.3	5,406	0.1	3,653,749
Minnesota	1,070,440	54.9	819,395	42	35,490	1.8	3,529	0.2	1,949,931
Mississippi	381,309	49.6	366,846	47.7	4,074	0.5	2,788	0.4	769,361
Missouri	998,387	51.1	927,443	47.5	29,029	1.2	0	0.0	1,953,600
Montana	149,259	45.4	173,703	52.8	0	0.0	0	0.0	328,734
Nebraska	233,692	38.5	359,705	59.2	9,409	1.5	1,482	0.2	607,668
Nevada	92,479	45.8	101,273	50.2	0	0.0	1,519	0.8	201,876
New Hampshire	147,635	43.5	185,935	54.7	4,095	1.2	936	0.3	339,618
New Jersey	1,444,653	47.9	1,509,688	50.1	32,717	1.1	9,449	0.3	3,014,472
New Mexico	201,148	48.1	211,419	50.5	1,161	0.3	1,110	0.3	418,409
New York	3,389,558	51.9	3,100,791	47.5	4,303	0.1	12,197	0.2	6,534,170
North Carolina	927,365	55.2	741,960	44.2	780	0.0	2,219	0.1	1,678,914
North Dakota	136,078	45.8	153,470	51.6	2,952	1.0	253	0.1	297,188
Ohio	2,011,621	48.9	2,000,505	48.7	58,258	1.4	8,961	0.2	4,111,873
Oklahoma	532,442	48.7	545,708	50	14,101	1.3	0	0.0	1,092,251
Oregon	490,407	47.6	492,120	47.8	40,207	3.9	0	0.0	1,029,876
Pennsylvania	2,328,677	50.4	2,205,604	47.7	50,584	1.1	0	0.0	4,620,787
Rhode Island	227,636	55.4	181,249	44.1	479	0.1	715	0.2	411,170
South Carolina	450,807	56.2	346,149	43.1	289	0.0	53	0.0	802,583
South Dakota	147,068	48.9	151,505	50.4	0	0.0	1,619	0.5	300,678
Tennessee	825,879	55.9	633,969	42.9	5,004	0.3	1,375	0.1	1,476,345
Texas	2,082,319	51.1	1,953,300	48	20,118	0.5	189	0.0	4,071,884
Utah	182,110	33.6	337,908	62.4	3,907	0.7	2,438	0.5	541,198
Vermont	80,954	43.1	102,085	54.4	4,001	2.1	0	0.0	187,765
Virginia	813,896	48	836,554	49.3	0	0.0	4,648	0.3	1,697,094
Washington	717,323	46.1	777,732	50	36,986	2.4	5,042	0.3	1,555,534
West Virginia	435,914	58	314,760	41.9	113	0.0	16	0.0	750,964
Wisconsin	1,040,232	49.4	1,004,987	47.8	34,986	1.7	3,814	0.2	2,104,175
Wyoming	62,239	39.8	92,717	59.3	624	0.4	89	0.1	156,343
District of Columbia	137,818	81.6	27,873	16.5	0	0.0	274	0.2	168,830
TOTALS	40,830,763	50.1	39,147,793	48.0	756,691	0.9	173,011	0.2	81,555,889

1976 ELECTION: STATE-BY-STATE RESULTS (CARTER vs. FORD vs. McCARTHY vs. MacBRIDE)

UNITED STATES
PRESIDENTIAL ELECTION OF 1980

THE ISSUES

THE ECONOMY

Who could best combat the stagflation of the US economy?

SOVIET AGGRESSION

Who could best combat Soviet aggression in the Third World?

The DEMOCRATIC CONVENTION

PLACE: New York, NY

DATE: August 11- 14, 1980

NOMINATED: Jimmy Carter,
of Georgia, for President

NOMINATED: Walter Mondale,
of Minnesota, for Vice President

President Carter and Vice President Mondale were routinely renominated at the 1980 Democratic convention in New York.

The REPUBLICAN CONVENTION

PLACE: Detroit, MI

DATE: July 14-18 1980

NOMINATED: Richard M. Nixon,
of California, for President

NOMINATED: Ronald Reagan,
of California, for Vice President

While a number of Republicans sought the Republican nomination in 1980, California Governor, Ronald Reagan, captured it on the first ballot.

PRESIDENTIAL CANDIDATES

James Carter (Democrat)

Ronald Reagan (Republican)

John Anderson (Independent)

Ronald Reagan
ELECTED

Governor Reagan ran in all of the Republican primaries winning against Howard Baker, John Connally, Robert Dole, and finally George Bush. Reagan entered the Republican convention in Detroit with the nomination all sewed up. President Carter was renominated at the Democratic convention in New York, after turning back a challenge from Senator Ted Kennedy. John Anderson ran as the first serious third party candidate since Henry Wallace in 1948.

Reagan campaigned for smaller government. He was an effective campaigner, but made a number of serious mistakes on the campaign trail, that ultimately forced the campaign to limit his access. Carter, on the other hand, attacked Reagan and was soon accused of being a "mean" campaigner.

There were very clear issues dividing the candidates in the campaign of 1980. Carter supported the Equal Rights Amendment, while Reagan opposed it. Reagan opposed S.A.L.T. II, while Carter supported it. Carter called for a National Health Insurance Program. President Carter and Reagan participated in a highly anticipated debate. Ronald Reagan did well in the debate, satisfying many that he was capable of being Commander in Chief.

Ultimately, however, it was not these issues, but the twin issues of the American Hostages in Iran, and what the Republicans called "The Misery Index" (inflation plus unemployment) that ended President Carter's chance of being re-elected.

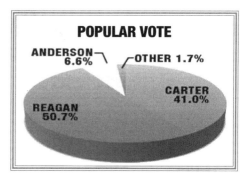

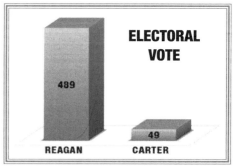

STATES	RONALD REAGAN		JIMMY CARTER		JOHN ANDERSON		ED CLARK		TOTAL VOTES
	VOTES	PERCENTAGE	VOTES	PERCENTAGE	VOTES	PERCENTAGE	VOTES	PERCENTAGE	
Alabama	654,192	48.8	636,730	47.4	16,481	1.2	13,318	1.0	1,341,929
Alaska	86,112	54.3	41,842	26.4	11,155	7.0	18,479	11.7	158,445
Arizona	529,688	60.6	246,843	28.2	76,952	8.8	18,784	2.1	873,975
Arkansas	403,164	48.1	398,041	47.5	22,468	2.7	8,970	1.1	837,582
California	4,524,858	52.7	3,083,661	35.9	739,833	8.6	148,434	1.7	8,587,063
Colorado	652,264	55.1	367,973	31.1	130,633	11.0	25,744	2.2	1,184,415
Connecticut	677,210	48.2	541,732	38.5	171,807	12.2	8,570	0.6	1,406,285
Delaware	111,252	47.2	105,754	44.8	16,288	6.9	1,974	0.8	235,900
Florida	2,046,951	55.5	1,419,475	38.5	189,692	5.1	30,524	0.8	3,686,930
Georgia	654,168	41.0	890,733	55.8	36,055	2.3	15,627	1.0	1,596,695
Hawaii	130,112	42.9	135,879	44.8	32,021	10.6	3,269	1.1	303,287
Idaho	290,699	66.5	110,192	25.2	27,058	6.2	8,425	1.9	437,431
Illinois	2,358,049	49.6	1,981,413	41.7	346,754	7.3	38,939	0.8	4,749,721
Indiana	1,255,656	56.0	844,197	37.7	111,639	5.0	19,627	0.9	2,242,033
Iowa	676,026	51.3	508,672	38.6	115,633	8.8	13,123	1.0	1,317,661
Kansas	566,812	57.9	326,150	33.3	68,231	7.0	14,470	1.5	979,795
Kentucky	635,274	49.1	616,417	47.6	31,127	2.4	5,531	0.4	1,294,627
Louisiana	792,853	51.2	708,453	45.7	26,345	1.7	8,240	0.5	1,548,591
Maine	238,522	45.6	220,974	42.3	53,327	10.2	5,119	1.0	523,011
Maryland	680,606	44.2	726,161	47.1	119,537	7.8	14,192	0.9	1,540,496
Massachusetts	1,057,631	41.9	1,053,802	41.7	382,539	15.2	22,038	0.9	2,522,890
Michigan	1,915,225	49.0	1,661,532	42.5	275,223	7.0	41,597	1.1	3,909,725
Minnesota	873,268	42.6	954,174	46.5	174,990	8.5	31,592	1.5	2,051,980
Mississippi	441,089	49.4	429,281	48.1	12,036	1.3	5,465	0.6	892,620
Missouri	1,074,181	51.2	931,182	44.3	77,920	3.7	14,422	0.7	2,099,824
Montana	206,814	56.8	118,032	32.4	29,281	8.0	9,825	2.7	363,952
Nebraska	419,937	65.5	166,851	26.0	44,993	7.0	9,073	1.4	640,854
Nevada	155,017	62.5	66,666	26.9	17,651	7.1	4,358	1.8	247,885
New Hampshire	221,705	57.7	108,864	28.4	49,693	12.9	2,064	0.5	383,990
New Jersey	1,546,557	52.0	1,147,364	38.6	234,632	7.9	20,652	0.7	2,975,684
New Mexico	250,779	54.9	167,826	36.7	29,459	6.4	4,365	1.0	456,971
New York	2,893,831	46.7	2,728,372	44.0	467,801	7.5	52,648	0.8	6,201,959
North Carolina	915,018	49.3	875,635	47.2	52,800	2.8	9,677	0.5	1,855,833
North Dakota	193,695	64.2	79,189	26.3	23,640	7.8	3,743	1.2	301,545
Ohio	2,206,545	51.5	1,752,414	40.9	254,472	5.9	49,033	1.1	4,283,603
Oklahoma	695,570	60.5	402,026	35.0	38,284	3.3	13,828	1.2	1,149,708
Oregon	571,044	48.3	456,890	38.7	112,389	9.5	25,838	2.2	1,181,516
Pennsylvania	2,261,872	49.6	1,937,540	42.5	292,921	6.4	33,263	0.7	4,561,501
Rhode Island	154,793	37.2	198,342	47.7	59,819	14.4	2,458	0.6	416,072
South Carolina	441,841	49.4	430,385	48.1	14,153	1.6	5,139	0.6	894,071
South Dakota	198,343	60.5	103,855	31.7	21,431	6.5	3,824	1.2	327,703
Tennessee	787,761	48.7	783,051	48.4	35,991	2.2	7,116	0.4	1,617,616
Texas	2,510,705	55.3	1,881,147	41.4	111,613	2.5	37,643	0.8	4,541,636
Utah	439,687	72.8	124,266	20.6	30,284	5.0	7,226	1.2	604,222
Vermont	94,628	44.4	81,952	38.4	31,761	14.9	1,900	0.9	213,299
Virginia	989,609	53.0	752,174	40.3	95,418	5.1	12,821	0.7	1,866,032
Washington	865,244	49.7	650,193	37.3	185,073	10.6	29,213	1.7	1,742,394
West Virginia	334,206	45.3	367,462	49.8	31,691	4.3	4,356	0.6	737,715
Wisconsin	1,088,845	47.9	981,584	43.2	160,657	7.1	29,135	1.3	2,273,221
Wyoming	110,700	62.6	49,427	28.0	12,072	6.8	4,514	2.6	176,713
District of Columbia	23,545	13.4	131,113	74.8	16,337	9.3	1,114	0.6	175,237
TOTALS	43,904,153	50.7	35,483,883	41.0	5,720,060	6.6	921,299	1.1	86,513,813

1980 ELECTION: STATE-BY-STATE RESULTS (REAGAN vs. CARTER vs. ANDERSON vs. CLARK)

UNITED STATES
PRESIDENTIAL ELECTION OF 1984

THE ISSUES

DEFECIT & TAXATION

Were the Reagan budget and taxation policies good for America?

The DEMOCRATIC CONVENTION

PLACE: Moscone Center San Francisco, California

DATE: July 16- 20, 1984

NOMINATED: Walter Mondale, of Minnesota, for President

NOMINATED: Geraldine Ferraro, of New York, for Vice President

When the Democrats opened their convention in San Francisco all of the talk at the convention was on Mondale's selection of Geraldine Ferraro, to be the first woman on a major ticket. Mondale was nominated on the first ballot. The greatest stir at the convention occurred when Mondale stated that both he and Reagan would have to raise taxes due to the rising deficit. Muskie stated that the difference between him and Reagan was that Reagan would not tell the truth, while Mondale had just done so.

The REPUBLICAN CONVENTION

PLACE: Dallas, TX

DATE: August 20-24 1984

NOMINATED: Ronald Reagan, of California, for President

NOMINATED: George Bush, of Texas, for Vice President

Reagan was renominated without opposition at the 1984 Republican convention.

Ronald Reagan **ELECTED**

PRESIDENTIAL CANDIDATES

Walter Mondayle (Democrat)

Ronald Reagan (Republican)

UNITED STATES PRESIDENTIAL Election of 1984

President Reagan faced no opposition to his renomination as the 1984 Republican Presidential candidate. Senator Walter Mondale, Jimmy Carter's Vice President, was the Democratic front-runner throughout the election campaign. Mondale's most serious opposition was Senator Gary Hart of Colorado, who ran on a theme of new ideas. Other opponents included: Senator Henry Jackson of Washington, and Reverend Jesse Jackson, the first serious Black candidate for President. Mondale was nominated on the first ballot at the Democratic convention, in San Francisco. Mondale selected Geraldine Ferraro to be his running-mate. Ferraro became the first women to be nominated as a vice presidential candidate by a major party.

The election campaign revolved mostly around the issues of deficit and tariff barriers. The traditional roles of the Democratic and Republican party were reversed. Democrats attacked the Republicans for their proposed budget deficit. The Democrats called for more tariff protection.

Two debates were held. During the first debate, Reagan did poorly. Though he recovered in the second debate by using humor to successfully parry one of Mondale's criticisms- (i.e. that he was too old). Reagan stating during the debate that he would not use age as issue. Reagan quipped he would refrain from criticizing Mondale's "youth and inexperience".

Ronald Reagan was re-elected by an 18 point margin. Ronald Reagan's re-election was one of the largest landslides in American History.

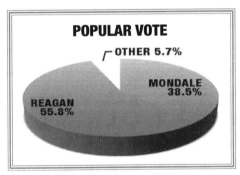

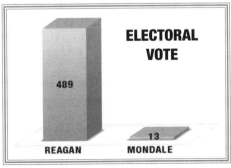

US MAP OF STATES CARRIED

STATES	RONALD REAGAN		WALTER MONDALE		DAVID BERGLAND		LYNDON LAROUCHE		TOTAL VOTES
	VOTES	PERCENTAGE	VOTES	PERCENTAGE	VOTES	PERCENTAGE	VOTES	PERCENTAGE	
Alabama	872,849	60.5	551,899	38.3	9,504	0.7	0	0.0	1,441,713
Alaska	138,377	66.7	62,007	29.9	6,374	3.1	0	0.0	207,605
Arizona	681,416	66.4	333,854	32.5	10,585	1.0	0	0.0	1,025,897
Arkansas	534,774	60.5	338,646	38.3	2,221	0.3	1,890	0.2	884,406
California	5,467,009	57.5	3,922,519	41.3	49,951	0.5	0	0.0	9,505,423
Colorado	821,817	63.4	454,975	35.1	11,257	0.9	4,662	0.4	1,295,380
Connecticut	890,877	60.7	569,597	38.8	204	0.0	0	0.0	1,466,900
Delaware	152,190	59.8	101,656	39.9	268	0.1	0	0.0	254,572
Florida	2,730,350	65.3	1,448,816	34.7	754	0.0	0	0.0	4,180,051
Georgia	1,068,722	60.2	706,628	39.8	152	0.0	34	0.0	1,776,120
Hawaii	185,050	55.1	147,154	43.8	2,167	0.6	654	0.2	335,846
Idaho	297,523	72.4	108,510	26.4	2,823	0.7	0	0.0	411,144
Illinois	2,707,103	56.2	2,086,499	43.3	10,086	0.2	0	0.0	4,819,088
Indiana	1,377,230	61.7	841,481	37.7	6,741	0.3	0	0.0	2,233,069
Iowa	703,088	53.3	605,620	45.9	1,844	0.1	6,248	0.5	1,319,805
Kansas	677,296	66.3	333,149	32.6	3,329	0.3	0	0.0	1,021,991
Kentucky	821,702	60.0	539,539	39.4	0	0.0	1,776	0.1	1,369,345
Louisiana	1,037,299	60.8	651,586	38.2	1,876	0.1	3,552	0.2	1,706,822
Maine	336,500	60.8	214,515	38.8	0	0.0	0	0.0	553,144
Maryland	879,918	52.5	787,935	47.0	5,721	0.3	0	0.0	1,675,873
Massachusetts	1,310,936	51.2	1,239,606	48.4	0	0.3	0	0.0	2,559,453
Michigan	2,251,571	59.2	1,529,638	40.2	10,055	0.3	3,862	0.1	3,801,658
Minnesota	1,032,603	49.5	1,036,364	49.7	2,996	0.1	3,865	0.2	2,084,449
Mississippi	582,377	61.9	352,192	37.4	2,336	0.2	1,001	0.1	941,104
Missouri	1,274,188	60.0	848,583	40.0	0	0.0	0	0.0	2,122,783
Montana	232,450	60.5	146,742	38.2	5,185	1.3	0	0.0	384,377
Nebraska	460,054	70.6	187,866	28.8	2,079	0.3	0	0.0	652,090
Nevada	188,770	65.8	91,655	32.0	2,292	0.8	0	0.0	286,667
New Hampshire	267,051	68.6	120,395	30.9	735	0.2	467	0.1	389,066
New Jersey	1,933,630	60.1	1,261,323	39.2	6,416	0.2	0	0.0	3,217,862
New Mexico	307,101	59.7	201,769	39.2	4,459	0.9	0	0.0	514,370
New York	3,664,763	53.8	3,119,609	45.8	11,949	0.2	0	0.0	6,806,810
North Carolina	1,346,481	61.9	824,287	37.9	3,794	0.2	0	0.0	2,175,361
North Dakota	200,336	64.8	104,429	33.8	703	0.2	1,278	0.4	308,971
Ohio	2,678,560	58.9	1,825,440	40.1	5,886	0.1	10,693	0.2	4,547,619
Oklahoma	861,530	68.6	385,080	30.7	9,066	0.7	0	0.0	1,255,676
Oregon	685,700	55.9	536,479	43.7	0	0.0	0	0.0	1,226,527
Pennsylvania	2,584,323	53.3	2,228,131	46.0	6,982	0.1	0	0.0	4,844,903
Rhode Island	212,080	51.7	197,106	48.0	277	0.1	0	0.0	410,492
South Carolina	615,539	63.6	344,459	35.6	4,359	0.5	0	0.0	968,529
South Dakota	200,267	63.0	116,113	36.5	0	0.0	0	0.0	317,867
Tennessee	990,212	57.8	711,714	41.6	3,072	0.2	1,852	0.1	1,711,994
Texas	3,433,428	63.6	1,949,276	36.1	0	0.0	14,613	0.3	5,397,571
Utah	469,105	74.5	155,369	24.7	2,447	0.4	0	0.0	629,656
Vermont	135,865	57.9	95,730	40.8	1,002	0.4	423	0.2	234,561
Virginia	1,337,078	62.3	796,250	37.1	0	0.0	13,307	0.6	2,146,635
Washington	1,051,670	55.8	807,352	42.9	8,844	0.5	4,712	0.3	1,883,910
West Virginia	405,483	55.1	328,125	44.6	0	0.0	0	0.0	735,742
Wisconsin	1,198,584	54.2	995,740	45.0	4,883	0.2	3,791	0.2	2,211,689
Wyoming	133,241	70.5	53,370	28.2	2,357	1.2	0	0.0	188,968
District of Columbia	29,009	13.7	180,408	85.4	279	0.1	127	0.1	211,288
TOTALS	54,455,075	58.8	37,577,185	40.6	228,314	0.2	78,078	0.1	92,652,842

1984 ELECTION: STATE-BY-STATE RESULTS (REAGAN vs. MONDALE vs. BERGLAND vs. LAROUCHE)

THE ISSUES

REAGANOMICS

Had the Reagan economic policies been fair to Americans?

The DEMOCRATIC CONVENTION

PLACE: Omni,
Atlanta, GA

DATE: July 18- 22, 1988

NOMINATED: Michael Dukakis,
of Massachusetts, for President

NOMINATED: Lloyd Bentsen,
of Texas, for Vice President

Governor Dukakis arrived at the Democratic convention with a lock on the majority of the delegates. He was nominated on the first ballot.

The REPUBLICAN CONVENTION

PLACE:New Orleans, LA

DATE: August 15-19, 1988

NOMINATED: George Bush,
of Texas, for President

NOMINATED: Dan Qualye.
of Indiana, for Vice President

Vice President Bush was selected on the first ballot. He gave a strong acceptance speech.

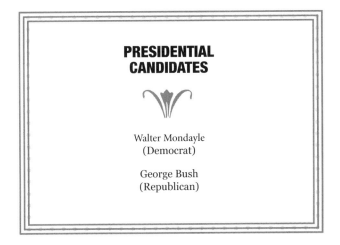

PRESIDENTIAL CANDIDATES

Walter Mondayle
(Democrat)

George Bush
(Republican)

George Bush
ELECTED

Vice President Bush faced challenges from both Senator Dole and Reverend Pat Robertson. While Bush finished an embarrassing third place in Iowa, he recovered. Bush forced his opponents to withdraw, after he won most of the contests on Super Tuesday. Thus, Bush was unopposed at the Republican convention in New Orleans. The only matter of contention at the 1988 Republican convention was Bush's decision to select Senator Quayle be his running mate. This decision was widely criticized.

Governor Michael Dukakis of Massachusetts quickly became the Democratic front-runner. Gary Hart withdrew due to allegations of sexual improprieties, and Mario Cuomo, of New York refused to run. One by one, Dukakis' opponents withdrew. When the convention took place in Atlanta, only Jesse Jackson was remained. Dukakis won on the first ballot, after receiving 2,876 votes, compared to Jackson's 1,218. Dukakis chose Senator Lloyd Bentsen of Texas as his vice presidential running mate.

When the campaign began, Governor Dukakis held a clear lead over Vice President Bush. Then, the Republicans successfully attacked Dukakis in a number of ways. One of the most notable criticisms was an attack on Dukakis surrounding the furlough release of Willie Horton, an African American convicted of murder. Horton was released on a weekend furlough from prison while Dukakis was governor. Bush stated: "Don't let murders out on vacation to terrorize innocent people... Dukakis owes the people an explanation of why he supported this outrageous program".

The Republicans then went on to sponsor a series of television ads with pictures of Horton and the related crime scenes, claiming it was Dukakis who had let that happen. The fact that the program was started by Dukakis'

Republican predecessor, and that while President Reagan had been governor of California it had been instituted there as well, was not mentioned. This and other attack ads were effective.

Governor Dukakis was not a very effective campaigner. He hurt his campaign badly when, at a debate, Dukakis stated he would not advocate the death penalty for someone who had raped and murdered his wife. Consequently, George Bush won by a large margin.

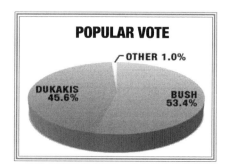

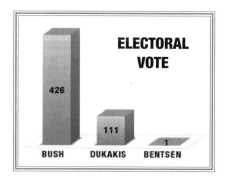

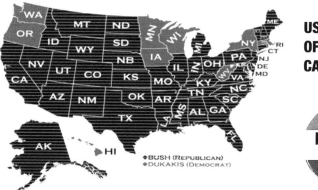

US MAP OF STATES CARRIED

UNITED STATES PRESIDENTIAL Election of 1988

STATES	GEORGE BUSH VOTES	GEORGE BUSH PERCENTAGE	MICHAEL DUKAKIS VOTES	MICHAEL DUKAKIS PERCENTAGE	RON PAUL VOTES	RON PAUL PERCENTAGE	LENORA FULANI VOTES	LENORA FULANI PERCENTAGE	TOTAL VOTES
Alabama	815,576	59.2	549,506	39.9	8,460	0.6	3,311	0.2	1,378,476
Alaska	119,251	59.6	72,584	36.3	5,484	2.7	1,024	0.5	200,116
Arizona	702,541	60	454,029	38.7	13,351	1.1	1,662	0.1	1,171,873
Arkansas	466,578	56.4	349,237	42.2	3,297	0.4	2,161	0.3	827,738
California	5,054,917	51.1	4,702,233	47.6	70,105	0.7	31,181	0.3	9,887,065
Colorado	728,177	53.1	621,453	45.3	15,482	1.1	2,539	0.2	1,372,394
Connecticut	750,241	52	676,584	46.9	14,071	1.0	2,491	0.2	1,443,394
Delaware	139,639	55.9	108,647	43.5	1,162	0.5	443	0.2	249,891
Florida	2,618,885	60.9	1,656,701	38.5	19,796	0.5	6,655	0.2	4,302,313
Georgia	1,081,331	59.8	714,792	39.5	8,435	0.5	5,099	0.3	1,809,672
Hawaii	158,625	44.8	192,364	54.3	1,999	0.6	1,003	0.3	354,461
Idaho	253,881	62.1	147,272	36	5,313	1.3	2,502	0.6	408,968
Illinois	2,310,939	50.7	2,215,940	48.6	14,944	0.3	10,276	0.2	4,559,120
Indiana	1,297,763	59.8	860,643	39.7	0	0.0	10,215	0.5	2,168,621
Iowa	545,355	44.5	670,557	54.7	2,494	0.2	540	0.0	1,225,614
Kansas	554,049	55.8	422,636	42.6	12,553	1.3	3,806	0.4	993,044
Kentucky	734,281	55.5	580,368	43.9	2,118	0.2	1,256	0.1	1,322,517
Louisiana	883,702	54.3	717,460	44.1	4,115	0.3	2,355	0.1	1,628,202
Maine	307,131	55.3	243,569	43.9	2,700	0.5	1,405	0.3	555,035
Maryland	876,167	51.1	826,304	48.2	6,748	0.4	5,115	0.3	1,714,358
Massachusetts	1,194,635	45.4	1,401,415	53.2	24,251	0.9	9,561	0.4	2,632,805
Michigan	1,965,486	53.6	1,675,783	45.7	18,336	0.5	2,513	0.1	3,669,163
Minnesota	962,337	45.9	1,109,471	52.9	5,109	0.2	1,734	0.1	2,096,790
Mississippi	557,890	59.9	363,921	39.1	3,329	0.4	2,155	0.2	931,527
Missouri	1,084,953	51.8	1,001,619	47.8	434	0.0	6,656	0.3	2,093,713
Montana	190,412	52.1	168,936	46.2	5,047	1.4	1,279	0.3	365,674
Nebraska	397,956	60.2	259,235	39.2	2,534	0.4	1,740	0.3	661,465
Nevada	206,040	58.9	132,738	37.9	3,520	1.0	835	0.2	350,067
New Hampshire	281,537	62.4	163,696	36.3	4,502	1.0	790	0.2	451,074
New Jersey	1,743,192	56.2	1,320,352	42.6	8,421	0.3	5,139	0.2	3,099,553
New Mexico	270,341	51.9	244,497	46.9	3,268	0.6	2,237	0.4	521,287
New York	3,081,871	47.5	3,347,882	51.6	12,109	0.2	15,845	0.2	6,585,683
North Carolina	1,237,258	58	890,167	41.7	1,263	0.1	5,682	0.3	2,134,370
North Dakota	166,559	56	127,739	43	1,315	0.4	396	0.1	297,261
Ohio	2,416,549	55	1,939,629	44.1	11,989	0.3	12,017	0.3	4,393,699
Oklahoma	678,367	57.9	483,423	41.3	6,261	0.5	2,985	0.3	1,171,036
Oregon	560,126	46.6	616,206	51.3	14,811	1.2	6,487	0.5	1,201,694
Pennsylvania	2,300,087	50.7	2,194,944	48.4	12,051	0.3	4,379	0.1	4,536,251
Rhode Island	177,761	43.9	225,123	55.6	825	0.2	280	0.1	404,620
South Carolina	606,443	61.5	370,554	37.6	4,935	0.5	4,077	0.4	986,009
South Dakota	165,415	52.8	145,560	46.5	1,060	0.3	730	0.2	312,991
Tennessee	947,233	57.9	679,794	41.5	2,041	0.1	1,334	0.1	1,636,250
Texas	3,036,829	56	2,352,748	43.3	30,355	0.6	7,208	0.1	5,427,410
Utah	428,442	66.2	207,343	32	7,473	1.2	455	0.1	647,008
Vermont	124,331	51.1	115,775	47.6	1,000	0.4	205	0.1	243,328
Virginia	1,309,162	59.7	859,799	39.2	8,336	0.4	14,312	0.7	2,191,609
Washington	903,835	48.5	933,516	50	17,240	0.9	3,520	0.2	1,865,253
West Virginia	310,065	47.5	341,016	52.2	0	0.0	2,230	0.3	653,311
Wisconsin	1,047,499	47.8	1,126,794	51.4	5,157	0.2	1,953	0.1	2,191,608
Wyoming	106,867	60.5	67,113	38	2,026	1.1	545	0.3	176,551
District of Columbia	27,590	14.3	159,407	82.6	554	0.3	2,901	1.5	192,877
TOTALS	48,886	53.4	41,809,074	45.6	432,179	0.5	217,219	0.2	91,594,809

1988 ELECTION: STATE-BY-STATE RESULTS (BUSH vs. DUKAKIS vs. PAUL vs. FULANI)

UNITED STATES
PRESIDENTIAL ELECTION OF 1992

THE ISSUES

IT'S THE ECONOMY, (STUPID!)

Which candidate could best respond to the America's economic recession?

The REPUBLICAN CONVENTION

PLACE: Astrodome
Houston, TX

DATE: August 17 to 21, 1992

NOMINATED: George Bush,
of Texas, for President

NOMINATED: Dan Quayle,
of Indiana, for Vice President

President Bush was renominated by the 1992 Republican convention body on the first ballot.

The DEMOCRATIC CONVENTION

PLACE: New York, NY

DATE: July 13- 17, 1992

NOMINATED: William Clinton,
of Arkansas, for President

NOMINATED: Albert Gore, of Tennessee,
for Vice President

William Clinton was nominated by the 1992 Democratic convention body on the first ballot.

ELECTED

PRESIDENTIAL CANDIDATES

William Clinton
(Democrat)

George HW Bush
(Republican)

UNITED STATES PRESIDENTIAL Election of 1992

As the election campaign of 1992 neared, the incumbent President, George Bush, held a commanding lead in the polls, over any and all potential rivals. Bush had been the Commander-In-Chief presiding over the Gulf War, the most decisive American military victory since World War II. Bush also directed US Foreign Policy as the Soviet Union fell apart. As a result, most leading Democratic candidates declined to run.

The Democrats held a long primary process. At the close of the primary process, Bill Clinton, the sitting governor of Arkansas, emerged as the leading Democratic presidential candidate. Bill Clinton was favored, despite charges he dodged the draft and was unfaithful to his wife. His wife, Hilary Rodham Clinton stood by him, throughout the barrage of allegations. As a result, Clinton was able secure and obtain the presidential nomination on the first ballot at the Democratic party convention.

From the time of the Democratic convention, Governor Clinton held a commanding lead in the polls over President Bush. Bush's campaign was hobbled by troubled economy. The campaign revolved primarily around economic issues. The ending of the cold war, for which Republicans took credit, perversely worked against them. No longer could they claim superiority by pushing Americans to question: "Do you trust the Democrats to stand up to the Russians?"

The third party candidacy of Ross Perot was a true wild card in the campaign. Perot, a self made billionaire, ran a one-issue campaign; deficit reduction. Early polls showed Perot as a leading candidate. However, his decision to first withdraw from the campaign and then reenter it, caused him to lose much of his early support. Bush ran a rather listless campaign that failed to connect with voters. He seemed completely disconnected from the needs of the average American.

Clinton's image of youth convinced enough Americans looking for change to vote for him. For the first time in a decade many voted for a Democrat, sealing Clinton's victory.

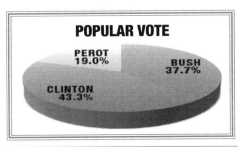

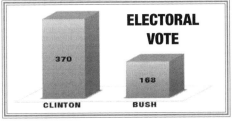

STATES	BILL CLINTON		GEORGE BUSH		ROSS PEROT		ANDRE MARROU		TOTAL VOTES
	VOTES	PERCENTAGE	VOTES	PERCENTAGE	VOTES	PERCENTAGE	VOTES	PERCENTAGE	
Alabama	690,080	40.9	804,283	47.6	183,109	10.8	5,737	0.3	1,688,060
Alaska	78,294	30.3	102,000	39.5	73,481	28.4	1,378	0.5	258,506
Arizona	543,050	36.5	572,086	38.5	353,741	23.8	6,759	0.5	1,486,975
Arkansas	505,823	53.2	337,324	35.5	99,132	10.4	1,261	0.1	950,653
California	5,121,325	46	3,630,574	32.6	2,296,006	20.6	48,139	0.4	11,131,721
Colorado	629,681	40.1	562,850	35.9	366,010	23.3	8,669	0.6	1,569,180
Connecticut	682,318	42.2	578,313	35.8	348,771	21.6	5,391	0.3	1,616,332
Delaware	126,054	43.5	102,313	35.3	59,213	20.4	935	0.3	289,735
Florida	2,072,698	39	2,173,310	40.9	1,053,067	19.8	15,079	0.3	5,314,392
Georgia	1,008,966	43.5	995,252	42.9	309,657	13.3	7,110	0.3	2,321,125
Hawaii	179,310	48.1	136,822	36.7	53,003	14.2	1,119	0.3	372,842
Idaho	137,013	28.4	202,645	42	130,395	27.0	1,167	0.2	482,142
Illinois	2,453,350	48.6	1,734,096	34.3	840,515	16.6	9,218	0.2	5,050,157
Indiana	848,420	36.8	989,375	42.9	455,934	19.8	7,936	0.3	2,305,871
Iowa	586,353	43.3	504,891	37.3	253,468	18.7	1,076	0.1	1,354,607
Kansas	390,434	33.7	449,951	38.9	312,358	27.0	4,314	0.4	1,157,335
Kentucky	665,104	44.6	617,178	41.3	203,944	13.7	4,513	0.3	1,492,900
Louisiana	815,971	45.6	733,386	41	211,478	11.8	3,155	0.2	1,790,017
Maine	263,420	38.8	206,504	30.4	206,820	30.4	1,681	0.2	679,499
Maryland	988,571	49.8	707,094	35.6	281,414	14.2	4,715	0.2	1,985,046
Massachusetts	1,318,662	47.5	805,049	29	630,731	22.7	9,024	0.3	2,773,700
Michigan	1,871,182	43.8	1,554,940	36.4	824,813	19.3	10,175	0.2	4,274,673
Minnesota	1,020,997	43.5	747,841	31.9	562,506	24.0	3,374	0.1	2,347,948
Mississippi	400,258	40.8	487,793	49.7	85,626	8.7	2,154	0.2	981,793
Missouri	1,053,873	44.1	811,159	33.9	518,741	21.7	7,497	0.3	2,391,565
Montana	154,507	37.6	144,207	35.1	107,225	26.1	986	0.2	410,611
Nebraska	216,864	29.4	343,678	46.6	174,104	23.6	1,340	0.2	737,546
Nevada	189,148	37.4	175,828	34.7	132,580	26.2	1,835	0.4	506,318
New Hampshire	209,040	38.9	202,484	37.6	121,337	22.6	3,548	0.7	537,943
New Jersey	1,436,206	43	1,356,865	40.6	521,829	15.6	6,822	0.2	3,343,594
New Mexico	261,617	45.9	212,824	37.3	91,895	16.1	1,615	0.3	569,986
New York	3,444,450	49.7	2,346,649	33.9	1,090,721	15.7	13,451	0.2	6,926,925
North Carolina	1,114,042	42.7	1,134,661	43.4	357,864	13.7	5,171	0.2	2,611,850
North Dakota	99,168	32.2	136,244	44.2	71,084	23.1	416	0.1	308,133
Ohio	1,984,942	40.2	1,894,310	38.3	1,036,426	21.0	7,252	0.1	4,939,967
Oklahoma	473,066	34	592,929	42.6	319,878	23.0	4,486	0.3	1,390,359
Oregon	621,314	42.5	475,757	32.5	354,091	24.2	4,277	0.3	1,462,643
Pennsylvania	2,239,164	45.1	1,791,841	36.1	902,667	18.2	21,477	0.4	4,959,810
Rhode Island	213,299	47	131,601	29	105,045	23.2	571	0.1	453,477
South Carolina	479,514	39.9	577,507	48	138,872	11.5	2,719	0.2	1,202,527
South Dakota	124,888	37.1	136,718	40.7	73,295	21.8	814	0.2	336,254
Tennessee	933,521	47.1	841,300	42.4	199,968	10.1	1,847	0.1	1,982,638
Texas	2,281,815	37.1	2,496,071	40.6	1,354,781	22.0	19,699	0.3	6,154,018
Utah	183,429	24.7	322,632	43.4	203,400	27.3	1,900	0.3	743,999
Vermont	133,592	46.1	88,122	30.4	65,991	22.8	501	0.2	289,701
Virginia	1,038,650	40.6	1,150,517	45	348,639	13.6	5,730	0.2	2,558,665
Washington	993,037	43.4	731,234	32	541,780	23.7	7,533	0.3	2,288,230
West Virginia	331,001	48.4	241,974	35.4	108,829	15.9	1,873	0.3	683,762
Wisconsin	1,041,066	41.1	930,855	36.8	544,479	21.5	2,877	0.1	2,531,114
Wyoming	68,160	34	79,347	39.6	51,263	25.6	844	0.4	200,598
District of Columbia	192,619	84.6	20,698	9.1	9,681	4.3	467	0.2	227,572
TOTALS	**44,909,326**	**43.0**	**39,103,882**	**37.4**	**19,741,657**	**18.9**	**291,627**	**0.3**	**104,425,014**

1992 ELECTION: STATE-BY-STATE RESULTS (CLINTON vs. BUSH vs. PEROT vs. MARROU)

UNITED STATES
PRESIDENTIAL ELECTION OF 1996

THE ISSUES

GOVERNMENT SHUT-DOWN

Which candidate could best respond to the America's economic recession?

The REPUBLICAN CONVENTION

PLACE: Astrodome
Houston, TX

DATE: August 12 to 15, 1996

NOMINATED: Bob Dole, of Kansas,
for President

NOMINATED: Jack Kemp, of New York,
for Vice President

Kansas Senator, Bob Dole received the nomination to be the 1996 Republican Presidential nominee on the first ballot.

The DEMOCRATIC CONVENTION

PLACE: Chicago, IL

DATE: August 26-30, 1996

NOMINATED: William Clinton,
of Arkansas, for President

NOMINATED: Albert Gore, of Tennessee,
for Vice President

William Clinton was renominated as the 1996 Democratic Presidential candidate on the first ballot.

William Clinton
ELECTED

PRESIDENTIAL CANDIDATES

William Clinton
(Democrat)

Bob Dole
(Republican)

President Clinton did not face any opposition in his bid to be renominated by the Democratic party. Senator Dole of Kansas made his third bid to obtain the nomination of the Republican party. This time he was successful. Dole defeated both magazine publisher, Steve Forbes, as well Pat Buchanan, to receive the Republican nod.

By the time the 1996 election took place the country was in the midst of an economic boom. Employment was rising, as was the stock market. The internet boom had begun. Given all of the positive economic indicators, President Clinton remained extremely popular-- despite continued minor scandals, revolving around his personal conduct.

Senator Dole turned out to be an ineffective campaigner. He was unable to connect with the American public. Furthermore, Dole's age was an issue during the campaign. He was 73. Had he been elected, he would have been the oldest President to take office.

William Jefferson Clinton became the first Democratic President to be reelected in the U.S. for a second full term since Franklin Delano Roosevelt.

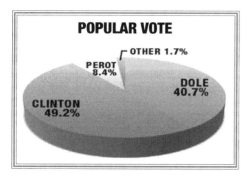

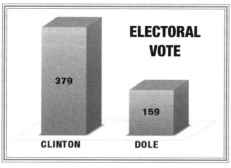

STATES	BILL CLINTON		BOB DOLE		ROSS PEROT		RALPH NADER		TOTAL VOTES
	VOTES	PERCENTAGE	VOTES	PERCENTAGE	VOTES	PERCENTAGE	VOTES	PERCENTAGE	
Alabama	662,165	43.2	769,044	50.1	92,149	6.0	0	0	1,534,349
Alaska	80,380	33.3	122,746	50.8	26,333	10.9	7,597	3.1	241,620
Arizona	653,288	46.5	622,073	44.3	112,072	8.0	2,062	0.1	1,404,405
Arkansas	475,171	53.7	325,416	36.8	69,884	7.9	3,649	0.4	884,262
California	5,119,835	51.1	3,828,380	38.2	697,847	7.0	237,016	2.4	10,019,484
Colorado	671,152	44.4	691,848	45.8	99,629	6.6	25,070	1.7	1,510,704
Connecticut	735,740	52.8	483,109	34.7	139,523	10.0	24,321	1.7	1,392,614
Delaware	140,355	51.8	99,062	36.6	28,719	10.6	18	0.0	270,845
Florida	2,546,870	48.0	2,244,536	42.3	483,870	9.1	4,101	0.1	5,303,794
Georgia	1,053,849	45.8	1,080,843	47.0	146,337	6.4	0	0.0	2,299,071
Hawaii	205,012	56.9	113,943	31.6	27,358	7.6	10,386	2.9	360,120
Idaho	165,443	33.6	256,595	52.2	62,518	12.7	0	0.0	491,719
Illinois	2,341,744	54.3	1,587,021	36.8	346,408	8.0	1,447	0.0	4,311,391
Indiana	887,424	41.6	1,006,693	47.1	224,299	10.5	895	0.0	2,135,431
Iowa	620,258	50.3	492,644	39.9	105,159	8.5	6,550	0.5	1,234,075
Kansas	387,659	36.1	583,245	54.3	92,639	8.6	914	0.1	1,074,300
Kentucky	636,614	45.8	623,283	44.9	120,396	8.7	701	0.1	1,388,708
Louisiana	927,837	52.0	712,586	39.9	123,293	6.9	4,719	0.3	1,783,959
Maine	312,788	51.6	186,378	30.8	85,970	14.2	15,279	2.5	605,897
Maryland	966,207	54.3	681,530	38.3	115,812	6.5	2,606	0.1	1,780,870
Massachusetts	1,571,763	61.5	718,107	28.1	227,217	8.9	4,565	0.2	2,556,786
Michigan	1,989,653	51.7	1,481,212	38.5	336,670	8.7	2,322	0.1	3,848,844
Minnesota	1,120,438	51.1	766,476	35.0	257,704	11.8	24,908	1.1	2,192,640
Mississippi	394,022	44.1	439,838	49.2	52,222	5.8	0	0.0	893,857
Missouri	1,025,935	47.5	890,016	41.2	217,188	10.1	534	0.0	2,158,065
Montana	167,922	41.3	179,652	44.1	55,529	13.6	0	0.0	407,261
Nebraska	236,761	35.0	363,467	53.7	71,278	10.5	0	0.0	677,415
Nevada	203,974	43.9	199,244	42.9	43,986	9.5	4,730	1.0	464,279
New Hampshire	246,214	49.3	196,532	39.4	48,390	9.7	0	0.0	499,175
New Jersey	1,652,329	53.7	1,103,078	35.9	262,134	8.5	32,645	1.1	3,075,807
New Mexico	273,495	49.2	232,751	41.9	32,257	5.8	13,218	2.4	556,074
New York	3,756,177	59.5	1,933,492	30.6	503,458	8.0	75,956	1.2	6,316,129
North Carolina	1,107,849	44.0	1,225,938	48.7	168,059	6.7	2,108	0.1	2,515,807
North Dakota	106,905	40.1	125,050	46.9	32,515	12.2	0	0.0	266,411
Ohio	2,148,222	47.4	1,859,883	41.0	483,207	10.7	2,962	0.1	4,534,434
Oklahoma	488,105	40.4	582,315	48.3	130,788	10.8	0	0.0	1,206,713
Oregon	649,641	47.2	538,152	39.1	121,221	8.8	49,415	3.6	1,377,760
Pennsylvania	2,215,819	49.2	1,801,169	40.0	430,984	9.6	3,086	0.1	4,506,118
Rhode Island	233,050	59.7	104,683	26.8	43,723	11.2	6,040	1.5	390,284
South Carolina	506,283	44.0	573,458	49.8	64,386	5.6	0	0.0	1,151,689
South Dakota	139,333	43.0	150,543	46.5	31,250	9.7	0	0.0	323,826
Tennessee	909,146	48.0	863,530	45.6	105,918	5.6	6,427	0.3	1,894,105
Texas	2,459,683	43.8	2,736,167	48.8	378,537	6.7	4,810	0.1	5,611,644
Utah	221,633	33.3	361,911	54.4	66,461	10.0	4,615	0.7	665,629
Vermont	137,894	53.4	80,352	31.1	31,024	12.0	5,585	2.2	258,449
Virginia	1,091,060	45.1	1,138,350	47.1	159,861	6.6	0	0.0	2,416,642
Washington	1,123,323	49.8	840,712	37.3	201,003	8.9	60,322	2.7	2,253,837
West Virginia	327,812	51.5	233,946	36.8	71,639	11.3	0	0.0	636,459
Wisconsin	1,071,971	48.8	845,029	38.5	227,339	10.4	28,723	1.3	2,196,169
Wyoming	77,934	36.8	105,388	49.8	25,928	12.3	0	0.0	211,571
District of Columbia	158,220	85.2	17,339	9.3	3,611	1.9	4,780	2.6	185,726
TOTALS	47,402,357	49.2	39,198,755	40.7	8,085,402	8.4	684,902	0.7	96,277,223

1996 ELECTION: STATE-BY-STATE RESULTS (CLINTON vs. DOLE vs. PEROT vs. NADER)

UNITED STATES
PRESIDENTIAL ELECTION OF 2000

THE ISSUES

TAXATION

Should tax rates be lowered?

ENVIRONMENT

How much resources should be placed on maintaining the quality of our environment?

The DEMOCRATIC CONVENTION

PLACE: Los Angeles, CA

DATE: August 14-18, 2000

NOMINATED: Albert Gore, of Tennessee, for President

NOMINATED: Joseph Lieberman, of Connecticut, for Vice President

Vice President Al Gore was nominated as the 2000 Democratic Presidential candidate on the first ballot.

The REPUBLICAN CONVENTION

PLACE: Astrodome
Houston, TX

DATE: July 31–August 3, 2000

NOMINATED: George W. Bush, of Texas, for President

NOMINATED: Richard B. Cheney, of Wyoming, for Vice President

In a well orchestrated campaign, Gov. George Bush received the 2000 Republican Presidential nomination on the first ballot.

George W. Bush
ELECTED

PRESIDENTIAL CANDIDATES

Albert Gore
(Democrat)

George W. Bush
(Republican)

Vice President Gore was the clear choice to succeed President Clinton. Gore had been challenged in the early Democratic Primaries by New Jersey, Senator Bill Bradley. Bradley failed, however, to win a single primary. Al Gore quickly secured the 2000 Democratic Presidential nomination.

Governor Bush of Texas, the son of former President Bush, was the choice of the Republican establishment. Governor Bush was challenged for the nomination by Senator John McCain of Arizona. When Bush won a bitterly fought primary in South Carolina, he became the presumptive Republican nominee. Both candidates broke with tradition and announced their vice presidential candidates. Bush announced that Dick Cheney, who had been Secretary of Defense, would be his vice presidential choice, thus, balancing Bush's limited experience with a very experienced Vice President.

Gore selected Senator Joe Lieberman, an Orthodox Jew, as his rumming mate. Lieberman was the first Jew to be selected on a major ticket. Lieberman had been critical of President Clinton over the Monica Lewinsky affair. Throughout the campaign, polls showed the race was very close. Bush initially stumbled, but regained his momentum during the three debates. The Republicans effectively defined the game of expectations. When Bush did better than expected, he won the debates.

On election night, the results were so close that neither candidate was declared the winner. Gore won the nationwide popular vote, but the outcome of a recount in Florida would determine the results of the Electoral vote. The initial numbers of votes, in an election marked with several irregularities, had given Bush a Florida lead of less than 1,000 votes. The Supreme Court intervened and stopped the recount. Thus, giving the election to Bush. The 2000 election was the fourth in American history when the winner of the popular vote was not the winner of the electoral votes.

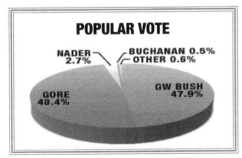

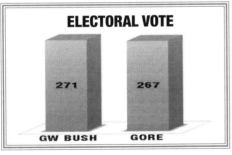

STATES	GEORGE W. BUSH VOTES	PERCENTAGE	AL GORE VOTES	PERCENTAGE	RALPH NADER VOTES	PERCENTAGE	PATRICK BUCHANAN VOTES	PERCENTAGE	TOTAL VOTES
Alabama	941,173	56.5	692,611	41.6	18,323	1.1	6,351	0.4	1,666,272
Alaska	167,398	58.6	79,004	27.7	28,747	10.1	5,192	1.8	284,492
Arizona	781,652	51.0	685,341	44.7	45,645	3.0	12,373	0.8	1,532,016
Arkansas	472,940	51.3	422,768	45.9	13,421	1.5	7,358	0.8	921,781
California	4,567,429	41.7	5,861,203	54.3	418,707	3.8	44,987	0.4	10,965,856
Colorado	883,748	50.8	738,227	42.4	91,434	5.3	10,465	0.6	1,741,368
Connecticut	561,104	38.4	816,659	55.9	64,452	4.4	4,731	0.3	1,460,177
Delaware	137,288	41.9	180,068	55.0	8,307	2.5	777	0.2	327,529
Florida	2,912,790	48.8	2,912,253	48.8	97,488	1.6	17,484	0.3	5,963,070
Georgia	1,419,720	54.7	1,116,230	43.0	0	0.5	10,926	0.4	2,583,208
Hawaii	137,845	37.5	205,286	55.8	21,623	5.9	1,071	0.3	367,951
Idaho	336,937	67.2	138,637	27.6	12,292	2.5	7,615	1.5	501,615
Illinois	2,019,421	42.6	2,589,026	54.6	103,759	2.2	0	0.3	4,739,935
Indiana	1,245,836	56.6	901,980	41.0	18,531	0.8	16,959	0.8	2,199,302
Iowa	634,373	48.2	638,517	48.5	29,374	2.2	5,731	0.4	1,314,395
Kansas	622,332	58.0	399,276	37.2	36,086	3.4	7,370	0.7	1,072,216
Kentucky	872,520	56.5	638,923	41.4	23,118	1.5	4,152	0.3	1,547,106
Louisiana	927,871	52.6	792,344	44.9	14,356	1.2	20,473	0.8	1,765,656
Maine	286,616	44.0	319,951	49.1	37,127	5.7	4,443	0.7	651,790
Maryland	813,724	40.3	1,143,888	56.5	53,763	2.7	4,247	0.2	2,021,987
Massachusetts	878,502	32.5	1,616,487	59.8	173,564	6.4	11,149	0.4	2,698,994
Michigan	1,953,139	46.1	2,170,418	51.3	84,165	2.0	1,851	0.0	4,232,501
Minnesota	1,109,659	45.5	1,168,266	47.9	126,696	5.2	22,166	0.9	2,438,685
Mississippi	572,844	57.6	404,614	40.7	8,122	0.8	2,265	0.2	994,184
Missouri	1,189,924	50.4	1,111,138	47.1	38,515	1.6	9,818	0.4	2,359,892
Montana	240,178	58.4	137,126	33.4	24,437	5.9	5,697	1.4	410,986
Nebraska	433,850	62.2	231,776	33.3	24,670	3.5	3,646	0.5	697,132
Nevada	301,575	49.5	279,978	46.0	15,008	2.5	4,747	0.8	605,655
New Hampshire	273,559	48.1	266,348	46.8	22,188	3.9	2,615	0.5	567,795
New Jersey	1,284,173	40.3	1,788,850	56.1	94,554	3.0	6,989	0.2	3,187,226
New Mexico	286,417	47.8	286,783	47.9	21,251	3.6	1,392	0.2	598,605
New York	2,403,374	35.2	4,107,697	60.2	244,030	3.6	31,599	0.5	6,821,999
North Carolina	1,631,163	56.0	1,257,692	43.2	0	0.0	8,874	0.3	2,914,990
North Dakota	174,852	60.7	95,284	33.1	9,486	3.3	7,288	2.5	288,256
Ohio	2,350,363	50.0	2,183,628	46.4	117,799	2.5	26,721	0.6	4,701,998
Oklahoma	744,337	60.3	474,276	38.4	0	0.0	9,014	0.7	1,234,229
Oregon	713,577	46.5	720,342	47.0	77,357	5.0	7,063	0.5	1,530,549
Pennsylvania	2,281,127	46.4	2,485,967	50.6	103,392	2.1	16,023	0.3	4,912,185
Rhode Island	130,555	31.9	249,508	61.0	25,052	6.1	2,273	0.6	409,112
South Carolina	786,892	56.8	566,037	40.9	20,279	1.5	3,309	0.3	1,383,902
South Dakota	190,700	60.3	118,804	37.6	0	0.0	3,322	1.1	316,269
Tennessee	1,061,949	51.1	981,720	47.3	19,781	1.0	4,250	0.2	2,075,753
Texas	3,799,639	59.3	2,433,746	38.0	137,994	2.2	12,394	0.2	6,407,637
Utah	515,096	66.8	203,053	26.3	35,850	4.7	9,319	1.2	766,697
Vermont	119,775	40.7	149,022	50.6	20,374	6.9	2,192	0.7	293,794
Virginia	1,437,490	52.5	1,217,290	44.4	59,398	2.2	5,455	0.2	2,736,640
Washington	1,108,864	44.6	1,247,652	50.2	103,002	4.1	7,171	0.3	2,487,433
West Virginia	336,473	51.9	295,497	45.6	10,680	1.6	3,283	0.5	648,251
Wisconsin	1,237,279	47.6	1,242,987	47.8	94,070	3.6	11,446	0.4	2,598,607
Wyoming	147,947	67.8	60,481	27.7	0	2.1	2,724	1.2	213,726
District of Columbia	18,073	9.0	171,923	85.2	10,576	5.2	0	0.0	201,894
TOTALS	50,456,062	47.9	50,996,582	48.4	2,858,843	2.7	438,760	0.4	105,363,298

2000 ELECTION: STATE-BY-STATE RESULTS (GW BUSH vs. GORE vs. NADER vs. BUCHANAN)

UNITED STATES
PRESIDENTIAL ELECTION OF 2004

THE ISSUES

TAXATION

Should tax rates be lowered?

ENVIRONMENT

How much resources should be placed on maintaining the quality of our environment?

The DEMOCRATIC CONVENTION

PLACE: Boston, MA

DATE: July 26-29, 2004

NOMINATED: John Kerry,
of Massachusetts, for President

NOMINATED: John Edwards,
of Tennessee, for Vice President

Senator Kerry was nominated on the first ballot. The convention was well organized with no real surprises.

The REPUBLICAN CONVENTION

PLACE: New York, NY

DATE: August 30-Sept 2, 2004

NOMINATED: George W. Bush, of Texas,
for President

NOMINATED: Richard B. Cheney,
of Wyoming, for Vice President

President Bush was renominated on the first ballot. The convention was well organized with no real surprises.

George W. Bush
ELECTED

PRESIDENTIAL CANDIDATES

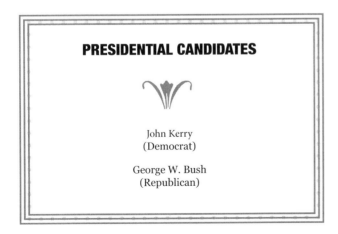

John Kerry
(Democrat)

George W. Bush
(Republican)

There were a large number of Democrats contending to become the party's presidential nominee in 2004. Initially, the leading contender was Governor Howard Dean of Vermont. Also competing were: Senator John Kerry, Senator John Edwards, Senator Joe Lieberman, Retired General Wesley Clark, Representative Dennis Kucinich, Senator Carol Mosley Braun, Senator Bob Graham, House Majority Leader Dick Gephardt and Reverend Al Sharpton. The Iowa caucus rearranged and narrowed the field. Senator Kerry won a decisive victory, with Senator Edwards coming in second. Governor Dean came in a distant third. Senator Kerry never looked back and secured the Democratic nomination. President Bush was renominated without opposition.

From the moment Kerry became the presumptive nominee of the Democratic party, the Republicans began an intensive attack on him. The Democrats made Kerry's Vietnam War service a major theme of their convention. Following the convention a group of Vietnam Veterans called the "Swift Boat Veterans" launched a major attack on Kerry's war record. The veterans claimed Kerry did not deserve his medals. Despite there seeming to be little truth in their allegations, the Swift Boat veterans received a great deal of publicity. Their attacks definitively hurt Kerry.

The Republicans had a successful convention, in which they repeatedly attacked Kerry. Republicans claimed Kerry was a "flip-flopper". They also asserted Kerry could not be trusted to fight the war on terror. The NY based Republican convention highlighted President Bush's qualities, which were well-suited to fighting terrorism. President Bush opened a significant lead in the polls following the convention.

President Bush's popularity rating shifted during the first debate. In that debate Kerry carried himself significantly better than the President. Bush performed better is subsequent debates. However, Kerry was considered the winner of all three. Events in Iraq in the last two weeks before the election seemed to favor Kerry. In the end, the Republicans were more successful than the Democrats in getting out their core voters. That, and the related lack of enthusiasm for Kerry, resulted in another Bush victory. Bush won almost the identical states he had in 2000. Though this time, he won the plurality of the popular vote.

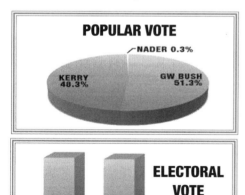

STATES	GEORGE W. BUSH		JOHN KERRY		TOTAL VOTES
	VOTES	PERCENTAGE	VOTES	PERCENTAGE	
Alabama	1,174,348	65.5	693,933	36.8	1,883,449
Alaska	190,889	61.1	111,025	35.5	312,598
Arizona	1,104,294	54.9	893,524	44.4	2,012,585
Arkansas	572,898	54.3	469,953	44.5	1,054,945
California	5,509,826	44.4	6,745,485	54.3	12,421,852
Colorado	1,101,255	51.7	1,001,732	47.0	2,130,330
Connecticut	693,826	43.9	857,488	54.3	1,578,769
Delaware	171,660	45.8	200,152	53.3	375,190
Florida	3,964,522	52.1	3,583,544	47.1	7,609,810
Georgia	1,914,254	58.0	1,366,149	41.4	3,301,875
Hawaii	194,191	45.3	231,708	54.0	429,013
Idaho	409,235	68.4	181,098	30.3	598,447
Illinois	2,345,946	44.5	2,891,550	54.8	5,274,322
Indiana	1,479,438	59.9	969,011	39.3	2,468,002
Iowa	751,957	49.9	741,898	49.2	1,506,908
Kansas	736,456	62.0	434,993	36.6	1,187,756
Kentucky	1,069,439	59.6	712,733	39.7	1,795,756
Louisiana	1,102,169	56.7	820,299	42.2	1,943,106
Maine	330,201	44.6	396,842	53.6	740,752
Maryland	1,024,703	42.9	1,334,493	55.9	2,386,678
Massachusetts	1,071,109	36.8	1,803,800	61.9	2,912,388
Michigan	2,313,746	47.8	2,479,183	51.2	4,839,252
Minnesota	1,346,695	47.6	1,445,014	51.1	2,828,387
Mississippi	684,981	59.5	458,094	39.8	1,152,145
Missouri	1,455,713	53.3	1,259,171	46.1	2,731,364
Montana	266,063	59.1	173,710	38.6	450,445
Nebraska	512,814	65.9	254,328	32.7	778,186
Nevada	418,690	50.5	397,190	47.9	829,587
New Hampshire	331,237	48.9	340,511	50.2	677,738
New Jersey	1,670,003	46.2	1,911,430	52.9	3,611,691
New Mexico	376,930	49.8	370,942	49.0	756,304
New York	2,962,567	40.1	4,314,280	58.4	7,391,036
North Carolina	1,961,166	56.0	1,525,849	43.6	3,501,007
North Dakota	196,651	62.9	111,052	35.5	312,833
Ohio	2,859,768	50.8	2,741,167	48.7	5,627,903
Oklahoma	959,792	65.6	503,966	34.4	1,463,758
Oregon	866,831	47.2	943,164	51.3	1,836,782
Pennsylvania	2,793,847	48.4	2,938,095	50.9	5,769,590
Rhode Island	169,046	38.7	259,790	59.4	437,134
South Carolina	937,974	58.0	661,699	40.9	1,617,730
South Dakota	232,584	59.9	149,244	38.4	388,215
Tennessee	1,384,375	56.8	1,036,477	42.5	2,437,319
Texas	4,526,917	61.1	2,832,704	38.2	7,410,765
Utah	663,742	71.5	241,199	26.0	927,844
Vermont	121,180	38.8	184,067	58.9	312,309
Virginia	1,716,959	53.7	1,454,742	45.5	3,198,367
Washington	1,304,894	45.6	1,510,201	52.8	2,859,084
West Virginia	423,718	56.1	326,741	43.2	755,887
Wisconsin	1,478,120	49.3	1,489,504	49.7	2,997,007
Wyoming	167,270	68.9	70,776	29.1	243,428
District of Columbia	21,256	9.3	202,970	89.2	227,586
TOTALS	**62,040,610**	**50.7**	**59,028,439**	**48.3**	**122,295,345**

2004 ELECTION: STATE-BY-STATE RESULTS (GW BUSH vs. KERRY)

UNITED STATES
PRESIDENTIAL ELECTION OF 2008

THE ISSUES

TIME FOR CHANGE

Was it time for America to embrace new directions with Obama, or stay the course with McCain?

IRAQ
How much resources should be placed on maintaining the quality of our environment?

The REPUBLICAN CONVENTION

PLACE: St. Paul, MN

DATE: September 1–4, 2008

NOMINATED: John McCain, of Arizona, for President

NOMINATED: Sarah Palin, of Alaska, for Vice President

Senator McCain was nominated on the first ballot. The original convention schedule was cancelled, due to hurricane Gustav.

The DEMOCRATIC CONVENTION

PLACE: Denver, CO

DATE: August 25-28th, 2008

NOMINATED: Barack Obama, of Illinois, for President

NOMINATED: Joseph Biden, of Delaware, for Vice President

Senator Obama was nominated by the 2008 Democratic Convention delegation on the first ballot.

Barack Obama
ELECTED

PRESIDENTIAL CANDIDATES

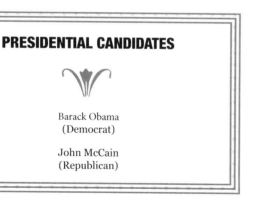

Barack Obama
(Democrat)

John McCain
(Republican)

UNITED STATES PRESIDENTIAL **Election of 2008**

Senator Barack Obama won the 2008 Presidential Election. His victory came at the end of the longest, and most interesting election in American history. The 2008 election was the first election in 50 years, in which there was no incumbent President or Vice President from either party competing for the Presidential nomination. The absence of any incumbent encouraged a large number of candidates from both parties to run.

On the Democratic side, the early assumptions were that Senator Hilary Clinton, wife of the former President Bill Clinton, would be the favorite to receive her party's nomination. Clinton entered the Presidential primary race with the highest name recognition of any candidate. She had an established political organization, inherited partially, from her husband, as well as built on her own. A large number of other Democrats announced their intentions to run. Most of the potential candidates were senators. One of the Senators was Barack Obama, a freshman Senator from Illinois. Obama was an African-American, who come to national attention when he gave the keynote address at the 2004 Democratic National Convention. Obama was the only African-American Senator. He was also the only candidate that had been on record opposing the war in Iraq, prior to its beginning. This was a strong draw among a Democratic primary electorate that was strongly against the war.

Obama won the first primary election battle, the Iowa caucus. Senator Clinton revived her campaign with a comeback victory in New Hampshire. The two battled in repeated primary states. Obama made an important strategic decision to compete heavily in many of the smaller caucus states; states that almost never voted for a Democrat in a general election. Securing victories in the smaller caucus states provided Obama with a significant lead in the delegate count in his favor. The Democrats appointed delegates proportionally. Thus, despite the fact that Clinton won many of the later primary contests in the biggest states, she was unable to catch Obama's delegate lead. In addition, Obama had a superior fundraising operation. He successfully used the internet to build a significant base of small donors.

The early Republican front-runner had been Senator John McCain. However, in the summer of 2007, his primary campaign nearly fell apart. McCain was forced to retrench and begin again. The early leader in the polls was the former mayor of New York, Rudolf Giuliani. "Rudy" Giuliani had high name recognition, due to his stewardship of the city through the tragedy of 9/11. Many questioned whether Giuliani, who was relatively liberal on social issues, could be nominated in the Republican primaries. Giuliani decided not to compete in the early caucuses and primaries. Governor Huckabee, a self-defined Evangelical, won the Iowa caucus. Though Senator McCain won the New Hampshire primary, where he had placed much of his effort. McCain then went on to win the North Carolina primary; the state from which his 2000 efforts against George W. Bush hit a wall. By the time McCain arrived in Florida, he had momentum and the endorsement of the popular Florida governor. McCain handily won the Florida primary. The Republican rule of "winner takes all" allowed McCain to swiftly build an insurmountable lead in delegates. As a result, he clinched the nomination.

Once both nominees had cemented their party's nominations, Senator McCain suggested that he and Senator Obama jointly conduct 10 Town Hall meetings throughout the United States. The Obama campaign deflected the invitation.

Both major parties held their conventions late in the season. The Democrats convened in last August. The Republicans held their convention in early September. Both parties wanted to schedule their elections as late as possible, in order not to limit their spending, in the event they chose to accept public financing. Senator Obama became the first major candidate not to accept public finances, since the campaign finance laws were first passed.

Senator Obama selected Senator Joe Biden, of Delaware, to be his running mate. The choice of Biden as a vice presidential candidate was well received. The Democratic convention was considered a success by all observers. At the conclusion of the Republican convention, Senator McCain announced his running mate. That selection was Alaskan Governor, Sarah Pallin. Choosing Pallin was successful, in that it generated enthusiasm with the Republican base (something McCain had not been able to do). However, others questioned whether Pallin had the experience to be President. This blunted much of the attacks on Obama, which centered on his lack of experience.

Coming out of the two party conventions, most observers believed the Presidential race was close. In mid-September the United States, and much of the rest of the world, experienced a severe financial crisis that required rapid government intervention. Obama's response to the crisis, was considered by many, better than McCain's response. That response put Obama ahead in the polls. The economic crisis, which had been building for over a year. A record number of Americans lost their homes. These losses made it nearly impossible for McCain to win. Going into the election campaign it was thought that one of Obama's advantages would be his opposition to the war in Iraq, but thanks to a surge of troops that McCain advocated, clear progress was taking place in Iraq. This did not work to McCain's advantage. Instead, it took the issue off the table. In the end, it was economic the issues that dominated the election.

Obama also benefited from his decision not to take public finances. He raised record sums of money. He was able to out spend McCain by a factor of nearly three to one. Finally, the Obama campaign was the first campaign that was truly successful in bringing out the youth vote. Obama won a decisive victory, carrying all of the swing states. He further won states that had not been won by a Democrat in a generation, such as Virginia and Indiana.

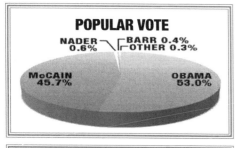

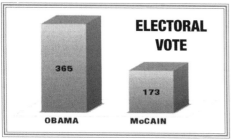

STATES	BARACK OBAMA		JOHN McCAIN		RALPH NADER		BOB BARR		TOTAL VOTES
	VOTES	PERCENTAGE	VOTES	PERCENTAGE	VOTES	PERCENTAGE	VOTES	PERCENTAGE	
Alabama	813,479	38.7	1,266,546	60.3	6,788	0.3	4,991	0.2	2,099,819
Alaska	123,594	37.9	193,841	59.4	3,783	1.2	1,589	0.5	326,197
Arizona	1,034,707	45.1	1,230,111	53.6	11,301	0.5	12,555	0.5	2,293,475
Arkansas	422,310	38.9	638,017	58.7	12,882	1.2	4,776	0.4	1,086,617
California	8,274,473	61.0	5,011,781	37.0	108,381	0.8	67,582	0.5	13,464,495
Colorado	1,288,576	53.7	1,073,589	44.7	13,350	0.6	10,897	0.5	2,401,361
Connecticut	997,772	60.6	629,428	38.2	19,162	1.2	0	0.0	1,646,783
Delaware	255,459	61.9	152,374	37.0	2,401	0.6	1,109	0.3	412,412
Florida	4,282,074	51.0	4,045,624	48.2	28,124	0.3	17,218	0.2	8,390,744
Georgia	1,844,123	47.0	2,048,759	52.2	1,158	0.0	28,731	0.7	3,921,693
Hawaii	325,871	71.9	120,566	26.6	3,825	0.8	1,314	0.3	453,568
Idaho	236,440	36.1	403,012	61.5	7,175	1.1	3,658	0.6	655,032
Illinois	3,419,348	61.9	2,031,179	36.8	30,948	0.6	19,642	0.4	5,513,635
Indiana	1,374,039	50.0	1,345,648	48.9	909	0.0	29,257	1.1	2,751,054
Iowa	828,940	53.9	682,379	44.4	8,014	0.5	4,590	0.3	1,530,386
Kansas	514,765	41.7	699,655	56.6	10,527	0.9	6,706	0.5	1,235,801
Kentucky	751,985	41.2	1,048,462	57.4	15,378	0.8	5,989	0.3	1,826,620
Louisiana	782,989	39.9	1,148,275	58.6	6,997	0.4	0	0.0	1,960,761
Maine	421,923	57.7	295,273	40.4	10,636	1.5	251	0.0	731,163
Maryland	1,629,467	61.9	959,862	36.5	14,713	0.6	9,842	0.4	2,622,549
Massachusetts	1,904,097	61.8	1,108,854	36.0	28,841	0.9	13,189	0.4	3,080,985
Michigan	2,872,579	57.4	2,048,639	41.0	33,085	0.7	23,716	0.5	5,001,766
Minnesota	1,573,354	54.1	1,275,409	43.8	30,152	1.0	9,174	0.3	2,900,873
Mississippi	554,662	43.0	724,597	56.2	4,011	0.3	2,529	0.2	1,289,865
Missouri	1,441,911	49.3	1,445,814	49.4	17,813	0.6	11,386	0.4	2,925,205
Montana	231,667	47.3	242,763	49.5	3,686	0.8	1,355	0.3	490,109
Nebraska	333,319	41.6	452,979	56.5	5,406	0.7	2,740	0.3	798,444
Nevada	533,736	55.2	412,827	42.7	6,150	0.6	4,263	0.4	961,581
New Hampshire	384,826	54.1	316,534	44.5	3,503	0.5	2,217	0.3	707,611
New Jersey	2,215,422	57.3	1,613,207	41.7	21,298	0.6	8,441	0.2	3,868,237
New Mexico	472,422	56.9	346,832	41.8	5,327	0.6	2,428	0.3	830,158
New York	4,804,701	62.9	2,752,728	36.0	41,248	0.5	19,595	0.3	7,590,551
North Carolina	2,142,651	49.7	2,128,474	49.4	1,448	0.0	25,722	0.6	4,296,847
North Dakota	141,278	44.6	168,601	53.3	4,189	1.3	1,354	0.4	316,621
Ohio	2,940,044	51.5	2,677,820	46.9	42,337	0.7	19,917	0.3	5,697,927
Oklahoma	502,496	34.4	960,165	65.7	0	0.0	0	0.0	1,462,661
Oregon	1,037,291	56.8	738,475	40.4	18,614	1.0	7,635	0.4	1,814,251
Pennsylvania	3,276,363	54.6	2,655,885	44.3	42,977	0.7	19,912	0.3	5,992,384
Rhode Island	296,571	63.1	165,391	35.2	4,829	1.0	1,382	0.3	471,766
South Carolina	862,449	44.9	1,034,896	53.9	5,053	0.3	7,283	0.4	1,920,969
South Dakota	170,924	44.8	203,054	53.2	4,267	1.1	1,835	0.5	381,975
Tennessee	1,087,437	41.8	1,479,178	56.9	11,560	0.4	8,547	0.3	2,599,749
Texas	3,528,633	43.7	4,479,328	55.5	5,440	0.1	56,116	0.7	8,077,795
Utah	327,670	34.4	596,030	62.6	8,416	0.9	6,966	0.7	942,678
Vermont	219,262	67.4	98,974	30.4	3,339	1.0	1,067	0.3	325,046
Virginia	1,959,532	52.6	1,725,005	46.3	11,483	0.3	11,067	0.3	3,716,905
Washington	1,750,848	57.7	1,229,216	40.5	29,489	1.0	12,728	0.4	3,036,878
West Virginia	303,857	42.6	397,466	55.7	7,219	1.0	0	0.0	713,451
Wisconsin	1,677,211	56.2	1,262,393	42.3	17,605	0.6	8,858	0.3	2,976,356
Wyoming	82,868	32.5	164,958	64.8	2,525	1.0	1,594	0.6	253,137
District of Columbia	245,800	92.5	17,367	6.5	958	0.4	0	0.0	265,853
TOTALS	69,498,215	52.9	59,948,240	45.7	738,720	0.6	523,713	0.4	131,032,799

2008 ELECTION: STATE-BY-STATE RESULTS (OBAMA vs. McCAIN vs. NADER vs. BARR)

UNITED STATES
PRESIDENTIAL ELECTION OF 2012

THE ISSUES

THE ECONOMY
Has President Obama does enough to create jobs in the economy?

TAXES
Should wealthy Americans pay more?

BUDGET
Should entitlements be cut to balance the budget?

The REPUBLICAN CONVENTION

PLACE: Tampa, FL

DATE: August 27–30th, 2012

NOMINATED: Mitt Romney,
of Massachusetts, for President

NOMINATED: Paul Ryan,
of Wisconsin , for Vice President

Senator Romney was nominated on the first ballot. The original convention schedule was postponed, (as the convention before), due to hurricane Isaac.

The DEMOCRATIC CONVENTION

PLACE: Charlotte, NC

DATE: September 4th-6th 2012

NOMINATED: Barack Obama,
of Illinois, for President

NOMINATED: Joseph Biden,
of Delaware, for Vice President

Senator Obama was renominated by the 2012 Democratic Convention delegation on the first ballot.

Barack Obama
ELECTED

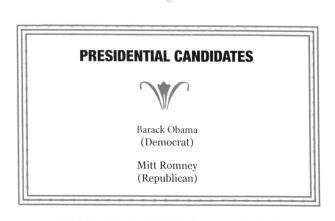

PRESIDENTIAL CANDIDATES

Barack Obama
(Democrat)

Mitt Romney
(Republican)

President Obama's bid for the Democratic Presidential nomination was not opposed. Conversely, the Republicans had a large field of candidates competing in their primaries for the nomination. The leading Republican candidate was former governor of Massachusetts, Mitt Romney. Romney had attempted to gain the 2008 Republican nomination. However, Senator John McCain bested Romney in 2008. As a result, in 2012 – in keeping with the tradition of the Republican Party – Romney was considered to be the leading candidate by the virtue of that fact that it was "his time".

Candidate Romney had a number of advantages, including his vast personal wealth, a relatively successful record as Governor of Massachusetts, as well as his Chairmanship of the Salt Lake City Olympics. Romney's weakness was the seemingly liberal positions he evidenced to hold while serving as governor of Massachusetts. The views Romney had purported made the Republican base wary of him. The role Romney's religion – Mormonism – played in determining his popularity remains an unknown factor in this race. Throughout the course of the Republican primary Romney had a number of opponents, including: Michelle Bachman, Rick Perry, Rick Santorum and Newt Gingrich. Each one of these opponents seemed to have his or her day in the sun. In the end, Romney (with his superior money and organization) would repeatedly come out on top.   In the end Romney emerged as the Republican nominee when the last of his opponents Rick Santorum conceded defeat.

As the primary campaign began winding down, and Romney became the presumptive Republican nominee, the expectation was that the presidential race would be very close. Romney had the fundamental advantage of the weak state of US economy. The unemployment rate in the United States stood at 8.2% in July 2012. No President had won reelection with unemployment rates so high since Franklin Roosevelt. It was Romney's hope to make the election both a referendum on Obama's stewardship of the Presidency (especially the economy), while at the same time touting his accomplishments as a successful businessman.

Unfortunately for Romney, he was vulnerable on a number of fronts. These same issues had been sources of personal attack against him on during the primary campaign. Romney's business experience had been with Bain Capital, a company that he had founded and headed. Bain's business was built purchasing troubled companies and extracting as much value from them as possible. Often part of the way Bain achieved its' success with these struggling companies was to fire some of the employees and move the work overseas. This practice, commonly known as "outsourcing" was not well received in the industrial Midwest, where residents had suffered greatly from the loss of work. Second, Romney refused to release his tax returns for more than one year. Romney's consistent refusal to disclose his returns allowed speculation on what he was hiding to run rampant. President Obama's election campaign exploited these facts. Throughout the late spring and summer the Obama campaign ran a relentless series of ads attacking Romney on these issues. As a result, President Obama developed a significant lead in the polls. This was a lead the President never really lost.

Governor Romney announced that Wisconsin Congressman Paul Ryan would be his nominee for Vice President. It was his hope that Ryan would energize the Republican base that had remained unenthusiastic about Romney's candidacy. Ryan's appointment did help somewhat to bring out the Republican base. However, Ryan's budget proposals, that included a substantial cut in Medicare, no doubt hurt Romney with Independent voters.

The Republican Party held their convention in Orlando. It seemed the Republicans could not get a break. The start of their convention had to be delayed due to a hurricane. The rest of the convention seemed to go down hill from there. Influential speakers seemingly chose to "toot their own horns" instead of discussing why the election of the Governor Romney was important. On the most important night of the convention, the night that the nominee is formally introduced to the country – due to a scheduling error – the nation watched an odd, albeit entertaining, monologue by Clint Eastwood, instead of the slick videos that had been prepared on the life of Governor Romney. By contrast, the Democratic convention went off without a hitch.

With the conventions over, the candidates moved to the General election campaign. The 2012 Presidential campaign was primarily held in 11 key states, the so-called "swing states" (those states whose electoral votes could possibly go to either candidate). The swing states included: Florida, Ohio, Virginia, North Carolina, New Hampshire, Wisconsin, Colorado, Iowa, New Mexico, Michigan, and Pennsylvania. The candidates spent almost all of their money and time in those states. The only exception the candidates made was to travel to raise money in other states.

In 2012 these candidates fundraised and spent in unprecedented amounts. President Obama and those parties directly associated with him raised $1,072,600,000, and spent $986,700,000. While Governor Romney and the Republican raised $992,500,000 and spent $992,000,000. It is estimated that an additional $60,000,000 was spent by groups that were not required to report their spending, almost all of it on behalf of governor Romney.

The only time the outcome of the race seemed to be at all in question was after the first debate. At that debate Governor Romney clearly bested President Obama, who appeared unengaged. However, in the two subsequent debates President Obama regained his momentum and outperformed Governor Romney.

President Obama won an unexpectedly large victory on Election Day, November 6th 2012. Obama beat Romney, by a margin of nearly 4% in the popular vote, and commanding a victory of 332 electoral votes to Romney's 206 electoral votes. Obama won all but 1 of the contested, so-called "swing states".

The Obama victory can be traced to several factors. First of all, Romney was a weak candidate. Romney continually made errors during the campaign, including a statement that "he did not have to worry about the 47% of the country who did not support him and were takers". Candidate Romney had been forced to take positions during the nominating process, (especially on issues such as immigration reform) that hurt him with segments of the population. Earlier attacks on the actions of Bain Capital and Romney's refusal to release his tax returns, as well as his earlier position opposing the government bailouts of the automobile companies did not resonate with voters.

Second, other Republican candidates making a number of extreme statements on issues such as rape hurt Romney. One Republican senate candidate stated that "in the case of rape the human body was able to block pregnancy" and as such, a rape exception to ban on abortions was unnecessary. These actions energized those opposed to Republican positions on social issues to get out and vote. This disparity was underscored by a number of actions taking by President Obama, both to support Gay & Lesbian rights, as well as supporting the rights of immigrants.

Third, the changing demographics of the US favored President Obama. The percentage of non-whites in the US continues to increase, and the number of the white male voters (the key supporters of the Republicans) decreased. Thus, the failure of the Republican Party to reach out to the non-white population of the US put its candidates at a distinct disadvantage.

Finally, as Election Day approached the US economy seemed to improve marginally. The unemployment rate fell below 8% for the first time in Obama's term. Consumer confidence rose and with it President Obama's chances of winning his second term.

All of these factors contributed to what became a decisive Obama victory in the election.

STATES	BARACK OBAMA		MITT ROMNEY		OTHER		TOTAL
	PERCENT	VOTES	PERCENT	VOTES	PERCENT	VOTES	
Alabama	795,696	38.36%	1,255,925	60.55%	22,717	1.10%	2,074,338
Alaska	122,640	41.21%	164,676	55.33%	10,309	3.46%	297,625
Arizona	1,025,232	44.59%	1,233,654	53.65%	40,368	1.76%	2,299,254
Arkansas	394,409	36.88%	647,744	60.57%	27,315	2.55%	1,069,468
California	7,854,285	60.24%	4,839,958	37.12%	344,314	2.64%	13,038,547
Colorado	1,322,998	51.49%	1,185,050	46.12%	61,169	2.38%	2,569,217
Connecticut	905,083	58.06%	634,892	40.73%	18,985	1.22%	1,558,960
Delaware	242,584	58.61%	165,484	39.98%	5,853	1.41%	413,921
DC	267,070	90.91%	21,381	7.28%	5,313	1.81%	293,764
Florida	4,235,965	50.00%	4,162,341	49.14%	72,895	0.86%	8,471,201
Georgia	1,773,827	45.51%	2,078,688	53.33%	45,324	1.16%	3,897,839
Hawaii	306,658	70.55%	121,015	27.84%	7,024	1.62%	434,697
Idaho	212,787	32.62%	420,911	64.53%	18,576	2.85%	652,274
Illinois	3,019,512	57.61%	2,135,216	40.74%	86,451	1.65%	5,241,179
Indiana	1,152,887	43.93%	1,420,543	54.13%	51,104	1.95%	2,624,534
Iowa	822,544	52.23%	730,617	46.40%	21,577	1.37%	1,574,738
Kansas	440,726	38.03%	692,634	59.77%	25,473	2.20%	1,158,833
Kentucky	679,370	37.80%	1,087,190	60.49%	30,652	1.71%	1,797,212
Louisiana	809,141	40.58%	1,152,262	57.78%	32,662	1.64%	1,994,065
Maine	401,306	56.44%	292,276	41.10%	17,471	2.46%	711,053
Maryland	1,677,844	62.16%	971,869	36.01%	48,826	1.81%	2,698,539
Massachusetts	1,921,290	60.78%	1,188,314	37.59%	51,611	1.63%	3,161,215
Michigan	2,564,569	54.21%	2,115,256	44.71%	51,136	1.08%	4,730,961
Minnesota	1,546,167	52.84%	1,320,225	45.12%	59,636	2.04%	2,926,028
Mississippi	562,949	43.79%	710,746	55.29%	11,889	0.92%	1,285,584
Missouri	1,223,796	44.38%	1,482,440	53.76%	51,087	1.85%	2,757,323
Montana	201,839	41.71%	267,928	55.36%	14,165	2.93%	483,932
Nebraska	302,081	38.21%	475,064	60.08%	13,517	1.71%	790,662
Nevada	531,373	52.66%	463,567	45.94%	14,208	1.41%	1,009,148
New Hampshire	369,561	52.17%	329,918	46.57%	8,920	1.26%	708,399
New Jersey	2,122,786	58.34%	1,478,088	40.62%	37,625	1.03%	3,638,499
New Mexico	415,335	52.99%	335,788	42.84%	32,634	4.16%	783,757
New York	4,018,385	60.41%	2,145,628	32.25%	488,261	7.34%	6,652,274
North Carolina	2,178,391	48.47%	2,270,395	50.52%	45,134	1.00%	4,493,920
North Dakota	124,966	38.70%	188,320	58.32%	9,646	2.99%	322,932
Ohio	2,827,621	50.67%	2,661,407	47.69%	91,803	1.64%	5,580,831
Oklahoma	443,547	33.23%	891,325	66.77%	0	0.00%	1,334,872
Oregon	970,488	54.64%	754,175	42.46%	51,332	2.89%	1,775,995
Pennsylvania	2,990,274	52.08%	2,680,434	46.69%	70,782	1.23%	5,741,490
Rhode Island	279,677	62.70%	157,204	35.24%	6,809	1.53%	446,049
South Carolina	865,941	44.09%	1,071,645	54.56%	26,532	1.35%	1,964,118
South Dakota	145,039	39.87%	210,610	57.89%	8,166	2.24%	363,815
Tennessee	960,709	39.10%	1,462,330	59.52%	33,799	1.38%	2,456,838
Texas	3,308,124	41.38%	4,569,843	57.17%	115,884	1.45%	7,993,851
Utah	251,813	24.76%	740,600	72.82%	24,595	2.42%	1,017,008
Vermont	199,239	66.57%	92,698	30.97%	7,353	2.46%	299,290
Virginia	1,971,820	51.25%	1,822,522	47.37%	52,901	1.38%	3,847,243
Washington	1,755,396	56.16%	1,290,670	41.29%	79,450	2.54%	3,125,516
West Virginia	238,230	35.53%	417,584	62.27%	14,742	2.20%	670,556
Wisconsin	1,620,985	52.78%	1,410,966	45.94%	39,483	1.29%	3,071,434
Wyoming	69,286	27.82%	170,962	68.64%	8,813	3.54%	249,061

2012 ELECTION: STATE-BY-STATE RESULTS (OBAMA vs. ROMNEY)

CHAPTER
6
Conclusion

As the evidence in the preceding pages shows,

Americans have gone to vote for Presidents every four years, since the end of the 18th century. Each of the elections has had its own flavor. Each has been influenced, both by the events and technology of the times. In the end, however, the only technology that ever counted was the decision of the voters who decided to vote. In the overwhelming number of cases, the will of the people was met. The candidate that received the most popular votes also received the most number of electoral votes and became President. In a few cases, most notably in the 2000 Gore vs. Bush election, the results differed. Yet, as always, even in this deeply disputed case, a peaceful transition transpired. The defeated candidate conceded the election and a new President was nominated.

As this book goes to the virtual press (the iBook Store) the United States is in the midst of an election campaign to determine if President Obama will be reelected. That election is taking place against the background of an end to one war, and a second war that is still raging in Afghanistan. This election is also taking place as the United States seems to be emerging from the worst economic downturn since the Great Depression. Will President Obama be reelected in November? Only the voters can determine the outcome.

ABOUT THE AUTHOR

Marc Schulman has authored 20 CD Roms on topics in American and World History,

including a multimedia biography of JFK, written almost 20 years ago. He is the primary editor

of Historycentral.com, the largest history web site. Marc has taught history in a very wide range

of schools; from Middle School to Colleges. Marc Schulman lives in Mamaroneck, New York with

his wife and children.

BIBLIOGRAPHY

Asher, Herbert. *Presidential Elections and American Politics Voters: Candidates and Campaigns since 1952.* Chicago: Dorsey Press. 2008.

Boller, Paul Jr. *Presidential Campaigns From Washington to Bush.* New York: Oxford University Press. 2004.

Gould, Lewis. *Grand Old Party a History of the Republicans.* New York: Random House. 2003.

Lenge, James and Shafer,Byron. *Presidential Politics, Reading on Nominations and Elections.* New York: St. Martins Press. 1983.

Mieczkowski, Yanek. *The Routledge Historic Atlas of Presidential Elections.* New York:Routledge. 2001.

Polsby, Nelson and Wildavsky, Aaron. *Presidential Election Strategies and Structures of American Politics.* London : Bowman and Littlefied , 2004.

White, Theodore. *The Making of the President 1960.* New York: Atheneum Publishers. 1961.

White, Theodore. *The Making of the President 1964.* New York: Atheneum Publishers. 1965.

Witcover, Jules. *Party of the People.* New York: Random House. 2004.

Printed in Great Britain
by Amazon.co.uk, Ltd.,
Marston Gate.